CHRISTOPHER POLHEM

*The Father
of Swedish Technology*

Christopher Polhem, painting, Klosterverken (Kloster Works), Långshyttan

CHRISTOPHER POLHEM

THE FATHER OF
SWEDISH TECHNOLOGY

TRANSLATED FROM
Christopher Polhem
(Minnesskrift utgifven af Svenska Teknologföreningen, 1911)

BY

WILLIAM A. JOHNSON, Ph.D.
Trinity College, Hartford, Connecticut

1963

Published by The Trustees of
TRINITY COLLEGE
HARTFORD, CONNECTICUT
Under a grant from
KARL WILLIAM HALLDEN, Sc.D.

© 1963, The Trustees of Trinity College
Printed in the United States of America by Connecticut Printers, Inc.
Library of Congress Catalog Card Number: 63–13636

FOREWORD

Some fell upon rocky ground . . . other seeds fell on good soil."
These words from the New Testament parable of the sower sum up
the long and eventful life of Christopher Polhem. Polhem, one of the
most ingenious and inventive individuals ever to grace the pages of
history, had an extraordinary ability to fashion new and creative con-
cepts. He was a man of many talents – one dares to call him a genius.
He was a man who passionately absorbed what was known in the natural sciences and engineering at his time. But to this deposit of understanding, he contributed his own discoveries and insights. At times his
ideas were brought to fruition, but too often he was considered a fail-
ure because there was no one to recognize him for what he was – a
scientific and technological giant, but someone who lived before his
time. This is, however, very often the fate of the genius.

Certainly he was honored and highly respected in Sweden during
his lifetime! Not the least among his admirers was the great sovereign,
King Karl XII. He was also known and revered abroad. But, as with all
great men, he had enemies, and there were those who were jealous of
him and attempted to deter him from changing existing conditions.
His reforming ideas were often resisted. Christopher Polhem insisted
that old-fashioned rituals and customs in the technical and social sciences be destroyed. He was an outspoken and honest man, and was
motivated by a desire to add to the well-being of mankind. Everything
he did was directed toward this end.

If one is interested in studying the more than 20,000 manuscripts
which have been preserved (all of which are authentically Polhem's),
one wonders if there is any phase of human activity which had not at
one time or other concerned this great reformer. Mining, iron and
steel manufacturing, the construction of waterways, theoretical and
practical mechanics, all branches of the natural sciences, the teaching
of technical materials, music, language, the nation's economy, military
strategy, the minting of coins, as well as the Biblical doctrine of creation, all concerned him and gave impetus to his revolutionary ideas.

Did his versatility cause him to be isolated from the thought-world
of his time? No, he was, as everyone else, a product of his time, a product of the assimilation of experience and knowledge of the period in
which he lived. He was typical of the most educated and learned of
men in his century. The latter part of the seventeenth century and the

first half of the eighteenth century was a period in which a great deal of progress had been made in Europe in the fields of mathematics, optics, mechanics, and chemistry. These areas of scientific knowledge have been enriched by present-day observations and discoveries. Nonetheless, much of the scientific knowledge of our time is dependent upon the discoveries of previous centuries. It is very easy to overestimate the achievements of the modern world and forget that they too are dependent upon the past. Only by understanding this fact will we be able to appreciate the contribution Christopher Polhem made to the history of Western civilization. We construct our world upon the same ideas and theories which in his time "fell upon rocky ground." Now, however, in the different soil of a different century, his ideas can take root and bear fruit.

There are very few Swedes who have been able to hold the attention of the mind of man throughout history as intensely as has Christopher Polhem. His creative imagination, his versatility and vitality command attention and generate excitement. Many Swedes who have at one time or another in their lives discovered or invented something (or who at least thought they did) identified themselves immediately with Christopher Polhem. It is for this reason that the memory of Polhem lives on in Sweden. That which is identified with the creative, the imaginative, the technical (and Sweden is a highly technical country) is also identified with Christopher Polhem!

Polhem's contemporaries considered him a wizard in technical matters, a man who could do anything. He too believed that he could succeed in many fields and for that reason he tackled any task. Probably he was motivated by the belief that, once given a task, he would find the strength and ability to perform it. As an engineer and an inventor of mechanical devices, he undoubtedly was at his very best. His contribution to the fields of economics, philosophy, cosmology, and other speculative areas was minimal, albeit interesting, and another indication of the breadth of Polhem's abilities. He was primarily a technician, an inventor, and a builder of machines used in the mining and metalworking industries. One of his talents is often overlooked, and that is that he was a pioneer in the mass production of replaceable machine parts, which he made with great precision and accuracy. He attempted to replace manual operations with machines. In this way, he felt the life of the worker would be made more meaningful. He believed in the dignity of man and sought to find ways to implement this belief. Many of his ideas were never realized, however, and were forgotten by entire generations of people. But in our time, Polhem is being recognized as the genius he really was – a genius who expressed

vi

himself in the technical fields, as well as in an affection for humanity.

Polhem used the idea of mass production for the first time when making cogwheels for a complicated clock mechanism. His first real accomplishment, while still a student at Uppsala University, was the repair of the sixteenth-century astronomical clock in the cathedral there. This experience meant that as a young man he came into contact with his century's most advanced mechanical apparatus, the mechanical clock. In addition, while still a young man, he speculated on some of the most complex philosophical and cosmological problems of his time. This fact made Polhem aware of problems which were not being discussed by his world and forced him to find answers to questions his colleagues were not even asking. His eyes were opened to the great possibilities which lay ahead for him and for all mankind.

Polhem was an incisive as well as a creative thinker. Whether as a technician, an engineer, the founder of a new industry, or a writer, the same characteristics of thought emerged. Similar to Olof Rudbeck and many other seventeenth-century figures in Sweden, Christopher Polhem was a broad-minded and liberal thinker. At the same time, however, he could be critical and was ready to discuss problems in any field which interested him. He was never afraid to defend what he believed to be right. He was able to bring about new solutions to old problems. In one of his manuscripts he devised a discussion between the proponents of theory and practice. In this, we see clearly his versatile, but always searching spirit, his desire to relate theoretical material to practical consequences and, as well, his insistence that one must relate the practical to its necessary theoretical counterpart. He always sought the Truth!

A biography of Christopher Polhem (which is to be found in this volume) was first published in 1911. Since that time, there have been many who have sought to discover the truth about this man. It is quite apparent that Polhem was a complicated individual, and, in addition, the nature of his work was extremely complex. There has been a need, therefore, to continue the research begun on Polhem in the early part of this century. Excellent results in modern scholarship have accomplished a great deal, but the image of Polhem which emerges from this recently translated work of a book fifty years old has not been substantially altered. The volume before us, of course, has undergone a number of corrections and additions, but these have been carried out solely to enrich the understanding of the contributions of the greatest man of Swedish technology, Christopher Polhem.

In order to enhance even more the picture we have of Polhem, I feel it is necessary to include a listing of the more important scientific publications which have appeared during the last decade which deal with Polhem and his contributions to the history of technology.

Polhem's handwritten manuscripts, preserved in the Royal Library, are very difficult to interpret because of an unusual handwriting style, an excessive use of abbreviations, and a strange manner of punctuating. Because of the initiative of Professor Johan Nordström of Uppsala, these manuscripts have been very thoroughly examined. Four Polhem scholars, Henrik Sandblad, Gösta Lindeberg, Axel Liljencrantz, and Bengt Löw, have analyzed them and put them into proper categories. This project has been sponsored by the Stora Kopparbergs Bergslags Aktiebolag (Great Copper Mountain Mining Corporation), an industry which Polhem helped build during the years 1700–1718. These published manuscripts, *Christopher Polhems efterlämnade skrifter* (*Christopher Polhem's Collected Papers*), are made up of five volumes with a total of 2,600 pages. Anyone who is interested in Polhem, his world, and his contributions to technology must immerse himself in these manuscripts. A reward far beyond one's wildest expectations will be the result.

Polhem had many disciples. Two of them, C. J. Cronstedt and Augustin Ehrensvärd, kept notebooks filled with drawings and outlines based upon Polhem's instructions during the year 1729. Four of these notebooks and about one hundred of the drawings have been found and have been placed in the Tekniska Museet in Stockholm. As a result of this material, we can now study in great detail and with a high degree of precision the nature of Polhem's technical discoveries. As well, these notebooks give us a good picture of Polhem's pedagogical techniques.

Professor Sten Lindroth has written a two-volume (a total of 1,200 pages) work entitled *Gruvbrytning och kopparhantering vid Stora Kopparberget* (*The Mining and Processing of Copper at the Great Copper Mountain Corporation*). Stora Kopparberget is Sweden's oldest corporation (and perhaps the world's oldest) with a history of 700 years of continuous operation. Polhem's contribution to the Falun mine is included in these volumes. A more detailed treatment of Polhem's contribution to Stora Kopparberget is found in Lindroth's *Polhem och Stora Kopparberget* (*Polhem and the Great Copper Mountain Corporation*). Lindroth has brilliantly presented a description of Polhem's machines and inventions, primarily those in the area of mine engineering. These inventions have been placed within their proper historical perspective. As well, Lindroth has indicated the tremendous contribution Polhem made to the mining industry of Sweden. This richly-illustrated book is one of the most important docu-

viii

ments dealing with Christopher Polhem in our time. We can see as never before the true nature of his work, the problems he faced, the opposition he encountered, as well as the major improvements he made in mining techniques.

Polhem's contribution to the realization of the ancient dream to build a canal across Sweden from the Baltic Sea to the North Sea was described by Samuel Bring in 1911 in his doctor's thesis which dealt with the Trollhättan Canal. The canal was finally finished in 1832, long after Polhem's death, and remains to this day a monument to the genius which was Polhem's.

In the yearbook of the Tekniska Museet, which is entitled *Daedalus* (and which has appeared every year since 1931), a series of articles have been published dealing with Polhem's mechanical inventions. These articles have appeared primarily in conjunction with a description of the experiments which took place in the *Laboratorium Mechanicum,* which was founded by Polhem in 1697, and which later became the Royal Model Chamber. The Tekniska Museet now exhibits most of the models of Polhem's mechanical inventions. It took ten years to reconstruct these models, and the claim can be justified that they form part of the largest and most varied collection of eighteenth-century items found in Europe today. There are also a great many items and machines from Polhem's factory, "Stjernsund," which was located in Dalecarlia. In the museum, one can experience the everyday life of a factory more than 250 years old. Here one is confronted with a concrete witness to Polhem's industry and spirit.

At Stjernsund there was also a clock factory which had machines designed and built by Polhem, which automatically cut cogwheels and other parts necessary for the construction of clocks. In Dr. Sten Lundwall's book entitled *Stjärnsundsuren Väggurtillverkningen vid ett 1700-tals bruk (Stjernsund's Clocks, the Manufacture of Wall Clocks in an Eighteenth-century Factory)*, there is a description of the structure and organization of Polhem's mill. The book also serves as a guide to the identification of the much sought after Stjernsund clock.

As we have said, Polhem was a pioneer in the mass production of machine parts. His techniques were used extensively in the Stjernsund clock factory. But he was also a pioneer in the use of gauges to control mass-produced articles. Professor Robert S. Woodbury, of the Massachusetts Institute of Technology, has dealt with Polhem's contribution to this field in his book *History of the Gear-Cutting Machine*. In another volume by Professor Woodbury, *The History of the Lathe,* the lathe Polhem built is considered to be one of the earliest lathes constructed anywhere. Woodbury has attempted to demonstrate in

ix

these books and in other publications how the Swedish people, and Christopher Polhem in particular, shared in the development of engineering techniques during the eighteenth century.

There was at Stjernsund a shop which Polhem built which made various household articles. This shop was equipped to make different kinds of plates and dishes. A number of the parts belonging to these machines are preserved in the Tekniska Museet in Stockholm. Dipl. Ing. Ernst von Wedel, in his thesis *Die Entwicklung des Umformens in Gesenken* (Technische Hochschuhle, Hannover, Germany, 1960), has described Polhem's contributions to this area of technical development.

In the journal *Transactions of the Newcomen Society for the Study of the History of Technology and Engineering* (London, Vol. VII, 1926–27), there is a short article by John G. H. Rhodin which deals with Polhem and his work. This article was quite significant because so relatively little was known in Great Britain about Polhem.

No one who deals with the history of technology in a scholarly way can overlook Polhem's work! His theoretical insights and practical knowledge are still alive in engineering techniques and industrial operations all over the modern world.

Very seldom in the history of civilization is an individual permitted to work at full capacity for seventy of his ninety years. Polhem said of Stjernsund: "even if this mill is little thought of by those who do not really understand it, nonetheless, it has significant value." He could have said the same thing about his life's work in its entirety.

Three hundred years have passed since this remarkable man was born and more than two hundred years since he died. In the long history of mankind, this is only a brief moment. However, Christopher Polhem, the father of Swedish mechanics, will always live among us, a figure worthy to be remembered and esteemed; a figure whose creative genius has given us much of what makes up our modern technological civilization.

The modern world brings new knowledge and technical achievements. Some of this too falls on rocky ground, some on good soil. This is always our expectation as one generation follows another. Let me in conclusion remind you of the words which are found on many of the clocks from Polhem's time, which even today, second by second, measure the passing of time – *Sic Volvitur Aetas*.

TORSTEN ALTHIN
Tekniska Museet
Stockholm, Sweden

PREFACE

WHY THIS BOOK WAS TRANSLATED INTO ENGLISH

A few years ago my wife and I were on a Caribbean cruise and were seated at dinner next to Chief Engineer Eric Olson. The subject at one particular dinner conversation was Emanuel Swedenborg, the Swedish philosopher and scientific theorist. Mr. Olson stated that Swedenborg was at one time engaged to the daughter of Christopher Polhem. As I was quite well informed about the life of Swedenborg, I expressed amazement at this statement. Not so well informed about Polhem, I began to ask questions about him. Mr. Olson informed me that the next time I visited Göteborg, he would lend me the book entitled *Minnesskrift av Christopher Polhem*.

The following year I went to Göteborg and Mr. Olson lent the above-mentioned book to me. As I read, to my amazement I found a description and print of a metal rolling mill built on the principle of the modern four high mill and found it was operating in Sweden already in the early part of the eighteenth century. For those who are not acquainted with the art of metal rolling, the four high rolling mill revolutionized the art of cold rolling steel.

After I investigated further into this book, I found that this technical improvement was only one among many which this remarkable man had developed at that early date and that only now, in the twentieth century, have we caught up with the technological principles which he had conceived. Mr. Olson allowed me to bring the book back to America where I had more time to study the contents carefully. I was enthused about its contents and described some of the things in the book to my wife Margaret. She made the remark, "Why don't you have it translated so we can all enjoy it?" That settled it! Off to Stockholm we went and contacted my friend Eric Jurehn, whom I had known in New York when he was associated with the Swedish Chamber of Commerce, and who now was a resident of Stockholm. Mr. Jurehn introduced me to Mr. Gunnar A. Hambraeus, editor of *Teknisk Tidskrift*, the descendant of the Svenska Teknologföreningen, which originally had published the Polhem book in 1911. Mr. Hambraeus gave me the right to translate and publish this book in English. I was also introduced to Dr. Torsten Althin, who was director of the Tekniska Museet (Technical Museum) in Stockholm, and who is the leading authority on Polhem in the world today. Dr. Althin personally took us through his very interesting museum where we were shown many of the models of Polhem's original inventions. After spending almost an entire afternoon at the museum, we were more convinced than ever that Polhem must be translated into the English language. We were very pleased when Dr. Althin graciously consented to write the Foreword for this book.

After returning to America, we had to find someone who was capable of translating Swedish into English, and I found to my delight that Dr. William A. Johnson, a member of the Religion Department at Trinity College, Hartford, Connecticut, my alma mater, not only had the requirements for the translation, but was about to go to Lund University in Sweden to complete work for his doctor's degree in theology. While in Stockholm, Dr. Johnson contacted Dr. Althin and both of these men carefully discussed Polhem and some of the additions and revisions which were to be included in the translation of the 1911 manuscript.

My only hope is that those who read this book will receive as much pleasure from the description of this very remarkable man, and what he has accomplished for civilization, as I have in bringing this book before the English-speaking people.

Dr. Karl William Hallden
President
The Hallden Machine Company
Thomaston, Connecticut

TRANSLATOR'S PREFACE

Christopher Polhem is among the very few men of greatness in the history of technology and scientific discovery. But Christopher Polhem is not at all known in the English-speaking world. The reason for this is that for centuries the Swedish language has been a cultural barrier. When there is an occasion to translate the writings of a Swede of the past, the world is amazed at the far-reaching consequences of his thought. The names of Swedenborg, Linnaeus, Nobel, Erikson, as well as Lagerlöf and Strindberg come to mind immediately. Christopher Polhem will surprise the contemporary reader. His contribution to the scientific and industrial development of Sweden has had no equal. In the creation of an early manufacturing mill, in Stjernsund, for example, we find industrial techniques which are still in use today. Even more than this, however, Polhem was a Swede who first envisioned the modern Sweden – a Sweden which would be looked up to by the rest of the world. Technically, what Sweden possesses today, and Sweden is among the leaders in technical advancement in our world, is in a very real way dependent upon Christopher Polhem and his dream for an industrial Sweden.

The task of translating any work is a difficult one. The task is made more difficult when a theologian attempts to step into the world of engineering. Nonetheless, I have attempted to be faithful to the ideas and techniques which were introduced to me in this Polhem volume. I have inquired of the volumes in the history of engineering and technology to determine how best to express the terms which Christopher Polhem used. I have conversed with engineers in the United States as well as in Sweden in an attempt to comprehend the nature of the devices and apparatus which Polhem created; that is, to determine how the machine operated!

Another difficulty, of course, is how to be faithful to the different literary styles of the authors of this volume. It is tempting to impose one's own mode of expression upon the various writers, in an attempt to add to the stylistic unity of the book. I have been conscious at all times of this temptation, and have resisted it as much as possible.

The volume *Christopher Polhem, Minnesskrift* was published in 1911. For this reason, the book, by definition, should be outdated. Fortunately, however, for this present project, there has been a great deal of Polhem research since this volume first appeared. Polhem's life, his world, and his contributions to science and technology are now better understood. Wherever possible, I have included the results of this modern scholarship. Where there should be alterations in the text, I have endeavored to make them, with the expressed intention of making this volume a useful scholarly work. This modernization would not be possible without the contribution of the man who knows more about Christopher Polhem than anyone alive today. He is Dr. Torsten Althin, director of the Tekniska Museet in Stockholm, Sweden. Dr. Althin has been responsible for keeping Polhem alive in Sweden. He has initiated and inspired hundreds of studies dealing with Polhem and his inventions. He, himself, has scoured all of Sweden to find models of machines which were made by Polhem, and his success in this endeavor may be seen in the Polhem division of the Tekniska Museet. Here there is assembled the technological achievements of Polhem's world – presented for all the world to see!

It is hoped, too, that this volume might add to the Swedish-American cultural exchange, and that by virtue of it, we in the United States might receive a more complete picture of our own heritage.

This translation and revision of *Christopher Polhem, Minnesskrift* has been a family project. The entire manuscript was read, and suggested alternate readings were given, by my mother and father, Ruth and Charles Johnson, both of whom taught me my first Swedish words. The manuscript in its earlier and later drafts was typed by my wife, Carol Johnson. In addition, Miss Carol Steiman, the secretary of the Religion Department at Trinity College, prepared the manuscript for the publisher.

Dr. Torsten Althin has read the entire manuscript and has offered valuable suggestions throughout. He has also provided many of the illustrations and drawings which are included in this volume.

However, the individual who is most responsible for this project is Dr. Karl William Hallden, president of the Hallden Machine Company, Thomaston, Connecticut. Without his initial discovery of the volume and his persistence in getting it to this, its final printed form, Polhem would still be an unknown Swede who belonged to the dark past. His many kindnesses to me, his encouragement, and his faith in my ability to do the job will always be appreciated.

One last thing *must* be said – I feel that it is appropriate that the volume be dedicated to Karl William Hallden, because he, more than anyone else, represents the Polhem genius and spirit in our world. Indeed, he is the Christopher Polhem of the twentieth century!

WILLIAM A. JOHNSON
Trinity College
Hartford, Connecticut

xiv

TABLE OF CONTENTS

LIST OF ILLUSTRATIONS

Frontispiece

Christopher Polhem, painting, Klosterverken (Kloster Works), Långshyttan

Chapter One: A Contribution to the Biography of Christopher Polhem

Figure

*Chapter Two: Polhem's Contributions to
Applied Mechanics*

Chapter Three: Polhem, the Mining Engineer

Figure

*Chapter Four: Polhem's Contribution to
the Art of Building*

Figure

CHAPTER ONE

A Contribution to the Biography
of Christopher Polhem

BY SAMUEL E. BRING

I. Polhem's Family, His Youth, and Study in Uppsala (1661–1690)

The Polhem family did not originate in Sweden. According to the most famous member of the family, Christopher Polhem,[1] the Polhems came from Hungary. A Hungarian nobleman whose name was Polheimer left his homeland for religious reasons and settled in Pomerania in about the year 1600. There is, however, another version of the story which says that the family came from Austria and that Baron von Polheim was the initiator of the Swedish line of the family.

Both of these versions of the origin of the Polhem family come from Christopher Polhem. However, it is apparent that he was not sure which account was authentic. In 1713, when it was proposed that he should be rewarded with the title of noble for his great accomplishments, Polhem wrote to his friend, Eric Benzelius (who was at that time librarian in Uppsala), and asked him if he could find out if there had ever been a family by the name of Polhaimer in either Hungary or Austria. He also wanted to find out what their coat of arms looked like. In his letter to Benzelius he wrote, "in my childhood I had learned that my grandfather escaped from Hungary or Austria for the sake of religion. As his situation did not permit him his former noble title, he changed his name by inserting a letter or two into it."[2] Unfortunately, Benzelius' answer has never been found, and has probably been destroyed. But from another of Polhem's letters to Benzelius, we learn that Benzelius, as he investigated Polhem's ancestry, found his name "in a printed Clerical Register or Book of Heraldry at Assessor Brenner's. It was determined that they had been barons, and possessed two coats of arms, one with three bands and three lions and the other with three bands and three eagles."[3]

The records which the famous authority on heraldry and assessor in the College of Antiquities, Elias Brenner, made available to Benzelius were undoubtedly part of J. Siebmacher's well-known work, *Wappenbuch*. From this source we learn that there are two branches of the family:[4] Baron von Pollheimb and Baron von Pollheimb of

---

[1] In this article we will use the spelling of Polhem which is most common. Before he became a nobleman he spelled his name Polhammar; for a time thereafter, Pol(l)heimer, and then later, Polhem.

[2] Polhem to Benzelius, Stjernsund, June 10, 1713. *Codex Bf.* 31. Linköpings stiftsbibliotek.

[3] Polhem to Benzelius, Stjernsund, July 18, 1716; cf. Swedenborg, *Opera de rebus naturalibus*, 1907, p. 255.

[4] Cf. the edition of 1655–57. The coat of arms reproduced here is taken from the 1734 edition.

3

1. *The Polhem coat of arms*

Partz, whose coat of arms corresponds very well with the above description.

The von Polheim family was at one time one of the oldest and most respected in Austria. The family castle, which is now in ruins, was located in Grieskirchen in the Archduchy of Upper Austria. By the year 1000, members of the family had attained to elevated and honored positions within Austrian nobility and were oftentimes allied (by virtue of marriage) with foreign dukedoms. In the period immediately thereafter, members of the family became distinguished soldiers and clergymen. In the sixteenth century, Wolfgang von Polheim was a governor in his ancestral province. This was an honorary position which was passed on to many of his descendants. Later, several members of the family were forced to leave their country because they were, as was the Austrian nobility in general, strong supporters of Protestantism.

In 1507, the baronial title was bestowed upon the family by Emperor Maximilian I. Another branch of the family was to receive the more elevated title of "Count" in September 1721 from Emperor Karl VI. The last male member of these families, Adolf Peter Graf von Polheim und Wartenburg, died in the month of March, 1900.[5]

Christopher Polhem believed that his ancestry could be traced back to this family line. His coat of arms is an exact reduplication of the coat of arms of his Austrian ancestors. He had chosen the figure of the lion to be included and used it in a manner which is most like the Swedish tradition. Assessor Brenner suggested that he also include the *theorema pythagoricum* and a few other mathematical figures. However, on the basis of the knowledge we have at present, it cannot be proved beyond any question that there is a direct association between the Austrian family von Polheim and the Swedish family Polhammar (which was also spelled Polhem and Polheimer).

In Pomerania, Polhem's ancestor changed his name to Polhammer when he became a civil servant. When he died in 1620 (probably in Stralsund), he left two sons, both of whom became Swedish citizens. The oldest, Wulf Christopher, born in 1610, was thought to have been shipwrecked off Gotland during a sea voyage. He settled in the old Hanseatic city of Visby. The younger son, Hans Adam, became a clerk in a Stockholm post office. It is not known when the brothers came to Sweden, but it was sometime after Pomerania became a Swedish province as a result of the Peace of Westphalia.

In Visby, Wulf Christopher Polhammar became "a prominent mer-

---

[5] *Historisch-heraldisches Handbuch zum genealogischen Taschenbuch der gräflichen Häuser*, 1855, pp. 710–712. *Gräfliches Taschenbuch*, 1904, p. 639, and 1911, p. 695.

chant, with many ships at sea." When he was 50 years old, he married Christina Eriksdotter Schening, who came from Vadstena.[6] A son was born to them about December 18, 1661, and was baptized with his father's name, Christopher. His birth date cannot be known with absolute certainty. Traditionally, it had been thought that the date was November 18. The basis for this conjecture was a remark made by Professor Samuel Klingenstierna, of Uppsala. In his "Christopher Polhem Memorial Address" given to the Royal Swedish Academy of Science in the Auditorium of the House of Nobles on June 25, 1753, Professor Klingenstierna indicated that Polhem was born on the 18th of November. Although he based his information on Polhem's own notes, it is apparent that he deviated from his sources. In Polhem's small autobiography which was written in 1740 in accordance with the regulations of the newly-instituted Academy of Science, Polhem gave his date of birth as December 18, 1661, and added that he was born in the city of Visby.[7] Klingenstierna's mistake was undoubtedly caused by a notice of Polhem's death in the *Stockholms Post*,[8] which erroneously gave the date of his birth as November 18. A letter written by Polhem's nephew, Anders Polhammar, to his parents (Johan and Elisabeth Polhammar) in November 1743, corroborates the claim that he was born in December rather than in November. The letter read, "Even in his old age dear uncle has good health; he will be 82 next December 20."[9] Additional support for the contention that Polhem was born in the latter part of December may be found in a portrait of Polhem at Stjernsund (Polhem's and Gabriel Stierncrona's famous manufacturing plant). The portrait was completed on July 12, 1703, and according to the inscription on the back, Polhem's date of birth was December 20. Still another portrait, this one completed in 1730 by J. H. Scheffel, gives December 16 as the date of birth. This portrait is possibly one of the four that Polhem ordered for his daughters.[10] It is clear from all of this that Polhem was most likely born in December, rather than in November as Klingenstierna maintained.

Strangely enough, there is no mention of the birth of a son to Wulf Christopher Polhem in the records of the city of Visby for 1661. Be-

[6] In another edition of Polhem's autobiography which was in the possession of G. Polheimer in Falun, Christina Schening was a sister to the circuit judge of Gotland and both were born in Vadstena of the Styra family.

[7] In another edition it reads, "at the end of the year 1661." *Biographi P.* Kungl. Biblioteket (KB).

[8] No. 69 (5–9).

[9] Nyberg, "När föddes Kristoffer Polhem?" in Gotlands *Allehanda*, 1910, No. 82 (12–4).

[10] Polhem's birth date is given as Dec. 18 in several foreign volumes; cf. Rotermund, *Fortsetzung und Ergänzungen zu Jöchers Gelehrten-Lexiko*, 6(1819) p. 513. *Nouvelle biographie generale*, 40(1862), pp. 602ff.

2. *Facsimile of Christopher Polhem's handwriting; from a manuscript in which Polhem described his parental background and early life*

cause of the complete records kept in that year, there is no possibility that a page is missing. The baptismal records, however, do indicate that a daughter, Anna Margareta, was born sometime in the beginning of 1661. She was baptized between the dates of February 17 and March 15, although it was reported that she had been "baptized at home," prior to this time. The fact of a child's birth early in 1661 would seem to support the argument that Christopher Polhem had to be born in December. However, as there is no record of Christopher Polhem's birth in Visby, one can question the claim that he was born there.

It has been suggested that Polhem was born in Ejsta.[11] A maternal aunt, the wife of Elias Torselius, lived there, and it is possible that Christopher Polhem's mother visited her at the time of his birth. This

[11] Nyberg, *op. cit.*

7

claim cannot be verified in any way because the records of the city are no longer in existence.

However, there exists the possibility of still another birthplace. Polhem's father had suffered great financial losses while in Visby and he was forced to give up his business interests. According to one report,[12] he moved to Tingstäde. Christopher may have been born while the family was there. Again, this claim cannot be verified, because the birth records for the city only begin in 1687.

Christopher Polhem's father died in 1669 when the boy was but eight years old. Shortly thereafter his mother married Jöran Silker, a builder. He was a miserly man and did not want to continue paying for his stepson's education. When Christopher's paternal uncle, Hans Adam Polhem, heard about the situation, he took Christopher to his home in Stockholm and enrolled him in the "Elementary School" which met in the German Church. However, two years later Hans Adam died, and his widow displayed a lack of concern "for her step-children, and particularly for her late husband's nephew." As a result, Christopher was forced to leave school. Alone and abandoned, the twelve-year-old boy had to go out into the world and earn his own livelihood. Soon after, however, he was employed by Margareta Wallenstedt, widow of the famous diplomat and senator, Mattias Biörenklou. At first he worked as a "common servant." Later, when his abilities in arithmetic and writing were recognized, he was given a responsible position at the Wallenstedt estate "Kungshamn" (which was located in the parish of Alsike, not far from Uppsala). He probably moved from there in the year 1675 to the Vansta estate, situated on the eastern shore of Lake Styran (Ösmo parish, Söderman-land). He was appointed revenue collector, or inspector, at Vansta, a job which involved keeping the accounts of the tenant farmers. He maintained this position for ten years.

It was during this time at Vansta that Polhem's mechanical skills became apparent. He seemed to be interested in little else than the operation of machines and mechanical apparatus. He built a work-shop all by himself which contained tools for carpentry work, a lathe, and, as well, some blacksmith's equipment. All of his free time was spent in this workshop. He built small and rather primitive machines which could make such things as knives and scissors, but which also could produce rather elaborate devices such as a turnspit and various kinds of clocks. As he worked, he realized more and more that without a formal education and a background of theoretical knowledge, his

[12] Klerckers genealogiska samling (KB).

8

practical abilities could not be used in a meaningful way. Often he came across problems which he could not solve, simply because he was unfamiliar with the principles of mathematics and mechanics. He tried to educate himself, but was frustrated in the attempt because the books were all in Latin. He recognized immediately that he had to find someone who could help him with this language. Only in this way, he believed, was he going to progress in his study of mathematics and mechanics. However, he was frustrated once again, for as he said, "I had no one to learn from; I had to depend solely upon myself."

His desire for further knowledge was intensified after meeting a young clergyman from the neighboring parish of Sorunda. He had come into Polhem's workshop to purchase a number of knives and scissors and was surprised to see the very complicated lathe Polhem was using. He suggested to Polhem that he attend school in Strängnäs where he would be able to receive training in mechanical subjects. However, the major problem in those days was how to finance an education. This did not have to be a concern for Polhem, the priest insisted, for his practical and inventive genius could be put to good use there. Polhem was further encouraged by a story of a shoemaker's helper who, to avoid military service, became a student in Strängnäs. Starting with a simple "ABC" book, he advanced so quickly that he eventually became a teacher.

So appealing did all of this sound that Polhem resigned his position in order to begin his formal education. His employer was reluctant to let Polhem go and ridiculed his ideas, hoping that he might change his mind.

At about this same time a land surveyor came to Vansta to make a map of the estate. Polhem became extremely interested in the surveyor's work and followed him everywhere. He quickly learned the practical aspects of the surveyor's trade, and was eager to learn more about map-making. However, he was eventually disappointed because he learned that the map itself was to be completed in Stockholm. In order to study the theoretical aspects of land-surveying and map-making, Polhem bought books on the topic written in both German and Swedish. Undoubtedly, the book in Swedish was Peder Nilson Raam's early work on surveying *Then svenske åkermätningen eller örtuga deelo book, item een lijten tractat om staaff och råå och thes beskaffenheet,* which had been published in 1670 in Strängnäs. This was one of the first books in Sweden on the subject of surveying.

But even in these books Polhem did not find what he was looking for. Subsequently, he came upon a number of ancient maps which were hanging in a room in the Vansta estate. One of these maps may

9

have been "Orbis arctoi nova et accurata delineatio," drawn by Andreas Bureus in 1626. This was the first reliable map of Scandinavia. Unfortunately for Polhem the inscription on the map revealed nothing, because it too was written in Latin. Curious about what was written there, and overwhelmed by a desire to study, Polhem went to visit the chaplain of the estate in hopes that the chaplain might help him get his formal education under way. He was given a Swedish-Latin dictionary, which Polhem began to memorize. He soon realized the impracticality of this method, for as he himself said, a language cannot be learned "simply by memorizing some names and phrases."

He complained about his situation to Lars Olof Welt, the son of the rector of the church in Ösmo. Lars Olof Welt was himself chaplain to Baroness Elin Fleming, the widow of Governor Nils Bååt of Fållnäs (located in the parish of Sorunda, a few miles from Vansta). Welt had come to Polhem to purchase a clock. Polhem immediately asked if he could study Latin with him. In exchange for these lessons, he promised to make him an unusual clock which would strike the quarter-hour, as well as give the date, the day of the week, and the phase of the moon. Welt accepted this proposal and came once a month to Vansta to teach Polhem "grammar and other things which would inform him in the Latin language." Polhem learned quickly, so quickly in fact, "that he was able really to understand Latin except when it was not too hard or complicated." The clock which Polhem made for Welt was placed in the Ösmo rectory and remained there for many years, as Lars Olof succeeded his father as rector of the Ösmo church in 1691.

To be closer to his teacher, Polhem finally left his position with Madam Biörenklou, although she was very reluctant to let him go. He was able to obtain the same kind of employment with Baroness Bååt on the Fållnäs estate. He continued his studies with even greater earnestness. Lars Welt was able to give him daily lessons in Latin during this time. Polhem's happiness was short-lived, however, because half a year later Lars Olof Welt was called to the church in Ösmo. His successor in Fållnäs, Lars Halenius[13] (who also became Polhem's teacher) was called after a very short period of time to become rector of a church in Helsingland. Fortunately, Polhem became friendly with the priest in Sorunda, Erland Dryselius, a very learned man, who was also interested in education. He took an interest in Polhem, and promised to teach him Latin and other subjects if he would come to Sorunda. Polhem was not discouraged by the fact that the distance was very great between Fållnäs and Sorunda. For a period of seven

[13] This does not agree with the report in Fant, *Upsala ärkestifts herdaminne.*

3. *Erland Dryselius*

months he traveled in the rain and snow to the priest's home for his lesson. Many times, after Polhem arrived, Dryselius could not see him because he was tied up with his duties as a parish priest. At the same time, Polhem did not forget about his responsibilities in Fållnäs. He worked so well there that "nothing was neglected; (he) even kept right on working during his mealtime."

Although Polhem possessed an insatiable desire to learn, it is not surprising to learn that he found this method tiring. Finally, Dryselius advised him to enroll at Uppsala University, where his unique talents could be better directed. With a recommendation from Dryselius to Anders Spole, Professor of Mathematics at Uppsala, Polhem left Stockholm. Spole was unable to accept him as a student at this time because of his university responsibilities, so Polhem had to return to Stockholm. He thought that he would try to get a job as a land-surveyor. While waiting for an opportunity to speak to the authorities in the office of the Department of Surveying, he read a manual which enumerated the requirements for entrance into the surveyors' guild. He realized immediately that he lacked the necessary university training required for the position. For that reason he returned to Uppsala and this time was able to speak to Professor Spole. To see what Polhem could do, Spole gave him two astronomical clocks to repair, one of which had never worked. Polhem was able to fix the clocks very quickly, and Professor Spole was convinced that he had a student of rare ability. He was invited to live in the Professor's home as a result. After being subjected to a number of initiatory ceremonies, which were oftentimes foolish and brutal, Polhem was admitted to Uppsala University. This took place on November 12, 1687, and according to the practice of the time he was "sponsored" by Professor Spole.[14]

Polhem remained at Uppsala for three years and quite naturally spent most of his time studying those subjects which interested him. Mechanics, of course, took first place. The rector of the University, Petrus Lagerlöf, in his *testimonium academicum* of 1694, said that Polhem had a natural aptitude for mathematics and physics, but that he excelled in mechanics. He was a good student in the humanities as well, Lagerlöf said.[15]

Polhem was not primarily concerned with theoretical problems in his studies, but rather with the practical application of theoretical

[14] Found in Uppsala Universitets matrikel. 5(1911), utg. af A. B. Carlsson and J. Sandström, for 12–11 1687, not 1686 which was published previously. It reads: "pro eo spondebat amplissimus professor Spole."

[15] *Testimonium academicum för Christophorus Polhammar Gotlandus,* Oct. 18, 1694. *Biographi P.* (KB).

principles. It was reported that he worked on the mechanism of the bells in the Uppsala Cathedral and improved it so much that only four men were needed to ring the bells, whereas before eighteen were necessary. As well, he made an astronomical clock which showed the time of the rising and setting of the sun, the phases of the moon, "and other unusual things." When Polhem died the clock was at Stjernsund, but was moved later to the observatory of the Royal Swedish Academy of Science.[16] Another extremely complicated clock comes from the period in Uppsala. Polhem immersed himself in his studies. From his autobiography, which was written in Polhem's later years, we learn that he never slept more than three hours a night during the time he was at the University. However, as he later said, "I grew accustomed to it, and found myself much more lively and quick to learn than ever before. . . . There is nothing which stunts the brain and spoils it for future use as too much sleep."

Most of his time during the student days in Uppsala was spent repairing the astronomical clock in the cathedral, a task which Polhem said himself "was the beginning of all of my good fortune."[17] It was on the basis of Professor Spole's recommendation that Polhem (then only 26 years old) was permitted to work on the clock. Nonetheless, the church officials had to be reassured that Polhem had the ability to repair the clock. Polhem was able to make the repairs, although the entire project took two years. He had to carry the heavy parts of the clock to his workshop so that they could be fixed, and then back again to the church. None of the work itself could be done inside the church. During the two years that he labored on the clock he received free board, but, as he reported, "no other payment." After the repair work was completed, Polhem received a scholarship of 60 copper daler. He was able to keep this scholarship for only one year as his absence from Uppsala for a term did not permit a renewal. It had always been thought that Polhem's work on the clock was finished in 1689, but according to Olof Rudbeck's letter to Chancellor Bengt Oxenstjerna, it was on July 7, 1688.[18] In the letter, Rudbeck described Polhem as "a mathematical genius," and related that "the clock was now working and had a pendulum which was 20 alnar or longer."[19]

In his work, "A Brief Description of the Most Important Mechanical Inventions," Polhem related that the clock in the Uppsala Cathedral was made by a monk from Vadstena by the name of Petrus Dasy-

[16] "Promemoria vid Polhems personalier." *Biographi P.* (KB).

[17] Polhem, *Kort berättelse om de förnämsta mechaniska inventioner,* 1729, p. 5.

[18] Published in *Bref af Olof Rudbeck,* utg. af Annerstedt, 1905, p. 323.

[19] Alnar, an obsolete measure. One aln corresponds to a British ell.

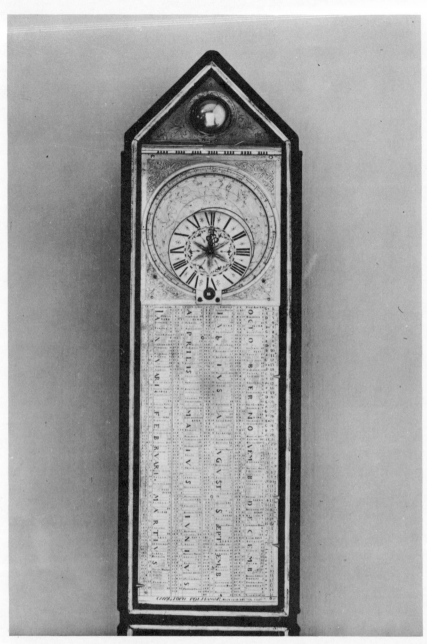

4. *Polhem's astronomical clock from the year 1690. In the possession of Kammarherre (Chamberlain) Harry Hedenstierna, Gothenburg*

podius. He went on to say that this same monk made a similar clock for the Strassburg Cathedral. Polhem is incorrect, however, on this point. The Uppsala clock was indeed made by a monk from Vadstena, but not the monk Polhem referred to. The monk who was also a clockmaker had received the name of Astronomus. He was a German by birth and lived in Uppsala in 1506. For a payment of 700 marks, he constructed the now-famous astronomical clock. It was probably placed initially in the area between the high altar and the Gustavian crypt.[20] The Strassburg clock was begun by Konrad Dasypodius, Professor of Mathematics, and was completed sometime in 1572 or 1574 by two brothers of the Habrecht family who came from Schaffhausen.[21] Polhem's error came about because he confused Petrus, the Vadstena monk, with Dasypodius, the Strassburg professor. Petrus Astronomus' clock was destroyed in the great fire of 1702, which demolished a great part of Uppsala. In 1710, while working at Stjernsund, Polhem made a new clock for the Uppsala Cathedral. In terms of the payment for this work, a "misunderstanding" arose. Many years later, Polhem asked his son-in-law, Ludwig Manderström, to inquire at the cathedral in Uppsala to determine how much was still due him in payment for his work.[22]

II. POLHEM'S FIRST INVENTION,
HIS MARRIAGE, AND FAMILY

Polhem's student days in Uppsala did not last long. He probably left the University in 1690[23] and settled in Stockholm where he began to construct a machine which would take ore out of a mine. A few months later a model of the machine was completed. It was nine alnar long and it required ten men to carry it to the King's castle. Karl XI studied it for a period of three hours with "great appreciation" for the work Polhem had done. It was subsequently given to the Bureau of Mines. Polhem's machine had many advantages over the machines which had been used previously. Furthermore, it was very simple in its construction. He had built the machine in such a way that it would take the ore from the working area in the mine to the shaft, then up

[20] Silfverstolpe, *Klosterfolket i Vadstena*, 1898, p. 153. (Skrifter och handlingar utg. genom Svenska autografsällskapet. 4.)

[21] Blumhof, *Vom alten Mathematiker Conrad Dasypodius*, 1796.

[22] Fredrik Alstrin to Polhem, Feb. 8, 1714. Manderström to Polhem, Feb. 1730. *Biographi P.* (KB).

[23] Polhem said upon one occasion that he was called by the Bergskollegium (Bureau of Mines) in 1689 to demonstrate his knowledge of mine engineering.

the shaft to the surface, to the furnace, where the barrels of ore were emptied. The barrels which carried the ore had an opening in the bottom which permitted the ore to be deposited easily. The bottoms were then closed, and the barrels were returned to the working area. Instead of the leather ropes which were usually used to hoist the ore, and which were expensive and not dependable, Polhem substituted wooden rods. The whole operation was powered by water. The only expenditure of human energy was in filling the barrels.[24]

As a reward for Polhem's "invention," the Bureau of Mines gave him a scholarship, the funds of which were to be used for study and travel within the country. During the summer of 1691, Polhem and Samuel Buschenfelt visited the most important mines in the mountain district of Sweden, "in order," as he wrote, "to gain knowledge and experience of everything pertaining to mining."[25] Just before his trip began, Karl xi gave him three hundred silver daler from funds held by the Bureau of Mines. At the same time, he directed that Polhem was to receive a yearly "allowance," or wage, of five hundred silver daler. These privileges were granted "because," as it was stated, "Polhem is a native Swede who has acquired great knowledge of mathematics and mechanics, who is gifted with an inventive and quick mind, who has discovered many useful things, and who will in time serve his country well. However, he will only be able to continue his promising work if he receives some support."[26] Polhem now believed that his financial problems were at an end, and that it was possible to get married. So on December 28, 1691, he married Maria Hoffman. The wedding took place on the Riksten estate in the parish of Botkyrka (an estate which was once owned by Eric Fleming). Polhem's bride was the daughter of a German architect who had come to Sweden. After the death of her father, Maria was brought up in the "Fleming House in Fållnäs."[27] L. Giöthe, a close friend of the bridal couple, composed a Wedding Song in the style of the time, entitled "Den Lilla Astrills Strek är Liufste Juhle-lek."[28]

[24] Polhem, *op. cit.*, pp. 10–14. "Promemoria vid Polhems personalier." *Biographi P*. (KB). Polhem, "Ett ödmjukt memorial, hvartill undertecknad blifvit brukad." Copy. *Teknologi*. (KB).

[25] Polhem and Buschenfelt to Bergskollegium, June 23, 1691. *Bref. till b:koll*. Passport for Polhem and Buschenfelt, June 23, 1691. *B:kolls registratur*. (RA).

[26] Karl xi to Bergskollegium, May 6, 1691 and to Statskontoret. *Riksregistraturet*. (RA).

[27] "Promemoria vid Polhems personalier." *Biographi P*. (KB). Cf. Carlen, *Polhem och hans verk*. in *Svea.*, Årg. 12(1856), pp. 154–155, where it mentions the fact that Polhem met Maria Hoffman in Vansta, where she was a maid.

[28] The poet Torsten Rudeen (who was later bishop in Linköping), wrote a poem to "det vackra och hedervärda brudparet," the last line of which went ". . . säng med tredje hjon är ökt, när månan tio hvarf sitt silfverhorn har krökt."

Han war ey sehn till wägz/ tog till sin Staf och Wingar/
Igenom Lufften fort sig nehr till Venus swingar/
   Begiärte at han straxt en af sitt Tärne-Tahl
   Tilskicka wille den/ som brann af Alskogs Owahl.
Ohet myste Venus äth/ såg på sin Nymphe-Skara/
Och frågad': hwem har Lust en Maka 'sig at para?
   Då steg en Jungfru up af swettigt/ blygsamt Sinn/
   From/ Ährbar/ dygdig/ kysk; det wiste hennes Miin/
Ty hon så sedig gick när Systrarn' henne ledde
Fram till den brede Steen; der hon sin Wän sig tedde/
   Och räckte Handen uth/ emot sin Kiärstes Hand/
   Då Hymen war till redz bandt stadigt Kiärleks-Band.
Så wart ett lika Par i lycklig Stund hoop bundne/
Jag önskar de mång Åhr tilsammans lefwa kunde
   J Sämia/ Kiärlek/ Friid/ i Frögd/ i Angla-Ro/
   Och se mång fager Owist uthaf sitt Läger gro. ²

5. *From Giöthe,* Den Lilla Astrills Strek är Liufste Juhle-lek, *the song composed for Polhem's wedding*

Ten children were born to Christopher and Maria Polhem, five sons and five daughters. Only one son and four daughters survived the father, however. The mother died in 1735 in Stockholm, where she had gone for her daughter's wedding. The oldest son, Christopher, who had inherited his father's aptitude for mathematics and mechanics, died in 1708 in Leipzig.[29] The youngest son, Gabriel, born in 1700 in Falun, was able to complete many of his father's mechanical experiments. During Polhem's last years he was his father's representative. Gabriel also accepted engineering assignments himself. A primary example of this was his plan for the Trollhättan Canal; another, his design for a mint in Kassel. He completed a canal lock for the city of Stockholm after his father's death, using his father's plans. However, in spite of all this, he seemed to have been only "his father's son." He became a member of the Royal Swedish Academy of Science in 1739 and received the honorary titles of noble and chamberlain. He never married. His death was recorded in Stockholm on August 1, 1772, and marked the end of the Polhem nobility.

[29] Anrep, *Svenska adelns ättartaflor*, 3, p. 217. According to "Promemoria vid Polhems personalier" it was the following year.

17

6. *Christopher Polhem, painting, Klosterverken, Långshyttan*

The oldest daughter, Maria, was born in 1698 and married Martin Ludwig Manderström who was "Counsellor of War" at that time. It was their great-grandson, Baron Carl Adolf Manderström, who, in 1878, gave the Polhem manuscripts to the Royal Library. Unfortunately, many of them had been destroyed in the Stjernsund fire of 1737. The second oldest daughter, Emerentia, born in 1703, was a romantic who was also a gifted poetess. She married Reinhold Rüdker, a district judge, who was made a noble in 1751. The family name was then changed to Rückersköld. It was Emerentia who at one time had been engaged to Emanuel Swedenborg. A story is told of their relationship which cannot now, of course, be verified.[30] However, as the story goes, Polhem and Swedenborg were working together on the Karlsgraf Canal, and Swedenborg was introduced to the beautiful Emerentia. He immediately fell in love with her, but it seems that she did not return his love. Polhem was very much impressed with Swedenborg and promised to persuade Emerentia to marry him. A marriage contract was drawn up which Emerentia had to sign. This caused so much grief in the family that Gabriel Polhem finally stole the contract from Swedenborg. When Swedenborg told Polhem about all of this, the elder Polhem wanted to renew the contract. However, out of consideration for Emerentia, Swedenborg refused to carry the matter any further. He left the Polhem home resolved never to think of a woman again, and certainly never to marry one. As an old man, Swedenborg assured the Rückersköld children that he could converse at any time with their deceased mother.

The second youngest daughter, Hedvig, was born in 1705 in Stjernsund. She married Carl Gripenstierna, who was a "forest superintendent." The youngest daughter, Elisabet, born in 1707, married Nils Stuwe, who became finance minister, and subsequently was elevated to the rank of noble with the name of Sandelhjelm. When Elisabet died in 1787, the last member of the Polhem family who was related to nobility also died.

Not too much more is known of the Polhem family. Christopher Polhem's oldest brother, Jonas, born in 1664, was a prominent landowner in Falköping. However, it is not known whether he left any descendants. Another brother, Johan (who was born in 1666 and died in 1749), was a farmer on the island of Gotland. He married Elisabeth Andersdotter Dominick, and two of their sons, Christopher and Johan, settled on Gotland. Their children did not retain the family

[30] Documents concerning the life and character of Emanuel Swedenborg by R. L. Tafel, 1(1875) pp. 50–51.

7. *Maria Hoffman, painting, Klosterverken, Långshyttan; photo SPA*

name, but added "son" to Polhem.[31] Polhem's brother Johan had two other sons, Lars and Anders. Nothing is known of Lars, but it is known that Anders became the director of the iron mill in Stjernsund. His wife, Anna Katharina Wiens, gave birth to ten children, all of whom took the name of Polheimer.

The first practical work which Polhem undertook was not success-

[31] See Nyberg, *Gotländsk släktbok*, 1911, pp. 464–468.

ful. In the autumn of 1691, he received an assignment from the Bureau of Mines to go to Hällestad (in Östergotland) to construct a water pump which would bring water out of the iron ore mine there. In the past, this operation had always necessitated a great number of people who "scooped, carried, pumped, and heaved the water" all by hand. A preliminary contract was drawn up in Finspång on December 14, 1691 with the owners of the iron mill, Louis de Geer and P. Rosen-stråle. The contract was confirmed by the mining authorities of Hällestad and Vånga, and Gustaf Danckwardt, who represented the mines. According to the contract, Polhem, aided by eight or nine "good" carpenters whom Danckwardt himself would pay, would complete the pumping machine in five or six weeks. Polhem was to receive three silver daler a day for his work, as well as his travel expenses. Half of this sum would be paid immediately, the other half when the machine was finished. The materials needed for the job were to be provided by the mining officials.

Late in the autumn of 1691, Polhem arrived in Hällestad with Knut Drefling, the director of mines for Södermanland. Polhem's description of the mine and the life about the mine (which Polhem included in a report to the Bureau of Mines in 1692) is an extremely interesting sketch of the culture and history of the period. However, Polhem's report did not tell the whole story. It appeared that Polhem had difficulty with the men he was working with. "As far as men are concerned," he wrote in one place, "there seemed to be the assumption everywhere that there was no God or government to fear. They quarreled and swore while working in the mine, and did so so vehemently that at times it would appear that the mountains were going to split in two. There was no order or system to their work. All they did was quarrel and swear: who is going to go down into the mine?; who shall remain on top?; who shall do that and that? They respected their boss as much as they did an old dog; what is more, he very often got drunk and went around in a crazy way. He deserved to be blamed as much as the miners. No one was in charge of the work here; everyone was his own boss. On Sunday they loitered about the church, and were everywhere, drinking, making a lot of noise, and as usual, swearing and disturbing everyone. At night they paraded about shouting like a swarm of evil spirits. The mine was in danger of filling up with water. The men fought with each other and tried to get more freedom, which they should not have. They were so jealous of one another and hated each other so much that before they could have helped anyone, they would have twice harmed themselves. They were the most quarrelsome, hateful, irritating, and offensive people that one could find. Nonetheless, there were a few honest and sober men, but they were so few, that they did not have any influence whatsoever."[32]

The work had begun early in the spring, but was never finished. The reason for this is difficult to ascertain, but it seemed that Polhem did not fulfill the obligations of the contract. In October of 1693, the owners of the mine took their grievances to the Bureau of Mines. From the minutes of the meetings of the mine owners, we learn that the project cost twice as much as Polhem had estimated, even though the materials he needed were always available. Furthermore, it was reported that the water pump, which had been tried seven times, never worked properly. It was charged that Polhem had demanded his pay before the work was completed, and, contrary to the directive from the Bureau of Mines, had left Hällestad and permitted his assistant, Silker, to do the same. Polhem had not, so said the mine owners, fulfilled the obligations of his contract. Polhem defended his actions by saying that he had not received good materials, that he was hindered by the workmen, who, among other things, put stones in the machine, which of course broke it. All of this happened, Polhem said, because the workers feared that they would lose their jobs if his machine was installed in the mine. Polhem believed that his pump would be able to do a great deal of work much more efficiently than a whole group of men and horses. His chief complaint was that he had not been paid adequately. This was the primary reason for the controversy, he believed.[33] Polhem was extremely frugal, and many times became involved in a hassle over what was adequate payment for his work. In reality, however, many times the controversy was caused by a confusion in the terms of the contract itself.

The Bureau of Mines called Polhem and asked him to explain the reasons for these complaints. Polhem rather vigorously rejected the claim of the Bureau to question him on this matter. He was instructed by the Bureau of Mines "to use milder language in the future when criticizing the mining profession." It was a long drawn-out affair, and the Bureau finally considered the matter of no great consequence, and

[32] Polhem to Bergskollegium, Hällestad, July 27, 1692. Bref till b:koll. (RA).

[33] Bergskollegium to Polhem, Sept. 27, 1692. *B:kolls registratur.* Bergslagsmännen to b:koll. Oct. 6, 1693, with a contract, protokoll, as supplementary. Polhem to b:koll., Stockholm, Aug. 15, 1692; Norrköping, Sept. 19, 1692; Oct. 25, 1692; May 18, 1693. *Bref till b:koll.* Bergskollegiums protokoll, April 1, May 18, Oct. 27, 1693. (RA). The above account deviates from what Polhem reported thirty-seven years later. Polhem's "Kort berättelse om de förnämsta mechaniska inventioner" is, as he says, an *apologia* "to show my innocence."

refused to take up good time listening to the "lamentations" of the miners. Then in October of 1700, Polhem was instructed to settle his legal problems.[34] A formal lawsuit was drawn up by the mine owners, with the result that Polhem was found guilty of the charge that he had failed to live up to the obligations of the contract. The Bureau of Mines felt that they too had to dispose of the case, and they did so quickly, adjudging him not guilty.

With good reason, Polhem feared that his "reputation suffered because of the Hällestad fiasco." However, he had good friends at the Bureau of Mines who stood by him. Assessor Peter Cronström, Assessor Harald Lybecker (who was also director of the Stora Kopparberg mine), as well as the president of the Bureau of Mines, Fabian Wrede, were his solid supporters. The matter seemed to be resolved in February of 1692, and Polhem was commissioned soon after by the Bureau to demonstrate his improved water-pumping device at the Blankstöten shaft in the Falun mine. After he had shown the advantages of this new pump and the new techniques he had developed for the whole mining industry, the Bureau decided that he was to have a horse during his employment in Falun. In addition, he was to receive one silver daler a day because, as they said, Falun was "a very expensive place in which to live." At the same time, however, a building contractor who accompanied him from Stockholm received six silver öre a day.[35]

Polhem had his problems at the Stora Kopparberg mine too. Olof Henriksson Trygg, the mining "engineer," opposed Polhem in every possible way. He refused to allow Polhem's machine to be used. Trygg was, of course, a representative of the old school which advocated manual labor for the operations of the mine. Polhem, on the other hand, wanted to improve the situation of the mine and the workers by constructing machines to do the burdensome work. There would be no rest until a contest was devised between the two men and their respective methods. This took place in the summer of 1694 in the presence of Assessor Lybecker, who described the event. "The public," he wrote, "could judge for itself from this contest which method was better." Lybecker continued, "The hoisting devices were set up in identical fashion. They both began with the same amount of water, and their

[34] Bergskollegiums protokoll, Oct. 27, 1693, Oct. 6, 16, and 24, 1694, Dec. 11, 1697, Nov. 7, 1706. B:koll to Polhem, Oct. 1, 1700. *B:kolls registratur.* (RA).

[35] Bergskollegium to Polhem, Feb. 20 and Sept. 14, 1692. *B:kolls registratur.* Bergskollegium protokoll, May 18 and 26, June 1 and 13, and July 5, 1693. B:koll to K. Maj:t June 1, 1693. *B:kolls skrifvelser.* K. Maj:t to b:koll., June 8, 1693. *K. Maj:ts skrifvelser.* (RA).

One silver daler equals 32 silver öre, and 1 silver daler equals 3 copper daler.

23

carriers were also of equal size. Polhem's machine took up twenty-two barrels of ore in an hour. Trygg, at the same time, with the traditional techniques, was only able to bring sixteen to the surface." Lybecker related that Trygg could have gotten one more to the surface if his machine had not broken down a number of times. A few days later, Lybecker asked Polhem to demonstrate his machine again. Operating it for three hours in the morning and two hours in the afternoon, he was able to bring one hundred and fourteen barrels of earth and granite to the surface. Polhem accomplished this, "without rushing or forcing the machine, and at the same time adding three barrels to the total number, which did not make the slightest difference in the speed of the operation of the machine." "If it had gone any slower," Polhem asked, "what would be its practicality and usefulness?"[36]

During his work at the mine, Polhem had time to "invent" several other extremely useful things. He replaced the leather lines which had been used in the hoisting operation with wooden rods, which greatly facilitated the work. Lybecker asked Polhem to demonstrate this several times during the period between July 20 and August 1 of that same year. Polhem was able to show that his machine did "function properly" and did not need to be repaired, whereas the device which had been used before had to be reinforced with new leather at least three times during its operation.[37] Polhem also made a new kind of sawing machine which he offered, for a reasonable price, to the "wood-mill in Falun." The sawmill was constructed in such a way that it could be driven by water power from a dam in the Dal River. With Polhem's sawmill, the wood could be cut much more economically. Polhem also conceived of a system of waterways which ships could use during the entire year as they traveled between cities.[38] There were other things as well – a boring or drilling machine which could be used to drill the barrel of the pump, a device to be used for blasting, and, in addition, the design for a kind of "grasping" tool.[39] In the spring of 1694, he traveled to Dannemora as a member of a commission, which included Assessor Peter Cronström and Assessor Robert Kinninmundt, to determine what could be done to make the mine there cleaner and safer.[40]

[36] Lybecker to Bergskollegium, Stora Kopparberget, Aug. 4, 1694. *Bref till b:koll.* Bergskollegium to K. Maj:t, Aug. 23, 1694. *B:kolls skrifvelser.* (RA).

[37] Lybecker to Bergskollegium, Stora Kopparberget, Aug. 4, 1694, and Bergskollegiums of Aug. 23, 1694.

[38] Bergslagens earliest letter to Bergskollegium, June 21, 1694, including Polhem's promemoria. *Bref till b:koll.* (RA).

[39] Polhem's memorial, Feb. 1, 1694. *Bref till b:koll.* (RA).

[40] Bergskollegium to Polhem, Feb. 3, 1694. *B:kolls registratur.* (RA).

Fodinæ ærariæ Falunensis, quâ orientem spectat, delineatio

8. *The mine at Falun, at the end of the seventeenth century, with hoisting and pumping apparatus; from Suecia Antiqua et Hodierna*

III. POLHEM'S TRAVELS ABROAD (1694–1696 AND 1707); THE LABORATORIUM MECHANICUM

Before Polhem's hoisting apparatus in the Falun mine was given official sanction, the Bureau of Mines decided to give him a scholarship to travel abroad. Polhem first heard about this when he was asked to appear at the Bureau in January, 1694. After telling the officials the kind of work he was doing, he was asked a number of questions by President Wrede:

"The President: Do you know algebra? Where did you learn it?

Polhammar: I learned some algebra in Uppsala and some from reading.

The President: Do you have any more inventions or are you speculating on anything at present?

Polhammar: Yes.

The President: Do you have a desire to travel?

Polhammar: Yes."[41]

The result of this brief and direct conversation was that the Bureau of Mines, with the aid of Karl XI, promised Polhem three hundred silver daler a year for a three-year period, plus his "annual allowance" of five hundred silver daler (which Polhem had received since 1691) for travel expenses.[42] Buschenfelt received a similar amount of money to accompany Polhem. During the summer of 1696 these figures were increased by one hundred silver daler.[43]

However, it was not until the autumn of the year that the trip took place. Karl XI made out the passport for Polhem. The passport read: "Noster Christophorus Polhammar studio bonarum artium, praesertim in iis, qua rem metallicam spectant." Approximately one month later the rector of Uppsala University issued the aforementioned *testimonium academicum*.[44] Rather than give Polhem and Buschenfelt travel plans, they were called to the Bureau of Mines where they received the necessary information verbally.[45] They traveled to Germany and then Holland, "where many strange and curious machines could be seen." They remained in Holland longer than they had anticipated because their money ran out. The money which they were to receive from

[41] Bergskollegiums protokoll, Jan. 27, 1694. (RA). The discussion contained here used the original spelling of Polhem's name.

[42] Bergskollegiums protokoll, Feb. 27, 1694. K. Maj:ts letter to b:koll, March 2, 1694. *K. Maj:ts skrifvelser*. (RA).

[43] Bergskollegiums protokoll, June 15, 1696. (RA).

[44] Both are in the original.

[45] Bergskollegium protokoll, Sept. 19, 1694. (RA).

9. *Fabian Wrede, painting by David Klöcker, Gripsholm; photo SPA*

Stockholm had not come as expected. A good friend from Stockholm was kind to them and lent them money to travel from Holland to England. While traveling from London to Oxford, Polhem met a businessman who, after a lengthy conversation, made him an extremely attractive offer. He wanted Polhem to supervise the construction of a brass factory. Before Polhem could even consider the offer, it was necessary for him to write and ask permission of the Bureau of Mines. It appeared that the Bureau did not think favorably of the offer.

In Oxford, Polhem became acquainted with John Wallis, who was professor of mathematics and geometry and one of the founders of the English Royal Society. It is difficult to know the extent of Wallis' influence upon Polhem. We do know that Polhem studied his mathematical theories. He learned of the latest methods for the construction of a pendulum clock. He also came to know Christian Huygen and his mathematical theories. Polhem wrote to Eric Benzelius while in Oxford and told him of his experiences there. Polhem, as before, was primarily interested in observing machines and their operation. He gained a great deal of "firsthand" experience in England simply by watching how the British did things. However, he wrote in his travel résumé that "unfortunately, because I was always poor, I did not receive the answers to the important philosophical problems nor the keys to the secrets of the arts from the learned men and masters of the trades whom I met." In spite of this, he acquired "a great deal of knowledge of the physical sciences and mechanics, which could lead to all kinds of inventions." In the travel résumé, he listed all of the machines, the water power mills, and the factories that he had seen. There were sawmills, mills which were used for drilling and polishing and for other functions, mills which produced oil and paper and cement and paint and gypsum; mills which could serve as forges; windmills for flour, grain, tobacco, mustard, and other things; "various kinds of saws for different kinds of materials; machines to make needles and thimbles; factories which wove cloth, velvet, ribbons, needle point, lace, stockings; as well as barges, canals, canal locks, drawbridges, dams; pile drivers and dredging machines; loading and building cranes; glass and mirror manufacturing; astronomical clocks and dials; musical clocks and chimes; mathematical, astronomical and mechanical instruments of every imaginable kind." "There were also many strange items, which," as Polhem related, "I could not describe." Polhem looked at all of these things "with great interest," but did not make any drawings or sketches of them. He did not have to do this, because when he saw a machine once, he could construct one, regardless of how complicated it was.

Polhem remained in England throughout the summer of 1695. He returned to Holland in the middle of September and wrote to the Bureau of Mines from Leyden for money because, as he said, "we live on credit here most of the time, but this does not make any sense because it costs so much more to live that way." Polhem used the time in Holland to devise a number of machines, which he believed he could put together later. The first was a machine he believed could be used in the war, which was inspired by the conflict between Ludwig XIV and the armies of the Grand Alliance. It was a machine which Polhem felt could be used to weaken severely an attacking army. With a few men and horses, thousands of stones could be cast from inside of a fort which could "kill the enemy that was approaching and storming the fortress." From this description, Polhem's war machine was undoubtedly some kind of catapult or ballista. His other ideas consisted of a "shock-proof" fort, as well as an "apparatus to be used on ships, so that one could quickly overcome pirates if they wanted to board your ship." Polhem never mentioned these elsewhere, so we do not know what they were, and it is possible that Polhem never tried to build them.

From Holland he traveled to Belgium and France. While in France, he visited Paris. His stay there was very brief, although, as was reported later, he did remain long enough to build a very complicated clock. This same clock was reduplicated by a Parisian clockmaker who presented it to the Turkish Sultan. A description of the clock was supposed to have been printed, but "so few copies were made that Swedish travelers could only get a written copy to take home." Polhem related this incident himself, and went on to say that the reason his work became known was because the Swedish ambassador in Paris, Daniel Cronström, insisted that his name be included on the description of the clock, as the creator of the clock, which would add "to the honor of the Swedish nation."[46] Polhem's claim to fame has never been supported by history, because it is known definitely that Cronström did not become ambassador in Paris before the year 1702. Polhem's reference to Cronström can be considered the result of a bad memory or a confusion of Cronström with Johan Palmquist, who was then the secretary of the Swedish delegation to the French Court. Palmquist's dispatches, however, as far as we are able to tell, said nothing of the sensation Polhem created among the learned of Paris. Perhaps, Polhem admitted later, his presence in Paris was not so noteworthy after all.

[46] Polhem, *op. cit.,* pp. 14–16.

Early in 1696, Polhem and Buschenfelt left Paris and traveled to Strassburg. They then decided to go on to Leipzig after their plans for a trip to Italy and Hungary had to be canceled because of a lack of funds. The war was raging at that time, and travel was unsafe, with the result that Polhem and his companion were forced to take a detour through Basel, Aarau, Schaffhausen, Ulm, Augsburg, and Nürnberg, before they came to Leipzig. Buschenfelt became ill soon after, and Polhem continued to Freiburg and Dresden alone. He wanted to visit Dresden because of the "great exhibition" which was located there. The journey back to Sweden was completed in the autumn of 1696.[47]

Polhem undoubtedly got ideas for some of his machines and "inventions" from what he had seen in other countries. It is impossible, however, to say for certain what were strictly his own, and which were copies of foreign models. Polhem said, in reference to a number of his machines, that they originated from his studies and experiences abroad.

In the report he gave to the Bureau of Mines, he proposed that a mechanical laboratory be established in Stockholm, which was to be used to construct and demonstrate "all kinds of machines and technical apparatus." Polhem was motivated by a desire to aid "many talented people who have the ability to speculate upon and to discover all sorts of things, but whose talents are hidden. . . . Mechanics is, after all, the foundation for philosophical speculation and should be given a chance to be *explored*." In addition to this purpose, Polhem maintained, machines could be built which eventually could be used by the government and by private persons. Furthermore, the king and "other high officials" would be pleased to see the valuable work which was going on in the mechanical laboratory. The eight or ten people who would be employed there, Polhem suggested, would always be available "to supervise similar institutions." Ultimately, Polhem believed that the mechanical laboratory would aid "foreigners, who had a poor conception of what the Swedish nation was capable of, and they would be able to see that a great deal had been done without outside assistance and instruction."

Polhem outlined a work program for the laboratory. He believed that it would serve as the best place to display his many machines which, as he said, could be used for "manufacturing, in war, as well

[47] *Ibid*. Polhem to Bergskollegium, Leyden, Sept. 17, 1695. Buschenfelt to Bergskollegium, Freiburg, May 21, 1696. *Bref till b:koll*. Bergskollegiums protokoll, Sept. 30, 1695, April 23, and June 15, 1696. (RA). Polhem to Bergskollegium, Oct. 26, 1696. Travel report. Copy, Jac. Troilius in a collection. *Teknologi* (KB).

as for mining." Every type of "experimental instrument in the area of physics and mechanics would be tested, such as air and water pumps," as well as instruments which could discover "the *gradus motus* of fire, water, and air." "Unusual technical instruments, astronomical clocks, globes, chimes, amusements for gardens and parks, and other things, could be developed," he continued. The laboratory could serve as a school on the one hand, and as an experimental center on the other, where theoretical and practical problems could be examined. At the same time, it could be a permanent exhibit for Polhem's own inventions. Polhem's idea was accepted immediately by the authorities. On April 20, 1697, upon recommendation of the Bureau of Mines, the Regency gave Polhem permission to establish a *laboratorium mechanicum*. From a special fund, the Bureau of Mines gave Polhem a sum of fifteen hundred silver daler annually for its support. Polhem was to receive three hundred silver daler of this as director. Three hundred would go to a skilful carpenter "who could work from a blue-print according to scale"; one hundred to his apprentice; three hundred to a blacksmith; and one hundred to his apprentice. Four hundred silver daler were held in reserve for tools and materials, for "wood, nails, glue, iron, steel, brass, lead, tin, solder, borax, charcoal, candles, as well as for any work which had to be done by others." The *laboratorium mechanicum* was to be housed in the Gripenhielm House on Kungsholm, for which purpose the government purchased it in 1694.[48]

Polhem's great plans were never fully realized. One of the reasons for this is that Polhem became extremely busy with a number of mining projects and with his manufacturing plant at Stjernsund. Polhem worked it all out, however, by making an agreement with Buschenfelt (who was "a competent blacksmith as well as a carpenter") that Buschenfelt, in his spare time, would do the work in the laboratory which Polhem wanted done. The Bureau of Mines agreed to this arrangement and granted Buschenfelt four hundred silver daler for his work. Buschenfelt was to concentrate on theoretical experimental work at first, and if this appeared to be of value, then to deal with its practical aspects. Neither a school nor an experimental laboratory was developed, however, and after Buschenfelt's death in 1706, the entire program died. Again, financial problems contributed to the demise of the laboratory. Polhem, however, developed a *laboratorium mechanicum* in Falun and did a great deal of work there, although even this did not continue for more than a few years. He sent a number of machines

[48] K. Maj:t to Bergskollegium, April 20, 1697. *Riksregistraturet.* (RA). Almquist, *Bergskollegium och bergslagsstaterna 1637–1857*, (1909), pp. 40, 48.

10. *The Gripenhielm house on Kungsholm, in which Polhem's* laboratorium mechani-cum *was located*

which he had built to Stockholm in 1704.[49] It was reported that by the year 1713, Polhem had established a substantial laboratory in Falun, which contained a great many of his tools and machines.[50] At about this time Polhem was called by Karl XII to come to Bender.[51] He was anxious that the original *laboratorium mechanicum* be established and directed funds to be used for this purpose. Furthermore, he wanted Polhem to receive a salary so that he could finish a number of machines he had been working on. For the position of assistant in the laboratory, Polhem suggested the name of Olof Telott who, was as he said, "an accomplished clockmaker, a master draftsman, and a carver." The laboratory was to be located at Stjernsund. As no records have ever been found of a *laboratorium mechanicum* at Stjernsund, it may be presupposed that one never came into existence. Probably the war at that time used all of the available capital. However, long after the death of Karl XII, an item remained in the budget for a *laboratorium mechanicum*. It is known that Polhem did receive some financial support for his work from the Bureau of Mines.[52]

In 1737 Polhem asked the government to support his experiments in the area of agriculture. An allowance was granted in 1739, the money coming from a "Manufacturers' Fund," to be used for "the construction of useful machines." Two carpenters and a blacksmith were hired and one hundred silver daler were provided for the purchase of the necessary materials. Polhem, in his request to the government, asked for permission to board with his relatives, where he felt he would receive the "best care." He could watch the workers better in this way too, he believed.[53] Permission was granted and he lived with his son-in-law, Carl Gripenstierna on the Kersö Estate on Ekerön. It is possible that Polhem established the *laboratorium mechanicum* there. However, it may have been brought back to Stockholm when Polhem returned there sometime in 1746 or 1747. The Parliament had decided at that time that Polhem should receive a financial grant for the work he was doing.[54] Models of his machines were placed in

[49] Polhem to Bergskollegium, June 16, 1700. *Bref till b:koll.* Bergskollegium to Polhem, Sept. 4, 1700. *B:kolls registratur.* Bergskollegiums protokoll, Feb. 28, 1703, Nov. 15, 1704. (RA).

[50] Bergskollegium to Bergskommissarien Peter Christiernin, April 13, 1713. Copy. *Biographi P.* (KB).

[51] See Chapter 4.

[52] Feif to Polhem, Feb. 9, 1712. Bergskollegium to Polhem, Dec. 20, 1712, April 13, 1713. *Biografi P.* (KB). Bergskollegiums protokoll, Jan. 12, 1713. K. Maj:t to Bergskollegium, Oct. 13, 1747. *Registratur i inrikes civila ärenden.* (RA).

[53] K. Maj:t to kammar-, bergs-, kommerskollegium and statskontoret, Nov. 14, 1738. *Reg. i inrikes civila ärenden.* Sekreta utskottets protokoll, April 4, 1739. (RA).

[54] K. Maj:t to Bergskollegium, Oct. 13, 1747. *Reg. i inrikes civila ärenden.* (RA).

11. *Olof Rudbeck (1630–1702), who was Polhem's teacher, and who was a pioneer in the development of Swedish technology during the seventeenth century. Engraving 1679*

the Royal Palace in 1748, and after a time were moved to the old royal house on Riddarholm.

The *laboratorium mechanicum* was reorganized in 1756 under the direction of Polhem's son, Gabriel. In 1761 he wrote that there were twenty-nine models of machines in the Royal Model Chamber which had been built in the *laboratorium mechanicum* "at different times."[55] In 1779 Jonas Norberg, who was director of the Royal Museum, published "An Inventory of the Machines and Models in the Royal Model Chamber in Stockholm." He listed fifty-five of Polhem's machines and three others which Polhem had improved upon. There was also a "mechanical alphabet" made up of eighty different pieces which represented all of the well-known mechanical motions. When a School of Mechanics was established in association with the Royal Artists' and Sculptors' Academy, Polhem's machines were brought to the Academy's attention. In 1813, the Academy of Agriculture became responsible for them, and they were displayed to the general public. When the Institute of Technology (Tekniska Högskolan)[56] was founded in 1826 the machines came under its jurisdiction. Today, the machines are handsomely displayed in the modern Tekniska Museet in Stockholm, located in a special Christopher Polhem wing of the building. The Tekniska Museet, too, has undertaken the task of determining which machines and models are authentically Polhem's. Contemporary interest in Christopher Polhem is initiated directly by the Tekniska Museet and its director, Dr. Torsten Althin.

Polhem's use of the laboratory facilities which were available during his time set the stage for later generations and their experimental work. How strange, therefore, that the Bureau of Mines in December of 1712 insisted that the *laboratorium mechanicum* could not be used for "individual projects but only for public ones,"[57] which was, of course, a direct reference to Polhem and his work.

Polhem attracted students from everywhere. The scholarships which the government gave for advanced mechanical study were placed under his direction. Among those who received this scholarship were Gabriel Polhem, Göran Wallerius (who later became as-

[55] Klingenstierna, S., *Åminnelse-tal öfver Kongl. Vetensk. Academiens framledna ledamot, commerce-rådet och commendeuren af Kongl. Nordstjerne-orden, herr Christopher Polhem*, pp. 17–18 refers to model no. 51 in the museum as of particular significance and of great practical value. It was an experimental machine to determine the power of water as it turned a water-wheel. Many experiments were made and statistical tables were formulated which were to be used by building contractors.

[56] Polhem, *Patriotiska testamente*, pp. 121–124. Norberg, *Inventarium*, 1779. Almquist, *op. cit.*, p. 42. Ferlin, *Stockholms stad.*, 1858, pp. 1666–1668.

[57] Bergskollegiums protokoll, Dec. 17, 1712. (RA).

35

12. *Kongl. Modell Kammaren (The Royal Model Chamber) at the Tekniska Museet in Stockholm, which houses most of the extant Polhem machines and models*

sessor in the Bureau of Mines), Daniel Menlös (who became professor of mathematics in Lund), and Samuel Sohlberg. It was Sohlberg who planned the Trollhättan Canal, although it was Polhem himself who drew up the original plans and supervised much of its work.

The scholarships were in great demand among students. However, they were usually given to relatives of the first students, rather than on the basis of aptitude and scholarly promise. Polhem complained about this to the Bureau of Mines as well as to Karl XII.

At Stjernsund, Polhem often tutored individuals privately. Emanuel Swedenborg studied with Polhem in 1710, and several years later became his assistant. Daniel Thunberg was another student who became an important construction engineer, particularly of docks and canals. Thunberg also assisted in the planning and construction of the Trollhättan Canal. Carl Johan Cronstedt became interested in mechanics during a summer's stay at Stjernsund in 1729. He later wrote of his experiences with Polhem and described in great detail some of Polhem's mechanical discoveries.[58] Augustin Ehrensvärd was also indebted to Polhem for all that he had learned.[59]

When Polhem returned to Sweden from abroad, he was appointed "Director of the mechanical operations of the Mines and second in authority after the Director of the Mines." He received no increase in salary, however. Polhem retained this position until his death in 1751. Undoubtedly, the title of "Director of the mechanical operations of the Mines" was conceived to reward Polhem for his many accomplishments and to give him an "honored title and rank."[60]

Two years later, when Polhem's old adversary Olof Trygg died, he was offered his position. Polhem accepted, and on March 29, 1700, he became the "mining engineer" at the Stora Kopparberg mine. It was inevitable, of course, that Polhem's two jobs would conflict with one another. A complaint was made to the Bureau of Mines in 1702 that Polhem was never at Stora Kopparberg. Assessor Cronström told Polhem that he had taken on more than he could handle, and that his work was going to suffer as a result.[61] Nevertheless, Polhem main-

[58] Anrep, *Svenska adelns ättartaflor*, 1(1858), p. 500.

[59] Ehrensvärd to Polhem, Jan. 10, 1730. *Biografi P.* (KB). "Huru stor orsak jag har att taga del däraf (Polhems välbefinnande), därtill kan intet större öfvertygande skäl vara än den ömhet herr commercierådet behagat betyga vid den reele information, igenom hvilken jag skattar min fördel större än alla andra timmeliga förmåner. Och som jag fördenskull ej annat kan än förvara en slik af herr commercierådet ertedd ogemena gunst i ett oupplåteligt tacksamt minne, så skall ock min högsta omsorg vara, huru jag i själva verket må kunna visa, med hvad synnerlig vördnad och förpliktelse jag alltid lefver till herr commercierådets tjänst."

[60] Bergskollegiums fullmakt, Feb. 17, 1698. *Biografi P.* (KB). Almquist, *op. cit.*, p. 78.

[61] Bergskollegium protokoll, Sept. 25, 1702. (RA).

tained his two positions. But the complaints continued. He was neg-
lecting his work was the charge. The situation got so bad that in 1714
Polhem almost lost his appointment. The Bureau of Mines requested
that another man come who would be content to stay at Falun.[62] Karl
XII gave his permission soon after to give Polhem's position to another
man. Subsequently, Magnus Lundstrom was appointed. Polhem was
fully compensated, and was made, thereafter, "Chief Inspector at Stora
Kopparberg mine, Salberg mine, and at other mines."[63]

Polhem's annual salary at this time was about twelve hundred silver
daler. The assessors at the Bureau of Mines received the same amount.

Polhem's improvement of mining techniques (particularly during
the years of 1697 to 1706) attracted great attention outside of Sweden.
Elector Georg Ludvig of Hanover (later George I, King of England),
who owned the Oberharz silver and iron mine, asked Polhem to come
and help him. Polhem received permission from Karl XII and the
Bureau of Mines to go to Harz for a period of three months. His primary contribution to the Harz mine was in terms of suggestions as to
how the whole operation might be improved. The mining officials in
Klausthal and the mine director himself, Albert von dem Busch, also
sought his advice. They used a number of his machines in their mines
with great success. A letter was sent to Karl XII telling him how completely satisfied everyone was with Polhem's work.[64] Polhem was invited to return to Harz any time he could receive permission to do so.
A mining official, Henrik Hartwig Knorre, wrote to Albert von dem
Busch of Polhem and said: "Hr. Polhem is indeed a *habiler Mechanicus;* he understands both the theoretical and the practical aspects of
mechanics, and has a complete knowledge of the operation of every
machine." Johan Valentin Pfeffer, another mining official at Harz,
related an incident in which Polhem, as he demonstrated one of his
machines for raising ore, so astounded the crowd of people watching
that they could not believe what they saw. Polhem, in fact, contributed a great deal to the technical improvements of the Harz mining
industry.[65]

Polhem was assured that as payment for his work at the Harz mine,

[62] Bergskollegium protokoll, April 15 and Nov. 11, 1714; February 7, 1715. (RA).

[63] Karl XII to Bergskollegium, Jan. 20, 1716. *Inrikes registratur.* (RA).

[64] Georg Ludvig wrote: "Nun ist solches mit aller dexteritet und geschicklichkeit zu
unser sonderbahren satisfaction von ihm geschehen und hat er gar wahrscheinlich
gezeiget, dass ein und andere nützliche veränderungen an beregten künsten und machi-
nen gemachet werden können."

[65] Calvoer, *Historisch-chronologische Nachricht . . . des Maschinenwesens . . . auf.
dem Oberharze,* 1763: 1, pp. 111ff. 2, p. 66.

he would receive a proportion of the savings which resulted from the use of his machines. This payment was to continue for a five-year period. Furthermore, Polhem and his son were to receive patent rights on all of the inventions. As had happened before, however, Polhem soon became involved in a conflict over the terms of payment. It seemed that Polhem had promised to take two young German boys to Sweden, "to feed and board them," and to instruct them in theoretical and practical mechanics, as well as in machine construction. For doing this, Polhem was to be paid four hundred thaler. Before he left for Sweden, Polhem asked for the money which had been promised him for the use of his machines. He was not given the money because he had refused to enter into what appeared to be an unfair contract. He was afraid that he would have to take care of the two young Germans without any payment, and at the same time he did not believe that he was receiving proper financial reward for his machines. The mining officials in Harz had hoped, of course, that their men might take their apprenticeships with Polhem, and when they returned could build exactly the same machines and apparatus that Polhem had in the mines in Falun and elsewhere.

It is not known how the whole matter was straightened out, but it seemed to be to Polhem's complete satisfaction. In one of Polhem's letters which referred to this incident, he remarked, "I received substantial payment for my trip and for the education of the two people who have stayed with me for two and one half years." The two men who accompanied Polhem on his return to Sweden were Bernt Ripking and Kristian Schwarzkopf.[66] One of them concentrated on the theoretical aspects of mining, the other on the practical. They returned to Harz after their apprenticeship and put their knowledge to good use.[67] Two more young Germans followed shortly after, one with the name of Bähr, the other, Johan Carl Hansen. They, too, based upon what they had learned, demonstrated that Polhem was a master of mining "engineering." Albert von dem Busch recognized Polhem as a leader in his field and, as he said, a dispenser of "true knowledge." Hansen corresponded faithfully with Polhem and very often asked his advice on questions which arose. He suggested that

[66] Bernt Ripking later became a machine director, Kristian Schwarzkopf, a mine engineer.

[67] Bergskollegium to Polhem, May 7, 1707. George Ludvig's guarantee, Ellingen, Sept. 15, 1707. Polhem's correspondence with berghauptman A. von dem Busch och det kurfurstliga bergamtet Klausthal, Sept. 27, 1707. Copy. A. von dem Busch's report, Klausthal, Sept. 28, 1707. Georg Ludvig to Karl xii. Copy. Polhem's memorial, Braunschweig, Nov. 16, 1707. Notes. *Biografi P.* (KB). Polhem, *Patriotiska testamente*, pp. 20–22.

39

Polhem finish his "siphon machine."[68] It was completed in 1747 and delivered to Klausthal.[69]

King George asked Polhem to come and settle in England with his whole family. He would receive great honors, and be given "a beautiful estate near London, a generous salary, and profits from his inventions, for himself and his family." A similar proposition was made by the Russian Czar, Peter. But, because he "loved his country," he declined both offers.[70]

IV. POLHEM, KARL XII
AND THE WARS OF THE NORTH

When Polhem was at the height of his creativity, Sweden was involved in a number of tragic wars. Polhem had no sooner returned to Sweden when the young King Karl went forth to protect his country against her enemies. During his absence from Sweden, a Council ruled the country from Stockholm. Karl never neglected domestic affairs and was always in contact with the Council during the eighteen years of the war. The defense of the kingdom, quite naturally, however, kept him away from Sweden for long periods of time. The Council was limited in its power for it was only an executive body and functioned only to carry out the King's programs. Because of this confused political situation, Polhem's projects could not always get official government sanction, although he was at this time Director of Mine Machinery, and the "mining engineer" at the Falun Mine, as well as the director of the manufacturing plant at Stjernsund. In the autumn of 1700 he devised plans for a gunpowder factory in Forsa and a drilling mill in Norrtelje. He was instructed to go to the gunpowder factory in Jönköping, as well as to the factory in Söderhamn to determine how "they could be used in a more effective way in the nation's service."[71] Karl XII, who learned of Polhem's many talents, encouraged him in his work.

[68] A machine that did not have a wheel and yet could raise water from a mine.

[69] Von dem Busch to Polhem, Dec. 22, 1727. Hansen to Polhem, Stockholm, Sept. 5, 1727, Hanover, Nov. 28, Dec. 19, Dec. 31, 1727; Jan. 16, July 12, 1728; Jan. 31, April 21, Aug. 4, 1729. *Biografi P.* (KB). Calvoer, *op. cit.*, 1, pp. 136ff.

[70] "Promemoria vid Polhems personalia." *Biografi P.* (KB).

[71] Krigskollegium to Polhem, Nov. 2 and 15, 1700; June 18, 1702. *Biografi P.* (KB). Bergskollegium to Polhem, March 5, 1701. *B:kolls registratur.* (RA). In November of 1669, Krigskollegium had requested Polhem to give his attention to the completion of the pontoon. Munthe, *Kungl. Fortifikationens historia*, 3:2 (1910), p. 313.

13. *Carl Cronstedt, painting by Scheffel, Gripsholm; photo SPA*

In the fall of 1709, the Danes invaded Skåne. From Helsingborg, Magnus Stenbock was able to drive them out of Sweden. As a result, an army was located in the southern part of Sweden to protect it from enemy attack. Stenbock was responsible for assembling this army and getting it prepared for combat. He reorganized and introduced many technical improvements into the field artillery. These were then put into operation by Lieutenant Colonel Carl Cronstedt. With Polhem's help, Cronstedt built a device which could aim a cannon instantane-

41

ously, and which also had a high degree of accuracy. Prior to this time, everything had to be done by hand and usually with extremely poor results.[72] Cronstedt ordered twenty-eight of these new "adjusting screws" from Polhem, which were to cost about nine silver daler each. Polhem later felt that this price was much too low, for, as he said, "when one considers the careful work which the King requires, and the great responsibility I have, it is necessary that the costs be increased." He suggested to Cronstedt that he get them elsewhere, but promised in the meantime to make an even better device.[73]

Stenbock, who commanded the armies during the Polish campaign, had been able by this time to initiate a great many savings, particularly in reference to supplies. Nonetheless, he had a very difficult time getting food to his armies. The mills which produced the food were very heavy and difficult to transport, and often could not be brought to the front where the army was fighting. Polhem constructed a simplified type of mill which could be carried easily by the armies as they moved from place to place. Cronstedt was sent to Stjernsund in 1711 to confer with Polhem about the purchase of such a mill. In September of that year, Polhem's mill was finished and was brought to Stockholm to be shown to the Council there. Later it was used by the Army in Skåne.

Polhem's mill had a great many advantages over the previous ones: "Rye and malt could be ground quickly and without difficulty," so said Stenbock. It was pulled by a pair of horses and when in operation, only one horse and two men were needed. Six barrels of rye and twenty-four barrels of malt could be ground in a twenty-four hour period. It could also be used to grind grain. Stenbock wanted every regiment to have a grain mill and as well, a malt mill, for every five thousand men.

The importance of Polhem's mills was highlighted by the fact that Sweden was at that time preparing to defend her western seacoast. Stenbock wrote to the Council in February of 1712, "highly recommending Polhem, the great craftsman and technician who, however, because of his poverty cannot continue his work; which is a great pity because he is a man whose abilities cannot be duplicated anywhere." As a result, the Council, upon Stenbock's recommendation, ordered Cronstedt to go to Stjernsund to arrange with Polhem for the construction of a number of his mills. Polhem's salary as the Director of

[72] Annerstedt, *Fältmarskalken grefve Magnus Stenbock,* Minnesteckning, (1906), pp. 159–163.

[73] Polhem to Cronstedt, Stjernsund, Nov. 18, 1711 with Stenbock's letter to rådet, Jan. 4, 1712. *Skrifvelser till Karl XII från generaler.* (RA).

the Falun Mine was to be paid immediately, so that, as it was reported, "he would not, because of hunger and thirst, lose his desire to continue exercising his knowledgeable and inventive mind."[74] Polhem was encouraged, and wrote to Johan Wallerius in Uppsala:[75] "I have been spirited to work again. My lethargy has been overcome, and I am encouraged to continue my speculations. I could do a great deal more, of course, if some of the promised allotments came through from the *collegium curiosorum*."

Polhem had planned to construct the mills from steel and to have six grinding devices in each for malt and rye. Later he used only four, two to grind malt, and two to grind flour. For flour, "a much smaller opening, finer grooves, and a wider outlet" had to be used. Flour could not be mixed with malt. Additional parts had to be kept in reserve for possible repairs.[76]

This mill was to cost five hundred silver daler: two hundred and thirty-nine daler for the salary of the workers, one hundred and twenty for materials, one hundred and twelve for the commission, and the remaining twenty-nine for extras.[77]

In October of 1711 the *collegium curiosorum* in Uppsala (an association which encouraged the study of mathematics and physics) sent a letter of recommendation on Polhem's behalf to Casten Feif, who was responsible to Karl XII for the administration of the government. The letter complained that Polhem was not able to carry to completion his mathematical and mechanical projects, "which were based upon a great deal of experimentation, profound calculations, and ingenious reflection." It would be a crime, the letter continued, for "such a genius as Pohlhammar, whom we consider one of the most able minds that Swedish science has produced, not to be able to continue his research and experimentation because of the lack of funds." Polhem wrote a letter to Feif too, with a description of many of his inventions.[78]

In this way, Karl XII came to know of Polhem and his accomplish-

[74] Stenbock's pass for Cronstedt, Jan. 28, 1711, letter to Cronstedt, April 15, 1711; rådet's pass for Erik Wendell, Aug. 1, 1711; Stenbock's letter to rådet, Jan. 4 and Feb. 28, 1712; rådet's answer, Feb. 30, 1712; rådet's letter to statskontoret of the same day – all copies in the collection of rector Jakob Troilius in Husby. *Teknologi*. (KB).

[75] Stjernsund, April 19, 1712. *Codex Bf. 31*. Linköpings stiftsbibliotek. Letter to the president of Bergskollegium Spens. 1711. Notes. *Biografi P*. (KB).

[76] Polhem's discussion of this mill. Stjernsund, Sept. 7, 1711, in a copy of J. Troilius. *Teknologi*. (KB). Polhem to Benzelius, Dec. 16, 1711. Copy. *Codex Bf. 31*. Linköpings stiftsbibliotek.

[77] A. Heyke's calculations, on the basis of Lieut. Col. Cronstedt's estimated costs of the mill. Copy. *Teknologi*. (KB).

[78] Letter, Upsala, Oct. 5, 1711, copy. *Codex Bf. 31*. Linköpings stiftsbibliotek. This letter arrived in Bender on Feb. 8, 1712.

14. *Karl* XII, *pencil sketch from c.1700. Kungl. Biblioteket*

ments. Feif wrote to Nicodemus Tessin, another member of the Council[79] that "His Majesty had not known that he had such a man in his kingdom and regretted the fact that he had not used him to good advantage before." As a result, requests were made of the authorities and of individual persons to support Polhem's work. The Treasury was directed to contribute in a substantial manner to the construction of Polhem's machines. The Bureau of Mines was instructed to make a

[79] Feif to Tessin, Feb. 30, 1712. In: *Handlingar ur v. Brinkmanska archivet*, D. 1(1859), p. 146.

44

contract with Polhem (at his terms!) for the construction of the new hoisting machine at the Falun mine, and to grant specific privileges to the manufacturing plant at Stjernsund. Quite obviously, as a result, Polhem's financial situation improved.[80]

Feif also wrote a letter recommending Polhem and his work to almost everyone on the Council. As a result, Count Nils Stromberg, who was director of the Treasury and the Internal Revenue Bureau at that time supported him. Stromberg's letters told of his relationship to "the noble and highly-esteemed director." At the same time, however, Polhem felt that the president of the Board of Trade, Jakob Reenstierna, was opposed to him, but the reason for this is not known. Feif himself, upon a number of occasions, asked Polhem's advice about his "Dylta" sulphur works (located in Axberg's parish in Örebro). He wanted to know about Polhem's hoisting device and whether it could be used to bring sulphur to the surface. He also inquired regarding the oven which was used within the plant, and even about how sulphur could be refined. They talked about their experiences with workers and the best way to obtain good workers.[81] Polhem was having his problems at Stjernsund, but nonetheless visited Dylta to talk to Feif about his difficulties. It was reported that Feif asked Polhem to make a clock for the King. Had this order been effected immediately, there perhaps may have been indications of a growing Swedish industry at Bender. Of course, this possibility was destroyed during the Turkish campaign.

Feif sent Polhem a number of sketches of the unusual machines and apparatus he had seen. There was a Turkish oven, which was constructed in such a way that one did not have to light it every time one wanted to bake, but once it was lit, it would continue for as long as was desired. There was also a plan for the heating of "a large room with cement walls, by using many barrels of water and a small fire under a large copper plate." This technique, said Feif, "could be used at the sulphur works." Polhem also received a clipping from a Vienna newspaper which told of a number of new machines that were being built in Dresden.

The fact that the King was personally interested in him meant a great deal to Polhem. Feif wrote on February 9, 1712 that "His Majesty has been extremely gracious and has read, with great interest, Polhem's papers on his inventions. As a result, His Majesty has requested that I write to him, asking that he complete his machines as

[80] Karl XII to Bergskollegium, Feb. 9, 1712, to rådet, March 13, 1712. Copy. *Biografi P.* (KB).

[81] Cf. Gabriel Polhem, *Kort berättelse om mitt lefnadslopp. Biografi P.* (KB).

45

soon as possible." In another letter he wrote, "The Director's letters can never be too lengthy, because the King reads them with great interest." Karl XII was, of course, interested in Polhem's ideas about windmills, threshing mills, and pontoon bridges, because these could be used effectively in warfare. He gave orders that Polhem's "machines which could be used for military purposes, were to be built immediately." Karl's interest in Polhem was motivated also by his own mathematical and mechanical interests. Feif wrote to Polhem on March 5, 1712, and told Polhem that "His Majesty is supporting your work because of its scientific character, of which he himself has great knowledge. For my part, I shall attempt to convince everyone that science and the arts are respected in our country." In still another letter, this dated November 4, Feif wrote: "If Herr Director has the opportunity to speak to His Majesty about mechanics, he will find that he possesses a remarkable genius in regard to mechanical theories."

Karl XII made a few changes in Polhem's mills so that they could be better utilized by his armies. Feif asked Polhem questions about the mills: "What was one to do if the rollers in the mills did not grind the grain?; what happened if the mills generated heat too quickly?; could an apparatus be made to fire glass?; what about the 'barrel-faucets'?" Polhem offered a suggestion as to how a musket could be constructed, but exactly what this was is not known. He also had some kind of an instrument which could be fastened onto the musket to increase the accuracy of its aim. Feif wrote about this too in a letter dated November 4, 1712: "A musket with such an instrument attached was made by Polhem, and sent to His Majesty; but one must fasten the instrument securely so that it cannot come off." A few days later, Karl XII asked the War Department to test Polhem's apparatus. Feif was instructed to ask Polhem "how the musket would shoot when aimed; would it shoot over or under their line of attack?"[82] The situation in Bender and Karl's imprisonment in Demotika and Timurtasch put an end to the correspondence with Polhem. The correspondence was resumed, however, as soon as the King returned home. He asked Polhem to come to Stralsund and bring his inventions with him, "and relate any ideas he felt were important."[83] Polhem left Stjernsund immediately "with three horses," and traveled to Stockholm, and then to Karlskrona, where he arrived early in the spring. Because of con-

[82] Feif to Polhem, Bender, Feb. 9, March 5, March 21, Nov. 4, Dec. 13, 1712. *Biografi P.* (KB).

[83] Feif to Polhem, Stralsund, Dec. 20–31, 1714. Karl XII to Polhem, Jan. 29–Feb. 9, 1715. *Biografi P.* (KB).

46

trary winds, which lasted all summer, it was impossible for him to travel to Stralsund. Then when Karl XII was forced to go to Skåne in December of 1715, it was necessary for Polhem to return to Stjernsund.[84] This period in Polhem's life remains a mystery – it is strange that he did not attempt to visit the king when he was in Skåne.

Karl wrote soon after (January 27, 1716) from Ystad, and addressed the letter to "Our beloved and faithful servant and assessor, noble and honorable Polhammar." He requested that Polhem go to Karlskrona to see Hans Henric von Liewens, who was chief of the Admiralty. To demonstrate his faith in him, the King appointed Polhem a member of the Board of Trade, with the same salary as he had received prior to this appointment. Two years earlier, he had received the title of Assessor. Finally, on December 15, 1716, he was "made a Nobleman and received a coat of arms."

Polhem's work was already very well known in Karlskrona. In June of 1712, the Navy Department had asked him to advise them on the construction of a dam in the Lyckeby River, on the shores of which a number of industries had already been developed. The work on the dam had begun earlier, but because of the death of two of the engineers and the great mass of ice in the river, the project was almost abandoned. Polhem remained in Karlskrona as long as was necessary. However, he was asked to return to Karlskrona the following summer, or send someone else "who could finish the job," or "to make a detailed drawing of what had been done so that the workmen could complete it." Polhem felt that it was too late in the year to travel (and furthermore that it would cost too much!). The foundation had been constructed so perfectly, he said, that "a competent engineer could finish the work without anyone's help; furthermore, it seems best to do the construction in the usual way." He did send a drawing of the dam, and affirmed that "if they worked according to his specifications, no difficulty would result and the dam would last indefinitely."

The Navy Department asked Charles Sheldon, a shipbuilder of Karlskrona, to finish the work. He wrote to Polhem, referring many times to his plans and drawings for the dam, and asked for his "learned opinion" on several details of the work.[85] Sheldon usually receives credit for this work, although it was Polhem who planned the entire construction. A book, *The Sheldon Family in Sweden*,[86] refers to

[84] Polhem's travel account. Liewens attest, Sept. 3, 1729. *Biographica* (Polhem). (RA). His expenses were four hundred and sixty-eight silver daler and his fare eighty-two silver daler and twenty öre.

[85] Amiralitetskollegiet to Polhem, June 21, 1712, July 11, 1713. Sheldon to Polhem, Jan. 12, 1715. *Biografi P.* (KB).

[86] Sheldon, *Tal om Sheldonska ätten i Sverige,* 1757, p. 14.

47

Charles Sheldon as "the initiator and executor of the Lyckeby dam, advised by the learned Trade Counselor and Nobleman Christopher Polhem, who was present when the dam was first conceived." In Polhem's time, an attempt was made to credit Polhem with the construction of the dam.[87] Sheldon, in actuality, did nothing more than carry out Polhem's plans for the dam.

Polhem was asked by Admiral Carl Hans Wachtmeister to assist the Navy in building a dock on the Island of Lindholm. The project was to be directed by Wachtmeister, who had as his assistants Gustaf Otto Lindblad, Christopher Polhem, and Charles Sheldon. Each was responsible for a specific aspect of the work. Polhem arrived in May of 1717, although it has been thought that Swedenborg (who was Polhem's assistant at that time) had already examined the area.[88] Although he did not work on this project more than the summer and autumn of 1717, his monthly salary had increased to one hundred and fifty silver daler.

Polhem built a "trap dam" for the purpose of keeping the working area dry while the dam was built. The dam was finished on December 17, 1717, but it was not until August of the next year that Wachtmeister was able to begin the construction of the dock itself. By that time, Polhem had indicated that he did not want to be part of the project any longer.

It is characteristic of the work methods of that time that when Wachtmeister contracted to have the work done, no mention was made of Polhem's dam. The reason for this was that he needed the assistance of the Navy, as well as "sixty or seventy vessels and eight hundred to one thousand men,"[89] to complete the work.

Karl XII settled in Lund in 1716 and remained there, with few interruptions, until the Norwegian campaign in 1718. The small university city, which at one time had been a busy Danish metropolis, now became the center of operations for the Swedish military forces. The Swedish diplomatic corps was also located in Lund. There was, however, no gay court life, and no brilliant receptions or expensive banquets. Life was necessarily much simpler. It was reported that the table settings were made of tin, and were a gift from Polhem, who brought them from Stjernsund. They consisted of "dishes, plates, spoons, knives, forks, oil and vinegar cruets, sugar bowls, candlesticks, shears, and large and small tankards for drinks." Hultman, a steward,

---

[87] *Den nya swenska Mercurius* (Utg. af Gjörwell), 1761, pp. 45–49.
[88] Cf. Swedenborg, *Underrettelse om docken, slysswercken och salt-wercket åhr 1719.*
[89] Admiral C. H. Wachtmeister's letter to K. Maj:t 1716–24. (RA).

48

related how these were taken along during the war with Norway.[90]

Karl XII, while in Lund, campaigned relentlessly for a new and more effective army. But, at the same time, he devoted himself to the reorganization of Sweden's industry and trade, which had suffered because of the war. Polhem suggested to the King that one of the ways to do this would be to build a canal between the Baltic Sea and the North Sea. Polhem's project came to a halt with the death of the King, although some preliminary work had been done in Karlsgraf in 1718. Polhem suggested a much more realistic project later, that of building a canal between Lake Vänern and the sea. The work was begun but never completed. One can see evidence still of this project, however. "Polhem's Lock" and its mighty waterfall remain as a memorial to this great genius, whose ideas are only now being fully appreciated.

Still another of Polhem's projects was never completed. In 1717 he suggested to the city of Lund that they build a saltworks on the west coast. When Sweden was at war, it was often impossible to get the necessary amount of food, including salt. The poorer classes suffered the most. One report said that during the war "Many people had to pay hundreds of daler for a barrel of salt." The saltworks in Strömstad was never able to produce enough salt for the population. Furthermore, the salt was never as good as the salt which came from Spain, France, or Germany. Polhem's plan was to build a saltworks in Gullmar's Fjord, which could easily be shielded from enemy attack. He would make the necessary evaporating apparatus, ovens, boilers, and what else was needed by himself, and planned to do this at the same time as he was building the canal at Karlsgraf. But in order to get water into the dam and then into the boilers, Polhem had to invent a windmill "which could stand in a pram and move with the pram in every kind of weather." Polhem also told how his salt could be prepared so that it would be as good as the imported kind. He explained, "As salt liquefies quickly when it is heated, a process similar to drying could be carried out (before the salt was refined and crystallized) which would reduce the cost of the salt. Blood from cattle could be used in the refining process because it draws out imperfections. Rain water could be used for the crystallizing process itself."[91]

On June 26, 1717, Karl gave his permission for Polhem to build a saltworks. To help finance it, a "shareholding company" or "corpora-

[90] *Handlingar till Karl XII:s historia*, 1(1819), p. 120.

[91] In the Royal Model Chamber, in 1779, there was a model of an "evaporating works" which had a mill, according to Norberg's *inventarium* (no. 165), whose arms could be used for an adjacent saltworks.

tion" was created. Two hundred thousand shares, each valued at one silver mark, were issued. The advantages of participation in the "salt-works corporation" were advertised – shareholders did not have to pay taxes on their holdings for a twenty-year period, and after this, they would have to pay only "one half" of the duty paid for foreign salt. There would be no other costs, "unless they agreed to it." Further-more, a law was passed which said that the workers would not have to serve in the military forces. To make the proposal more appealing it was stated that anyone who wanted to sell his shares would not be forced to sell them for the same price he had paid for them, but at their "present value."

Even though there was public notice of the sale of stock in the com-pany, nothing happened. Undoubtedly, the reason was that there was no money available, and certainly not for a saltworks which was only in the planning stage. Polhem resided in Karlskrona during the sum-mer and fall of 1717 and wrote about his experiences there: "There are those in Karlskrona who want to pay for their shares with 'token money' and if this is not possible for them, they want to be taken off the list. If everyone does this, it will be the beginning of the end and we shall have no company." "God knows," he added, "that it shall be a tragedy for Sweden if every project ends this way. I believe she is bewitched, because neither will nor knowledge can overcome her diffi-cult situation."[92]

The death of Karl xii destroyed Polhem's desire to continue with the project. Swedenborg and Professor Lars Roberg attempted to fol-low up Polhem's work, but with no success. Swedenborg wrote about it with the hope of awakening interest, but this too was to no avail.[93] An Irishman asked in 1723 if he could construct a saltworks in Swe-den. Polhem was asked about it, and he discouraged further discussion of the project.[94]

Polhem was asked by the Department of Commerce (which, during Karl xii's last years had unlimited control over the nation's finances) to assist them in making a copper coin which would be worth one silver daler. He had already protested against the proposed changes in

[92] Polhem, *Patriotiska testamente,* pp. 37–38. Swedenborg, *Underrettelse om docken, slysswercken och salt-wercket år 1719.* Polhem's memorial (Nov. 25, 1717), tr. in: *Troll-hättan, dess kanal-och kraftwerk,* utg. af Kungl. Vattenfallsstyrelsen, 1911, p. 326. Pol-hem's letter to "Välborne h. sekreter," Karlskrona, Dec. 19, 1717. *Biographica.* Privile-gium för ett saltsjuderi, June 26, 1717. *Riksregistraturet.* Among Polhem's manuscripts dealing with economic matters, there are a few which describe a saltworks.

[93] Stroh, *Grunddragen af Swedenborgs lif,* 1908, p. 36. Swedenborg had already by 1717 made a note about this topic, and it is possible that they were collaborating on this project.

[94] Kommerskollegium to Polhem, Nov. 22, 1723. *Biografi P.* (KB).

15. *Christopher Polhem, painting by Scheffel. In the possession of the Cronstedt family,*
Fullerö

the value of the nation's money, because, as he said, "such changes are either childish folly or outright deception." It is the same, he said, "as if a poor and common person received a noble title; the individual never becomes more noble as a result, rather, the title is degraded and is of less value."[95] Nonetheless, Polhem made a number of designs for the coins. He received instructions from the authorities at Avesta (where the nation's money was minted) that the "coins must be evenly rolled and cut." They requested that he construct a machine "which could stamp out the coins, and do this quickly and safely."[96]

While Polhem was working on the canal between Vänern and the sea, it was suggested to him that he construct a bridge over the Göta River at Rånnum. At this point there was a highway which went between Västergotland and Uddevalla, and which continued on to the Norwegian border. Polhem constructed a suspension bridge which connected directly with the roadway, and which allowed for passage even while it was under construction. This was very important to Karl because there was never any interruption of the march of his army.

Polhem wrote to Benzelius[97] about Karl XII: "If we can obtain the peace, and the return of our King unharmed, then we have a chance to develop and become a great nation. No other nation in Europe has a better opportunity to become wealthy. We can hope for happiness once again, if we can win the peace and have our beloved King returned to us." Karl was able to escape from the "crumbling walls" in Stralsund and the "angry waves" of the Baltic to his home, after being away for eighteen years, but without winning the peace. Nonetheless, Polhem continued to support the King in his various programs; in turn, Karl encouraged Polhem to continue with what he was doing.[98]

When Karl XII was killed at Fredrikshall, Polhem disappeared from the scene for a time. The new regime, which differed in its policies from Karl's, did not think too much of Polhem. The Karlsgraf canal was considered "nonsense," and thought to have been motivated solely by self-interest. Many other plans were rejected because the ad-

[95] Chydenius, *Politiska skrifter*, 1880, pp. 273, 275.

[96] Upphandlingsdeputationen to Polhem, June 14, 1716. *Biografi P.* (KB).

[97] Polhem to Benzelius, Stjernsund, Dec. 10, 1715. *Codex Bf. 31*. Linköpings stiftsbibliotek.

[98] Cf. the following incident: In the summer of 1717, Polhem requested that Herman Mallmin, who was a district judge, should be made an *ordinarius*, because Polhem's daughter, Maria, "did not want him until he became one." Judge Lindblom asked Polhem to suggest another person for this position: "Således gör Eders Majestät mig en välgärning, som är kapabelt göra Eders Maj:t tjänst många tusendalers nytta tillbaka medelst ett friare och nöjsammare sinne vid mina anbetrodde sysslor." Polhem to Karl XII, no date. *Biographica*. (RA). There was no resolution of this and no marriage between Maria and Mallmin either.

16. *Eric Benzelius (1731–1742), painting by Scheffel; photo SPA*

ministration did not appreciate Polhem's potential influence. Polhem hinted in his writings that he had enemies in the government who underestimated his work and abilities, who opposed him at every turn, and who even persecuted him. However, Polhem had a tendency to exaggerate the facts, and it seemed that this was the case at this time.

V. Polhem and Sweden's First Learned Society

Sweden's first learned society was formed in Uppsala in the fall of 1710. Eric Benzelius, the learned and brilliant librarian at the University of Uppsala, took the initiative in getting the society together. He convinced some of the best scholars at the university to meet at his home or at the library once or twice a week "to discuss important subjects." The group became known as the *collegium curiosorum*. Among the eight initial members were Harald Wallerius, professor of mathematics, and Pehr Elvius, professor of astronomy. Wallerius' sons, Johan and Göran, were also members. Johan was an adjunct in mathematics at the University, and famous as a musician and an orator. Göran studied mining and became a mine surveyor and eventually mine director in Uppland in 1714. Polhem and Emanuel Swedenborg were included as corresponding members. The *collegium curiosorum* did not have any specified organization at first and no records were kept. For this reason, it is difficult to learn how much Polhem contributed to the group. There is a fragment of the minutes from the meetings in 1711, but this does not reveal too much. It seemed that the group discontinued its activities in the autumn of 1711. In November of 1719, the society was resuscitated with the new name of *societas literaria*. Between the years of 1711 and 1719, Benzelius maintained a correspondence with the members of the group and in this way was able to keep the society alive.[99]

The main interests of the *collegium curiosorum* were in the areas of mathematics, physics, and economics. Theoretical questions in the natural sciences were discussed. Benzelius wrote in his autobiography[100] (in reference to Polhem): "In order to have material to discuss in our meetings, we corresponded with Polhem, who answered many of our questions and proposed further problems in mathematics and

---

[99] Cf. *Kungliga vetenskaps societetens i Upsala tvåhundra-årsminne*, 1910, pp. 6ff.

[100] Published in: *Brefwäxling imellan E. Benzelius och G. Benzelstierna*, utg. af Liden. 1791, p. XXII.

54

physics." Polhem's letters and writings from this period[101] display his broad scientific understanding and the contemporaneity of his ideas. He usually illustrated his scientific theories with their practical relevancy. His experiments were always related to the most modern of mechanical problems. His scientific interests were wide. He studied the structure of the mountain ranges in Switzerland and the geological formations in Harz, Germany and Harwich, England. He even took part in paleontological investigations. He theorized that England, Scotland, Ireland, and other islands in the same area were once under water, and that the English Channel had at one time been part of the land. He observed a number of mooring rings fastened high above the water on the coast of Gotland, and from these he concluded that the surface of the land had been raised or the level of the water had been lowered. He tells us that upon one occasion he regretted the fact that he was not too well acquainted with chemistry, "which was an extremely important subject." "But then," he added, "who is perfect in everything?"[102] Hans Forssell once said that Polhem's desire for knowledge and his capacity for work "elevated him above the scientific world of his time."[103] Polhem's manuscripts alone are worth while for the picture they give us of Swedish scientific and intellectual life in the first half of the eighteenth century.

Sometime in the late summer of the year 1710, Benzelius wrote to Polhem, and asked him for some ideas or theories to work with in their forthcoming meetings in Uppsala. Polhem responded in his letter of September 10 in the following way: "As experimentation continues, many of Descartes' ideas will be rejected, although others will be accepted. It is remarkable how nature can be understood on the basis of mathematical and mechanical principles, and how scientific experimentation seems to verify this fact more and more. . . . If at any time the group has a question regarding a problem in physics which cannot be answered, I will try to give a correct and satisfactory answer." Polhem then enumerated those properties of nature with which he would like to work "with the aid of mathematical and me-

[101] The letter may be found in *Codex Bf.31*. Linköpings stiftsbibliotek. In the autumn of 1710 there were 18 letters, all copied by Benzelius because he wanted to retain the most important of the contents. Polhem, for some reason, wanted to have the originals returned. In 1711, they were written by someone else, but are not always comprehensible because the writer could not always decipher Polhem's handwriting. From 1712 – Nov. 1722, the letters are original, but are only addressed to Benzelius and Swedenborg. A great many of the letters have never been located.

[102] Letter to Elvius, Oct. 15, 1710.

[103] Forssell, *Minne af erkebiskopen doktor Erik Benzelius in:* Svenska akademiens handlingar ifrån år 1796. D.58 (1883), pp. 289–291.

chanical insights."[104] It was a project which encompassed almost all of the branches of natural science.

Polhem is of particular interest in the history of Swedish science because of his response to Newton's Law of Gravitation. Newton's theories had not been generally accepted in Swedish scholarly circles. Elvius, a representative of the time, called the theory a "pure abstraction." It was Polhem, and later Swedenborg, who popularized Newton's ideas in Sweden. However, the older idea, that gravitation was caused by the pressure of the atmosphere,[105] was the more popular one. Polhem had written earlier[106] that a falling body was not caused by "the motion of the poles but solely by the pressure of the ether." In the meantime (April 1712), Polhem had read Newton's classic *Philosophiae Naturalis Principia Mathematica*[107] which had been published in 1687. Polhem felt that Newton "wanted to display his knowledge rather than teach others . . . and this is the same technique which Wallis employed." He went on to say, "but Wallis was never as obscure as is Newton." Polhem nonetheless understood the nature of Newton's theories, even though he had not, as he said, "exhausted himself over them as perhaps they deserve." He constantly sought for ways to explain Newton's method in "simpler and easier ways."[108] In a letter to Elvius, Polhem suggested a little problem based on Newton's ideas which he might work on, and added these words: "If Newton were in Uppsala, I would have more questions to ask him than he would have time to answer." He compared Newton's experiments with his own,[109] and sent Elvius "A brief explanation of Newton's theory of centripetal and centrifugal forces." He characterized Newton as "a great mathematician, although at times a little immature because he chooses to explain something with a great deal of noise

[104] "1) Compressio och vis elastica aëris, utan att han ramosus och plumosus, som strider emot dess fluiditet, refraction, igenomskinlighet etc.

"2) Jordens och planeternas aequilibrium in aethere, så ock dess rum, lopp och rörelser.

"3) Att gravitas icke orsakas af jordenes polarrörelse, ty då kommer månen att lida; item att gravitas är störst vid superficies terrae, men minskas högre och nedre ifrån.

"4) Orsaken till barometerns stigande och fallande; item regn, storm, blixt, dunder etc.

"5) Skillnad emellan materia fluida och fixa och på hvad sätt den ena af den andra formeras kan; item orsaken till alla mineralers och metallers olika tyngd och egenskaper.

"6) På hvad sätt generation sker i alla örter och trän, jämväl lefvande etc."

[105] Annerstedt, *Upsala Universitets historia*, D.2:2 1909, p. 323.

[106] Letter to Benzelius, Sept. 30, 1710.

[107] See letter to Elvius, Oct. 15, 1710.

[108] Letter to Elvius, Stjernsund, April 19, 1712. Original. Letter to Benzelius the same day. Copy.

[109] Letter to Johan Wallerius, Stjernsund, May 24, 1712. Original.

and fancy demonstrations, rather than in a simple way. Wallisius does the same thing – but he is never as bad as Newton. The two of them together, however, Newton and Wallis, are good men to work with. particularly if one wants to sharpen his mind."[110]

Polhem's position regarding the problem Newton introduced may best be seen in the following quotation: "The material of which the planets are made cannot possibly be as light as ether. It follows therefore that all planets are hollow and filled with fire, which is lighter than ether, in the same way that ether is lighter than matter. Because a hollow lead ball can float in water, so therefore, the earth and the planets can float in the air without any gravitational force. Whether the planets are moved by their 'natural impulses' which do not stand in opposition to mechanical forces when there is no weight, or whether they are propelled by the ether which surrounds them, like a whirlpool, or driven by their inner fire (which is related to the whirling fire around the sun or to a lesser fire around a larger planet) is a question I leave for the scholars to work out. I, myself, believe the last hypothesis best explains the phenomenon of motion. Only *regulae motus* can be maintained in this way, and it demonstrates *motum polarem*. Where there is no *resistentia media,* there is *motus infinit* without proportion." It is not known whether Polhem later accepted Newton's theory of gravitation.

In addition to these speculative questions, Polhem, in his correspondence with the members of the *collegium curiosorum,* dealt with practical matters. He discussed music and problems dealing with musical theory. For example, one of the questions which interested him was the effect of temperature on a harpsichord, and he talked of this with Harald and Johan Wallerius.[111] (It was Harald who later became director of music at the University.) Polhem wrote a manual on musical theory, "On Linea Musica," sometime in 1710 or 1711. In it, he devised a new way to divide the twelve intervals between the octaves "so that all half tones would be the same; all whole tones, thirds, quarters, and fifths, etc., would be equal, with the result that an octave would be made up of three whole thirds." Harald Wallerius later showed the absurdity of this division, as did Johan Cahman, "the reformer of Swedish Organ Building," some years later.[112] In addition to all of this, Polhem exchanged letters with Benzelius regarding the measure-

[110] Letter to Elvius, Stjernsund, May 31, 1712. Original.

[111] Letter to H. Wallerius, without a date, but probably the end of the year 1710. Letter to J. Wallerius, March 6, 1711.

[112] *Codex N.12.* Linköpings stiftsbibliotek. Contains Wallerius' comments and Cahman's letter. April 15, 1732.

ment of the speed of light, as well as other problems in physical theory, and with Johan Wallerius on the laws of different kinds of motion.

Polhem developed a number of cosmological theories.[113] On November 19, 1710, he wrote to Benzelius (and in his letter we have a preview of the theory of evolution): "If I dared to speculate on the matter, it would not seem impossible to me that the earth was once a sun, and that after many hundreds of thousands of years, it became the earth as we know it today. Eternity gave us time and space, although we conceive of the world in such small terms. When we think of time and the interminable nature of space, the center of which is God Himself, we must realize that He is much greater than we usually conceive Him to be." Polhem took it for granted that the earth did not always have its present form. Mountains were caused by earthquakes, he maintained. To prove this thesis, he described two mountains he had seen in Switzerland. They were located at great distances from one another, but their shapes indicated that at one time they had been very close together. The geological formations in the mountains near Harz showed, so he claimed, that they too had been formed by earthquakes. Polhem said, "the foliated rock (schist) on the ocean floor, made by earth falling into the muddy water, which encloses the forms of fish, demonstrates this thesis rather clearly." Earthquakes, Polhem believed, were caused by a "slow underground movement of the four elements: fire, air, water, and earth." In the center of the earth there was fire, then a layer of stone approximately two hundred and fifty miles wide, then a layer of water of the same width, and finally the ground and the mountains. Within the earth, there were great hollows filled with "hot steam." When these caverns became larger as sulphur, salt, and other minerals are taken from the mountains, water finally flows into them, and steam escapes. However, when the steam is displaced, its escape is very often impeded, and it is compressed into some of the earth's cavities. It remains there until enough steam is built up. When this happens, and if the earth is not strong enough, an earthquake occurs.

In another letter to Benzelius, dated November 26, 1710,[114] Polhem sets forth "Rules for Alchemy based upon mechanical demonstrations." "It seemed," he said, "that the earth and the planets began this way: in the beginning they were suns, but after a long time they absorbed so much matter from the other planets that a shell was

[113] Cf. Fredrik Wilhelm von Ehrenheim, *Samlingar i allmän physik*, D.1 (1822), pp. 226–227.

[114] "Förklaring pa det förra bihanget"; reference by Benzelius to this letter of Nov. 26; it can be possible that it ought to have referred to Sept. 1712.

formed around them, over which the air and water began to gather." Soon the water became so deep and so heavy that it formed a solid mass. This occurred first in those places where the shell was the thinnest. When more and more matter gathered, its surface began to buckle. Concave surfaces were formed by cold and hot water being released. Thereafter, "the steam, like rising dough, shot up into the highest mountains and down into the deep valleys." The low mountains were crushed in the passage of time by the continual motion of the rocks against each other and became "stones, sand, and so forth."

It is difficult to ascertain the importance of Polhem's contributions to the history of cosmology, but it is clear that he had a great influence upon Swedenborg.[115] His work, "On Living Spirits" was particularly important to Swedenborg.[116] In this work Polhem described "every living creature, including man, as an infinite number of charged particles or atoms, whose size and shape cannot be determined." He continued: "To these particles there is to be ascribed a specific kind of form and motion." The infinite motion is God Himself. Similarly to Swedenborg, Polhem divided his particles into six different kinds: the elemental, vital, vegetative, and the three mineral, salt, sulphur and mercury "from which all earthly bodies receive their composition."[117] "Human reason and the principles of mechanics" tell us, said Polhem, that these living spirits were created in the area between the bottom of the oceans and the fire in the center of the earth, "from which all matter and life are derived."[118] The particles are round so that they can "move more swiftly." Polhem developed these theories further in his work "On Habit or Nature," and described the size, shape, weight, and motion of the particles in the air, water, and in other "terrestrial matter." Both of these works by Polhem were written in the autumn of 1710; Swedenborg's "Prodromus principiorum," which dealt with the same topic, was not published until 1721.

In another work, "Thoughts about Spiritual Beings,"[119] Polhem explained how motion influenced man's mind, his thinking, and the functioning of his brain. Polhem explained that sympathy and antipathy, and many other emotions which appear to be supernatural,

[115] Stroh, *Grunddragen af Swedenborgs lif,* 1908, pp. 50–51.

[116] Manuscript. *Filosofi.* (KB). "Lifander kallar man de oändeliga små lif, som äro i naturen, utom hvilka intet lif och lefnad kunde bestå i djur och fänad, ja, icke i örter och trän."

[117] "Discurs om forma och figura spatium et materia in genere." Manuscript in copy. *Teknologi.* (KB).

[118] Letter to Benzelius, Dec. 17, 1710.

[119] Manuscript. *Filosofi.* (KB). These works by Polhem are referred to in: Manuscript in copy. *Teknologi.* (KB). Cf. letter to Benzelius, Dec. 31, 1710.

17. *Emanuel Swedenborg, engraving*

could not be understood without "the principle that thought and its external manifestations possess a real existence." As a sound wave can go through a wall, and "a light through the hardest diamond," so nothing can prevent thought from expressing itself. For example, said Polhem, two good friends can sense the presence of the other, even though they are many miles apart. He continued, "When one partner experiences sorrow and the agonies of death, and even great joy, the other partner can sense exactly his emotion." Dreams therefore are thought waves which move through the air. The fact that we do not dream all the time and do not always dream the same dream can be explained in terms of external impressions upon the mind. Dreams about another person's fortune or misfortune can also be explained by these thought waves.

Polhem's theory of the origin of the earth was opposed to the traditional idea presented in the book of Genesis. In his time, no one dared doubt the Biblical account of creation. However, like Newton, Polhem believed in a personal God, who revealed himself in creation. Polhem explained how he felt about all of this: "The words of Moses, which were supposedly dictated to him by the Holy Spirit, cannot be doubted by the Christian, any more than the Christian can question the words of Christ. The Genesis account of creation, however, should not be taken literally, but should be understood as a parable. To assert that 'The world has been created out of nothing' is a correct assertion, when one considers that air is made of nothing. Furthermore, there are things which our crude senses cannot comprehend which, in respect to God, are fully comprehensible. To assert, therefore, that God used the infinite to create the finite is quite understandable in terms of God's powers." Polhem suggested a number of criticisms of the Biblical account, however. The sun and the stars must have existed at least since the time of creation. It is difficult to understand, he said, how the days and nights were ordered before the sun and moon were created.[120] He wrote in a letter dated November 6, 1710: "How remarkable it is that all of nature hangs together like the links of a chain, and that one part cannot move without the other."

Polhem suggested that perhaps Moses and his account of creation referred to "the origins of the Jewish people and their world, which Moses took to be the whole world, which fact continued as late as the Apostolic period. Certainly there was no knowledge of geography at that time as we know it today. . . . If God created everything good, why are there so many useless things in existence, such as mountains,

[120] Letter to Benzelius, Nov. 19 and 26, 1710.

marshes, and swamps, which obviously came about because of changes in the earth's surface. To this list we may also add worthless vermin, animals, plants, and other such things."

The Genesis account of creation was significant, Polhem believed, because it taught man that: "1) There was a creator God; 2) He was omnipotent; 3) He had created man; 4) He insisted upon obedience; 5) He would punish the disobedient." For this reason, the story should be "revered as an article of faith." People could easily understand it, and it would make a lasting impression upon man, much better than "most of the trained orators could do." It would be difficult for man to believe in God if they did not have a number of stories about Him. "It is better, therefore, to preach to the common man and tell them that God has eyes and ears that see and hear what they do and say, particularly when it is evil. The preacher should also tell them about hell, burning with brimstone, where God sends those he punishes; this is necessary because it is obvious that the people are not overly concerned with Heaven." It would have been interesting to see the reaction of Benzelius to these unorthodox theological ideas. During Polhem's time, Benzelius became a leader in the spiritual and cultural life of Sweden. In theological matters, however, after he became bishop, he represented a hard and fast orthodoxy. Nothing is known of Benzelius' response to Polhem's theological ideas. Characteristically, Polhem requested that Benzelius not distribute "these discourses to the simple people, because God's being is hidden in so many ways from them." He apologized to Benzelius in a letter for his bold theological statements. He wrote, "My reverence and praise for God can never be diminished. The awe and wonder which I feel when I think of God and His creation can never be taken from me." In a letter to Benzelius in November 1713, Polhem wrote: "My last letter did not delight you, I am sure, and I am surprised that I can be so crude at times, and say things which are beyond my competence. But, if it so please the learned librarian, I would very much like to be corrected."[121] He continued, saying that he wrote what he did because so many young priests were ignorant of these things. "They make a mockery of their pulpit by their preaching and example." Such practices can only lead to "barbarism." Rather than this, physics, mathematics, and all of the sciences should form the basis for religion, and particularly for the account of creation, which, as Polhem said, "is the foundation for everything important." Polhem admitted that his earlier explanation was a little presumptuous, but asserted that there is "no real difference between the account in Genesis and my account

[121] "Ne sutor supra (ultra) crepidam" equals "skomakare blif vid din läst."

18. *Christopher Polhem, painting. In the possession of Överingeniör (Superintendent)*
Carl Hammarsköld

of the origins of the earth." This would be so clear if one would only use his reason, "which faculty separates man from all dumb animals." Later, in a little essay entitled "A Natural History of Creation," Polhem modified his position so that it became more Biblical. In another letter, however, Polhem insisted that he was not a Biblical critic.

Polhem became involved in a theological controversy between Johan Konrad Dippel, a German "Schwärmer," and Benzelius, who represented the Swedish church. Dippel had lived in Stockholm for a few years and preached his doctrines, which were made up of a strange mixture of piety, mystical theology, and astrology. He created a great deal of confusion in Sweden and was driven from the country sometime in 1728. Polhem wrote two articles on the problem of "Dippel-ianism," one entitled "Thoughts on Dippel's Philosophy," and the other, which was never finished, "Glasses for Hr. Dippel."[122] In these articles, Polhem went directly to the heart of the controversy and discussed Dippel's thought on the basis of the difference between worldly and spiritual wisdom, or the difference between philosophy and theology. Philosophy "is made up of mathematics, physics, and ethics; theology of revelation, miracles, and the will of God (which should be the basis for man's life)." The difference between philosophy and theology can be defined in still another way[123] he wrote: "when the philosopher cannot account for some phenomenon without faith, then he is not a philosopher any longer but a theologian. The basic difference is that one possesses a childlike faith and the other reason and experience. For example, if a man believes that iron floats, then he is a theologian, but if he asserts that it will sink, then he is a philosopher." Dippel's theological position would "impress the simple working people," said Polhem, "but not those who use their reason." "Our time," he said, "is based upon the ancient Aristotelian philosophical tradition. It is easy, therefore, to understand why new philosophies are held in contempt." Dippel received a favorable response because he based his teaching on "spirits and the occult" and not upon mathematical and mechanical principles. Polhem wrote in "Thoughts of Dippel's Philosophy," that, "if I were as experienced in speaking as Dippel and were as bold to bandy about the names of learned and honest men as he is, then I would challenge him. I am glad that destiny has not permitted me to do so."

From the minutes of the *collegium curiosorum* for 1711,[124] we learn

[122] Manuscript. *Filosofi*. (KB).

[123] "Tankar om världens upphof." Manuscript. *Filosofi*. (KB).

[124] *Kungliga Vetenskaps societetns i Uppsala tvåhundraårsminne*. 1910, pp. 57–67. Cf. pp. 15–17.

that the group discussed a book Polhem had written, entitled "General Housebuilding, dealing with the construction of mills and houses; containing comments of the mathematical, mechanical, and physical aspects of construction; with directions and dimensions; collected and published by the *collegium curiosorum* of Uppsala, to be used for the benefit of our beloved country."[125] Specific questions were asked at the meeting: "Is it better to place the stove in a wall or not; which way is least dangerous?" "How can one build a stove which opens into one room, but has its chimney in another?" "How can a balcony be constructed?" Other questions dealt with such construction problems as dockbuilding, the preparation and use of bricks, the malt-brewing process, and so forth. All of these indicated the practical-mindedness of the *collegium curiosorum* at this time.

The members of the *collegium curiosorum* discussed Polhem's plan for a scientific expedition to Lapland at their meeting on May 8. Polhem's program was very detailed and included twenty different points. Lars Roberg, professor of anatomy and practical medicine, led the discussion.[126] First, observations and measurements were to be made from the top of the highest mountains, as well as in the valleys, to determine the "height of the atmosphere," and "the weight and resistance of the wind." This he believed could be done with a number of pendulums and "measuring gauges." The speed of sound was also to be measured, and Polhem devised the following way to do it: "measure the time between the firing of a gun and its report, at both long and shorter distances; as well, measure the differences between the report of a shot fired from a high elevation and a low elevation." The strength of gunpowder might also be measured at high and low elevations. The sun itself could be a subject of investigation to determine if it could be seen more clearly when the barometric pressure was high. Polhem also suggested that measurements be made of the latitude in Lapland and then compared with that of France. He urged that the expedition study the plants and animals on the highest mountains and bring back specimens of the plants for chemical examination to determine how much "salt and sulphur they contain." The different trees could be examined to see if charcoal could be made from them. An expedition did reach Lapland in 1711 and many of Polhem's proposals were realized. It was reported that Eric Benzelius' younger brother, Henric, took part in the expedition.[127]

[125] *Codex E.3.* Linköpings stiftsbibliotek.

[126] "Förteckning på några experimenter som på lappfjällen och i dess dalar voro nödige att verkställas." Stjernsund, April 15, 1711. *Codex Bf.31.* Linköpings stiftsbibliotek. In Latin in: *Acta Literaria,* 1(1720–24), pp. 285–289.

[127] *Kungliga Vetenskaps Societetens i Uppsala tvåhundraårsminne,* 1910, p. 16.

DÆDALUS HYPERBOREUS.

Eller

Några Nya

MATHEMATIſka och PHYSICALIſka

Förſök

Och

Anmerckningar

För åhr 1716:

Som

Welborne Herr Aſſeſſ. Pollheimer

Och

Andre Sinrike i Swerige

hafwa giordt

Och

Nu tid efter annan til almen nytto lemna.

DÆDALUS en auras carpit, ridetqve ſuperne
Quos ſibi Rex Minos ſtruxit in orbe dolos.
Auras *Arte tuâ* ſic tu, mi Dædale! carpe,
Atqve dolos ride quos Tibi turba ſtruet,

Förſäljes af Bokföraren.

UPSALA/

hos Kongl. Maj:tz och Upſala Academiæ Bokt.

JOHAN. HENR. WERNER 1716.

19. *The title page of* Daedalus Hyperboreus

In the meeting in June of that year, excerpts from Polhem's paper dealing with "Motu et Resistentia Mediorum" were read. The paper dealt with the following topics: curved lines, the motion of a pendulum, and wind resistance.[128]

The first scholarly journal published by the *collegium curiosorum* was the *Daedalus Hyperboreus*. There were six issues in all, and they came out during the years 1716–1718. Already by 1710,[129] Polhem had suggested that the society publish its papers. When he realized, however, that it was impossible to publish them all in a "collected works," he advised them to purchase a page, or at least half a page, of the *Stockholms Post,* and publish the papers in that way. There was a tradition behind such a practice, for there had been a series, "Relationes Curiosae," which appeared in 1682, and again in 1700–1701, and which included popular essays on physical, zoological and geographical topics.[130] To do it this way, Polhem thought, would involve no financial risk, "because," as he said, "no profit could possibly be anticipated from such a project in our land." The articles, written in Swedish, were always to carry the name of the *collegium curiosorum.* The society would gain "recognition from the common man" in this way, Polhem believed. He was convinced that the venture would be successful, because, as he said, "there are many who would fancy such a thing, and everyone who reads the newspaper does not mind paying a few copper coins for half a page which he can read easily, much more easily than a whole scientific treatise. . . . If any profit comes from these articles, it could be used to expand this kind of work as well as the experiments which are being done by the group."

Initially, a great deal of the material Polhem sent in to the journal was published; in particular, a number of experiments in physics which, as he said, "formed the basis for all knowledge." There were also articles on the management of "malt and brewing processes," on the techniques of building, and so forth. Polhem summarized the intentions of his publication: "we will attempt to respond to others, particularly those in other countries, and although we are not popular with the masses, perhaps, with God's help, we can bring forth something new and not simply give excuses for the antiquity of our ideas. If I myself cannot construct something, I can tear down what has already been built. . . . So much of what has been said in other lands in-

---

[128] Cf. *Codex N.13.* Linköpings stiftsbibliotek.
[129] Letter to Benzelius, Dec. 17, 1710. *Codex Bf.31.* Linköpings stiftsbibliotek.
[130] Cf. Key, *Försök till svenska tidningspressens historia,* 1(1883), pp. 52–59.

dicates that they are not well grounded in the fundamentals of physics, mathematics, and mechanics. I will attempt to show what is fundamental and what belongs to guesswork."

Benzelius undoubtedly did not think that Polhem's plan could be realized immediately. In November and December of 1711, Polhem brought up the matter again, though this time he had a different proposal. He thought to begin with a number of his papers on clockmaking, which, if "financially popular" could pay for subsequent articles of a more scholarly nature. It seemed, however, that these were only selections from a larger work, which was to deal with: "1) all of the mechanical crafts; 2) the kinds of materials to be used; 3) practical mechanics for the common man, which would deal with all kinds of powered machines used in the country and elsewhere."[131]

Polhem finally gave up the idea of a scholarly supplement to the weekly newspaper. In December of 1711, he decided that it would be best if all of the articles from the *collegium* were translated into Latin, printed in Uppsala, and distributed at one time. A suggestion that the work should be printed outside of the country was rejected, because he felt that it would decrease "the honor of the Swedish nation, and it would make it appear that Sweden could not do this herself."[132] Polhem insisted that all printed material must have the name *collegium curiosorum,* "so that it would receive greater prestige and a better market for its journal." He asked the members of the *collegium* to criticize his manuscripts before they were printed, "because," as he said, "I do not have the disposition to do so." In reference to his manner of working, Polhem said: "When I write a little at a time, without any order or method, then it is not difficult for me to write." He wanted his speech to be criticized because, as he said, "I am not an eloquent speaker, and even though proper speech is popular at this time, I have never learned how to use it."[133] Polhem's speech was undoubtedly a bit rough and lacked the polish which belonged to his time, although, by means of his use of metaphors, he was extremely articulate.

A number of Latin translations of Polhem's works were sent to Stjernsund, even though they had not been published. They were probably "proof sheets" for some of Polhem's later works.

---

[131] Letter to Benzelius, Nov. 3, 1711. *Codex Bf.31.* Linköpings Stiftsbibliotek.
[132] Letter to Benzelius, Dec. 16, 1711. *Codex Bf.31.* Linköpings stiftsbibliotek. Polhem had suggested to printer Peter Momma to attempt to cast Swedish letters.
[133] Letter to Elvius, Oct. 15, 1710, May 31, 1712; to J. Wallerius, Nov. 6, 1710; to Benzelius, April 19 and Nov. 4, 1712. *Codex Bf.31.* Linköpings stiftsbibliotek. Letter to Benzelius, without a date. Notes. *Biografi P.* (KB).

Polhem's plan for the publication of the papers of the *collegium curiosorum* was never carried out. It is difficult to understand why. The possibility exists that there was not enough financial support for the printing of the manuscripts. Polhem, as we have already seen, was a very thrifty man and never thought to pay for the printing himself. At this time, unfortunately, no benefactor was found.

Then Swedenborg appeared on the scene. He wrote to Benzelius from Rostock in September, 1714, and told him that he planned to return home and publish a description of every one of Polhem's inventions.[134] Between 1716 and 1718, six issues of his journal *Daedalus Hyperboreus* appeared. Polhem greeted Swedenborg's plan to pay for the periodical with his own money "with great pleasure and satisfaction." He wrote: "Swedenborg printed and paid for the journal himself. The journal publishes articles dealing with learned and useful theories in physics, mathematics, and mechanics, which I and the *collegium curiosorum* in Uppsala have collected." He thanked Swedenborg for the words of praise in his introduction to the periodical, and promised that as long as he lived and had his health, he would contribute something to the periodical which had been given to the "learned world." Swedenborg often sent Polhem a manuscript to read before it was published. During the period of the life of the journal, Swedenborg, Polhem, and Benzelius corresponded frequently with one another. In this way, Polhem was always in contact with them and could ask their advice regarding his inventions. In one of his letters, Swedenborg asked Polhem to explain a little more about an airplane he thought to construct. This seemed to be as difficult, Polhem said, as making a perpetual motion machine or manufacturing gold. If a machine could be built which was large enough to carry one person, then the job would be done!, so Polhem believed.[135]

The *Daedalus Hyperboreus* carried several articles written by Polhem which dealt with very different subjects: a hearing-aid, a special kind of faucet, the hoisting machine at the Falun mine, experiments

---

[134] Swedenborg to Benzelius, Sept. 8, 1714 in Swedenborg, *Opera*, 1(1907), pp. 224–228. The journal *Daedalus Hyperboreus* was printed with four different title pages, and on three of them Polhem's name was spelled differently, Polhammar, Pålheimer, Pollheimer. See the facsimile in *Kungliga Vetenskaps societetens i Uppsala tvåhundraårsminne*. The Latin poem on the title page is reproduced in Swedish by Achatius Kahl:

"Daedalus sträcker sin flykt
mot aethern. Han ler uti höjden,
När med ränkornas makt Minos vill stänga hans väg.
Stig, min Daedalus! så på konstens vingar mot ljuset,
Och öfver hopens svek skämta, som Daedalus, du!

[135] This exchange of letters (between Polhem, Benzelius, and Swedenborg) is printed in Swedenborg, *op. cit.*, pp. 235–274.

in sound, observations on the resistance of air to falling objects, a way to figure compound interest for many years by means of "a simple triangle," and many other subjects. During the period of 1710–1711, Polhem undoubtedly sent a great number of manuscripts to the *collegium curiosorum*, but they did not always appear in Polhem's original form. Swedenborg edited Polhem's works before they were published in the *Daedalus Hyberboreus*. In one place, Swedenborg called Polhem "the Swedish Archimedes."

The original *collegium curiosorum*, as we have seen, was disbanded in the autumn of 1711. The group was called together again by Benzelius, Swedenborg, and Polhem a number of years later. It was felt that an astronomical observatory could be built as part of the society's program. To finance this project,[136] Polhem suggested that in the future the society should obtain patents for all of their inventions. Polhem offered his threshing machine for this purpose, which, he said, could be used at "manor houses and large villages, all over the country." The income received from the threshing machine would be divided in the following way: one half would be allotted to the society, one third to the inventor, and one sixth to the individual who arranged the transaction. Although Polhem was unable to get a patent on his threshing machine, a number of years later, in 1723, his son-in-law, Ludwig Manderström, was successful in doing so.[137]

The astronomical observatory in Uppsala was built in 1739. Twenty years previous to this time, the *societas literaria* had been organized. Polhem was asked to become a member of this society too. Although he did not take part in any of the meetings, he did, as before, correspond with members of the society. In 1722, he informed the society that he had "comprehended the causes of nature's functions and motions, all of which can be demonstrated mathematically, without any conjecture." The society was especially interested in his papers on the subject of the economy and trade of Sweden, as well as his paper on a proposed waterway between Stockholm and Gothenburg.[138] The journal of the society, *Acta Literaria Sueciae* was published in Latin, so that Swedish scholarship would be known in other lands. This journal published two smaller articles by Polhem, as well as a report of his proposed expedition to Lapland.

The period after 1719 and 1720, when Sweden was at peace, was a time when science and culture flourished. Interest in scholarly matters was not limited to professors and students in the university cities, but

[136] Letter to Swedenborg, Sept. 1716 in Swedenborg, *op. cit.*, pp. 259–262.
[137] Fredrik I's *privilegium för Manderström*, Aug. 13, 1723. *Biografi P.* (KB).
[138] Forssell, *op. cit.*, p. 309.

20. *The Polhem medal*

every class of society became conscious of the possibilities of knowledge. The ruling classes were enthusiastic about scientific and cultural expression, and many became "patrons of the arts." The "Royal Swedish Academy of Science" was founded in 1739 in Stockholm, and it specialized in mathematics and the natural sciences, but also included economics, commerce, and manufacturing among its interests. The intention which formed the basis for the Academy's existence was to disseminate scientific knowledge among the people of Sweden.

Polhem was not among the founders of the Academy, but the seventy-eight-year-old "Scandinavian Archimedes" was the fifth president elected by the Academy. He filled this honorary position from July to September of 1744. Most of the meetings of the Academy were held in his home. In accordance with the regulations of the Academy, he had to address the group. He prepared a speech on the topic of the steps necessary to make Sweden a progressive nation. Because of his illness, however, his speech was read by Anders Johan von Höpken. In this address, Polhem asserted that the price of raw material should remain high and that manufactured goods should be sold as cheaply as possible. In order to regulate prices and to supervise the manufacture and sale of iron products, he suggested that a "Corporation of Iron Masters" be established. He emphasized, furthermore, the freedom of everyone to improve his product. He also felt that the "Corpo-

71

ration of Iron Masters" should be the purchasing agent for iron products.

Another address was directed to "The highly esteemed gentlemen of the distinguished Royal Swedish Academy of Science in Stockholm."[139] In this address, Polhem concerned himself with the problem of the instruction and training of children, a topic which interested him a great deal. He considered it necessary that all books which dealt with "the education and training of young people" should be "carefully read and sanctioned by the Academy." All published textbooks should include the name of the Academy. Polhem felt that in this way only valuable books would be read by the young people. Books should be written, he said, "with the interests of the young people in mind." They would then be saved from bad books, "which are printed more for the publisher's profits than for the good of the youth."

Included in the first seven volumes of papers published by the Royal Swedish Academy of Science are twenty articles by Polhem. Most of them deal with mechanical and technical problems, although some of them have more of a practical concern. In one of the papers, he demonstrated how ale and wine could be pumped from the cellar; another showed how a horse could be prevented from bolting when in harness; still another described iron and steel manufacturing in Sweden; another dealt with farming, and still another with handicrafts. Polhem, in these papers, displayed the very practical side of his nature.

VI. A Few Annotations to Polhem's Manuscripts

There are only a few published works of Polhem[140] in addition to the papers published in the volumes of the Royal Academy of Science and the *Acta Literaria*. However, Polhem left a tremendous number of manuscripts which until recently had never been published. Many of his papers, unfortunately, were destroyed in a fire at Stjernsund in

[139] Manuscript. *Ekonomi*. (KB).
[140] Cf. the following: "Twenne betänkande, det förre angående oeconomien och commercen uti Swerige; det senare öfwer segelfartens inrättande emellan Stockholm och Giötheborg" (1721); "Åtskillige allmänne hushålds förslag" (1726); "Kort berättelse om de förnämste mechaniska inventioner" (1729); "Samtal emellan en swär-moder och son-hustrun om allehanda hus-hålds förrättningar" (1745); "Tal öfver den vigtiga fråga: Hvad som vårt kära fädernesland hafver nu mest af nöden"; "Wishetens andra grundwahl," and "Patriotiska testamente, eller underrättelse om järn, stål, koppar, mässing, tenn och bly" (1761).

1737, but those that remain give a good insight into the life and work of the man, Christopher Polhem. A great many of the manuscripts are incomplete. Some do not have a beginning or an ending. In addition to these manuscripts, there are a great number of letters, memoranda, and records which are stored in the Royal Archives. When we look at all of these, we can only be amazed at his scholarly productivity. It would be an extremely rewarding project to go through all of Polhem's manuscripts and compare his theories and ideas with those of the contemporary world.

Much of Polhem's writings belong to "Dissertationes Academiae," but because he was not classified officially as a scholar, and because he would have had to pay for his own printing, not too much of his writing was published. Polhem did not always write for the general public, either. Many of his manuscripts give the impression that they were written down when Polhem was an old man, and that they were written only as a form of diversion.

Polhem's manuscripts give evidence of his innumerable talents and breadth of interests. There is hardly a subject within the range of man's understanding which did not command his attention. Polhem and others of his time were "versatile scholars," who refused to be limited to specified areas of research. Nothing was so sacrosanct that it could not be examined. For this reason, many of Polhem's manuscripts are only fragmentary, suggesting the method of investigation he employed, rather than a conclusion he had discovered.

Many of his manuscripts deal with the subject of the nation's economy. Such a topic was not discussed extensively until after 1730, when Sweden was enjoying her period of peace. However, it can be assumed that many of Polhem's manuscripts came from an earlier time than this. In September and October of 1716 he wrote, "A Discourse on the Economy and Commerce of Sweden."[141] In this work, Polhem took the point of view that "a nation which does not have a good economy is in danger of losing its well-being and its freedom." He rejected an economic theory which permitted raw materials to be sold to other countries, where they were used to manufacture goods which were then returned to the original country. In another work, "A Discourse on the Nation's Trade and Administration,"[142] written in 1719, Polhem maintained that the nation's economic development was to accompany its recently-won political freedom. These and other articles and papers are conclusive proof of the fact that Polhem was one of the first commentators on the national economy of Sweden.

[141] Copy. *Westinska samlingen 361*. Uppsala universitetsbibliotek.
[142] *Statshushållning*. (KB).

Åtskillige
Allmänne
Hushålds
Förslag/

Såsom:

1. Om Järnbergslagernas Förening, at dymedelst slippa taga främmande Förlag, samt/ altid hålla Järnet uti skiäligt Prijs.
2. Om *Monopoliernas* afskaffande utan någons *Prejudice.*
3. Om Upstädernas *Cultur* och Tilwäxt.
4. Om Åkerbärgningen.
5. Om Lijns Bråkande och Beredande.
6. Om Giödselns Förökande.
7. Om Kiärr och Måsars Beredande til Åker och Äng.

Wid
Närwarande Rijksdag
Andras mognare Ompröfwande underkastade,

Af

CHRISTOPHER POLHEM.

STOCKHOLM,
Tryckt hos Biörkman, Acad. Boktr. i Åbo, 1726.

21. *The title page to Polhem's work,* Åtskillige Allmänne Hushålds Förslag

George Schauman, in a book published in 1910 entitled *Studies in the Economic Literature of Peace Time,* very clearly showed Polhem's influence on the economic and political situation of his time. Schauman pointed out that Polhem was very much opposed to the mercantile system which was popular at that time. He spoke out in favor of unlimited free trade, because, as he said, "one has always found that as long as free trade is permitted, then a nation can become great, as some ancient and modern countries have discovered. But as soon as there is any interference with trade, a nation begins to decline." Polhem did not believe in monopolies or a privileged class. He advocated the abolition of a class structure in his country, for he felt that only in this way could an economy develop. "To have monopolies in a country," he said, "is as healthy as gangrene for a person. . . . This does not really have to be proved, because all one has to do is see the lack of revenue which results from such a situation."[143] In the same reference, he suggested "how monopolies can be abolished without injury or prejudice to anyone." Polhem also attacked the larger towns (primarily Stockholm) for the exceptional privileges which its citizens received. "Every citizen," he said, "has the right to earn a livelihood." In a little paper entitled simply "Two Thoughts,"[144] he wrote: "an inhabitant of one town should not be taxed more than another. Justice and Christian love demand this. The 'unity of the country' is dependent upon everyone having the necessities of life. . . . Revolutions and insurrections are always caused by self-seeking individuals, who are envious and jealous of others." Polhem insisted upon the right of the smaller towns to sell their produce wherever they pleased, rather than to the nearest large city. He discussed this problem in his work, "A Conversation Between a Town and a City."[145] He compared the city to a number of large pickerel living in a pond with a lot of little fish. A representative of the town said, "the cities want to drain us dry, even though we are poor. . . . If there were no farms, however, there would be no food, and we would be miserable creatures, not citizens." Polhem believed that the main objective of the country should be the creation of an industrial Sweden. This was the only way, he felt, that the nation could become rich and powerful. "Trade without any industry," he said, "is not really trade; it makes the nation into a kind of warehouse, such as is found in some countries in the East and West Indies."[146] Without an industry, trade becomes meaningless. Pol-

[143] "Åtskillige allmänne hushålds förslåg."
[144] "Twenne betänkande."
[145] *Statshushållning.* (KB).
[146] Polhem, "Twenne betänkande."

hem referred to the Dutch who, he said, "built their commerce upon an industrial basis. Without this, they would never have been capable of destroying the trading monopoly held by the Spaniards and Portuguese in the East Indies."[147] Polhem knew that farming was also necessary for the nation's well-being. Farming must precede manufacturing, he once said; "This is so apparent that it is almost unnecessary to write it down on paper."[148]

The branch of industry which interested Polhem the most, and the one to which he devoted most of his scientific energies was, of course, mining. Polhem believed that the price of iron should be as high as possible. For this reason, the miners needed an association "which would permit every member to receive the same benefits." This trading and exporting "association" should have its headquarters in Stockholm and have a representative in every seaport and town who could direct the flow of exports.[149]

Schauman, in his book, demonstrated that Polhem, in his political and economic thinking, was very strongly influenced by Johan Joachim Becher, an Austrian doctor and economist. Becher's book, *Politischer Discurs,* appeared in 1667, and undoubtedly was a source for Polhem's ideas. Schauman also showed how Polhem completely reworked Becher's ideas for the specific Swedish situation. Polhem was also influenced in his thinking by two Germans, Johann Adolph Hoffman and Julius Bernhard von Behr, and by the French jurist, Jean Badin.

Schauman wrote an article for the newspaper *Aftontidningen* in 1910, which was entitled "Polhem as a Journalist." In it he called attention to a number of letters Polhem had written to "My dear *Argus,"* which were directed to a rather satirical weekly journal published by Olof von Dalin during the years 1732–1734. However, after reading these letters, one must concur with Schauman that they were not published in the *Argus* magazine. Polhem's writing style is much too turgid "for the caustic and humorous journal which Dalin introduced into Swedish life." One of Polhem's articles was undoubtedly refused by Dalin. However, the reason for Dalin's rejection was not, in this instance, because of the writing style, but rather because of the content of the article. In the next to the last issue of the magazine for the year 1733, the editor listed the names of the correspondents whose letters he could not answer. Included in this list is one individual de-

---

[147] *Samtal mellan krig och frid och fred. Historia Sv.* (KB).
[148] *Svar på den gångbara frågan, om manufakturer bör gå före landtbruket eller landtbruket före manufakturer. Statshushållning.* (KB).
[149] Polhem, "Åtskillige allmänne hushålds förslag," pp. 1–13.

22. *Christopher Polhem, lithograph from an engraving by J. F. Martin*

scribed as "a right-minded patriot who writes with great understanding about commerce and navigation." Polhem responded to this by writing a paper entitled "A conversation between a disciple of *Argus* and a correspondent concerning the material found in the fifty-first edition of *Argus*." Polhem had two individuals, "a disciple of *Argus*" and "a patriot of commerce," discuss the reasons for refusing the article sent in by a "right-minded patriot." The "patriot of commerce" said, in response to a remark made by the "disciple of *Argus*": "It

77

would seem to be unnecessary to answer the disciple, because the master does not answer correspondents. But even though the master does not consider the correspondent worthy of a public reply (because his arguments were not good enough), I, nonetheless, would respond to the disciple." From this it is clear that one of Polhem's articles which dealt with a political matter was rejected by Dalin, even though he considered it "reasonable." The real reason for the rejection of the article probably was that Polhem's political thinking was in sharp opposition to the interests of the ruling mercantile class. Polhem, in his article, made the point that "commerce needed complete freedom of expression." The "disciple of *Argus*" remarked, in Polhem's article, "But if you choose to come again, put your commerce and trade on a completely different footing. Never bring any goods into your country which cannot make a profit for your own people, and never take anything out of the country which could be used to make a profit for your people. Let your need and your pride serve as a guide so that everything will be made in your own country. If you bring in material from abroad and send out manufactured goods, then you have a good commerce." The "disciple of *Argus*" went on to say that the letter contained "such things which could only be understood by the ruling class – the common man could never understand them." He went on to relate that the letter was too long to fit on a page, "and therefore *Argus* did not have enough space for his criticism."

Although Dalin did not print any of Polhem's articles, Dalin was unquestionably influenced by Polhem. It is quite possible that some of Polhem's papers dealing with economic matters, the problems of teaching, and other subjects, were edited by Dalin and published in *Argus*. Polhem may never have been credited with what was really his. Polhem wrote to Dalin once and requested that he revise his articles: "your mode of expression and sense of propriety permits you to alter my material, which is so simple and short." In another letter to Dalin, Polhem said that he did not want his material published, because he would rather reveal his thoughts than change anybody's mind.

Schauman has theorized that the much-discussed letter of the 20th edition of *Argus* from the year 1733, which dealt with "assecurance contoir," was written by Polhem. The letter is signed with the initials V. P., which Schauman translates as "Verus Patriota." There are two other articles in the periodical *Sedo lärande Mercurius* (which was published by the Carlson brothers) which are also signed with V. P. Such a thesis appears plausible, as Polhem had already referred to himself in the *Argus* correspondence as "a right-minded patriot."

Polhem did not take an active part in politics, although he wrote a great deal on political subjects, particularly as they related to the nation's economy. He lived through some of the most important events in Sweden's history, and he was always conscious of the significant issues of his time. He often wrote about these issues. Two of Polhem's works dealt with the problems of government: "A Debate Over the Different Forms of Government," and "The Construction of Government."[150] Polhem never fully understood the reason for the different ranks of nobility, although he was a nobleman himself. In his paper, "A Conversation Between a Nobleman and a Priest at Parliament,"[151] Polhem seemed to identify himself with the commoners. His "Address to the House of Lords,"[152] which dealt with monetary matters, may have been given at one of the meetings of the Parliament in the 1720's, although it has been thought that this address is fictitious, as is "An Address by a Member of the Assembly."[153]

The Parliament which met in 1738 and 1739 had to make major political decisions: one dealt with a proposed military alliance with France and the other with the Russian war. Many pamphlet writers were active during this time, and attempts were made to influence political thinking. Polhem too contributed a number of pamphlets. He allied himself with those groups which advocated peace. Peace must be achieved, he believed, if Sweden was ever to have a chance to develop herself in an economic way. He wrote something entitled "A Conversation Between War and Peace,"[154] and let the pacifist respond to the questions of the militarist: The militarist felt that Sweden should show her gratitude to France for all the help she had given to Sweden. The pacifist replied: "To be thankful to one's benefactor is a very proper response, but to assist him when it is difficult and expensive, and when one puts himself in danger of complete destruction, then the desire to reciprocate is nonsensical." There are two other manuscripts[155] which deal with the subject of peace negotiations, which can be dated sometime after the death of Karl XII.

A number of Polhem's manuscripts discuss medical subjects. He was not very scientific in these; rather he expressed what was the "popular" understanding of the cause and cure of an illness. Polhem's intention in these articles, however, was to advise people in the simple rules of health and diet. A little article of his entitled, "Some of the

---

[150] *Historia Sv.* (KB).
[151] *Ibid.*
[152] *Statshushållning.* (KB).
[153] *Historia Sv.* (KB).
[154] *Ibid.*
[155] "Om fred med riksens grannar. Quaestio om krigets framhärdande med ryssen kan försäkra bättre fredsvillkor framdeles än nu för tiden?" *Historia Sv.* (KB).

Causes for Illness" appeared to be a supplement to a kind of almanac. Polhem never claimed to be a doctor. It was the task of the "learned doctor and anatomist" to diagnose illness. "I am not familiar with the science of the medical profession," he wrote. "What I have recommended to people, on the basis of the observations I have made, should not be taken seriously. My advice was simply an inducement to go to other individuals who can do it better."[156] "What I have said," he continued, "must be understood in light of my serious reflection on the subjects, as well as on the basis of the experiments which I and others have performed."[157]

However, not all of Polhem's medical knowledge came from his own experience. In his writings he quoted from many learned authorities. In anatomy, for example, he referred to the Italian, Giovanni Borelli, and his work *De Motu Animalium,* which attempted to explain the nature of the movements of the muscles, as well as the circulation of the blood, in mechanical terms. In microscopy, he used the work of the Dutchman, Anton van Leeuwenhoek, who had perfected the microscope, and with this instrument, had investigated the nature of blood. Polhem utilized van Leeuwenhoek's discoveries in his own work on "The Different Speeds and Beats of the Pulse," as well as in his discussion of the properties of blood and in his diagnoses of many different kinds of sicknesses.[158]

Polhem wrote concerning sickness: "The common people believe that God gives them their sickness. Their faith comforts those who suffer. However, those who have more insight and knowledge about nature cannot accept such a point of view."[159] In a number of works he states the reasons for the different kinds of sicknesses. Most of these can be traced back to a bad diet. Smallpox and measles were caused by too much meat. He told of the people in Dalecarlia who hardly ever ate meat and who never got smallpox.[160] Tuberculosis was one of the most common of illnesses. He found that it occurred more among the rich than the poor, who, on the other hand, suffered most from "pains and aches."[161]

The best remedy for all of these illnesses was "daily exercise" and a simple and natural kind of life. In "A Conversation Between Nature

[156] Work dealing with medicine, no title. *Medicin.* (KB).
[157] Work dealing with medicine, no title. *Medicin.* (KB).
[158] "Pulspändel, bekvämlig för dem, som ej hafva tid vara sjuka." *Medicin.* (KB).
[159] "Discurs om hälsa och sjukdom," *Medicin.* (KB).
[160] "Tankar om koppors och mässlings upphof. Fråga, hvad månde orsaken vara till barnmässlingen eller kopporna," *Medicin.* (KB).
[161] Notes on health. *Medicin.* (KB).

23. *Christopher Polhem, engraving by C. Bergquist*

and the Art of Health and Long Life,"[162] Polhem made nature empha-
size "moderation, sobriety, and temperance in food and drink," as the
best way of life, rather than gluttony and drunkenness, "which have
become so predominant in our land." "If people's stomachs and con-
stitutions were made of iron and steel, they would still suffer." Instead
of hot and spicy foods, Polhem recommended vegetables as well as
"cooled, uncooked herbs and fruits, which are planted, bear fruit, and

[162] *Medicin.* (KB).

81

only then are ready for eating." In the same work there is an exhortation to mothers to nurse their children, because, as he said, mother's milk is like a medicine and serves to cleanse "the stomach and intestines from phlegm."

Polhem often dealt with the topic of the consumption of alcoholic beverages. He did not want to forbid the use of alcohol, for he felt that there were times when it was necessary and proper to drink. However, drinking was always to be done in moderation. A little brandy, he believed, was good for older people who, when traveling, could not always maintain a proper diet. "But if a habit is formed, then alcohol no longer serves a purpose," but is very destructive. He suggested that brandy was more beneficial before meals than after, because "the effects of the alcohol do not occur so quickly at that time." A constant use of tobacco was detrimental to digestion. If, as he said, the person who used tobacco was forced to be without it, he would be "far worse off than the one who had never used tobacco."[163]

Many of Polhem's medical ideas appear strange to us today. We must realize, however, that not too much was known about medicine in the beginning of the eighteenth century. Medicine was usually mixed with a lot of superstitions and "old wives' tales." For example, during the period of the plague in Sweden, between the years of 1710 and 1711, amulets and dried toads and spiders were used to drive away the evil spirits.[164] It is quite natural that some of this should appear in Polhem's writing. In "A Conversation Between a Patient with a Toothache and a Doctor," the following remedy was offered: "cut off the bark from a young tree, and with a little splinter of the wood, poke the affected tooth, and then return the splinter of wood to the tree." If this remedy worked, Polhem said, it was simply because the sufferer had faith in the remedy, and nothing else.

In other things in this general area, Polhem was far beyond his time. For example, he recommended that the Royal Academy of Science obtain permission from the government to perform medical experiments on prisoners and condemned individuals. He suggested that research take place among people of several generations to determine the influence of meat and vegetables on mankind. Polhem could be called a vegetarian, and he described the advantages of such a diet. In addition, he constructed an apothecary for his workmen at Stjernsund.[165]

---

[163] "Discurs emellan naturen och konsten om människornas hälsa och lifslängd," *Medicin.* (KB).

[164] Broberg, *Om pesten i Stockholm 1710,* 1854, p. 45.

[165] "Notes on health," *Medicin.* (KB).

Many of Polhem's manuscripts dealt with the subject of child care. But, he said, "a woman who has the job of caring for children will not think too well of a man who tells her what to do."[166] He advised mothers not to bind babies and suggested that they feed their children at specified times. He urged young mothers to protect their children and not to punish them at the wrong time. Infant mortality was very great during his time and Polhem suggested ways to correct this situation. Natural processes of life must be studied, he insisted, and answers to problems must be found in nature rather than in old-fashioned practices. In addition, he asserted that parents were not to bring children into the world if they could not feed and care for them.[167]

Polhem was also interested in the nurture and training of young people to become good citizens.[168] "The young people of the nation," he said, "form the basis for the Sweden of tomorrow." As we have seen, Polhem was, for the most part, self-taught. Therefore he could speak directly to the educational situation of the young person. He emphasized very strongly the need of a formal education for every person. Polhem developed this theme in "A Conversation Between a Father and a Preceptor about His Son and His Studies."[169] The boy was first to learn to read Swedish and Latin, then to study geography, the structure of the earth, its genesis, its location in the solar system, and then to learn that the earth "is not flat like a *plane* but rather round like a ball or globe, and that it is suspended in the air like the moon and the stars." The student should also be taught about the days and the nights, about the division of the stars into "seven planets and over one thousand known fixed stars." Such a program was strange to the educational principles of Polhem's day. Polhem made his preceptor say: "For such an education, 'a full professor is required,' and not only a student. I can offer my services for Latin lessons, but I cannot teach philosophy or any other such subject."

Polhem disapproved of learning by rote. To permit students "to learn a language in a mechanical way is like giving books to an illiterate man, and tools to an unskilled laborer; it is the same as giving eyeglasses to a blind man."

Education, he said, should be directed toward practical goals. In an educational program which he set up for his grandsons,[170] he main-

---

[166] "Om barnuppfostran," *Undervisning*. (KB).

[167] "Samtal emellan swär-moder och son-hustru om allehanda hushålds förrättningar," 1745, pp. 42–46. Fragments.

[168] Schauman, *op. cit.*, indicates that Polhem was influenced by the British philosopher Locke and his work *Thoughts on Education* which appeared in Swedish in 1709.

[169] *Undervisning*. (KB).

[170] *Ibid.*

tained that woodworking was an extremely good thing for boys to learn. He believed that every province in Sweden should have a trade school which would be an addition to the high school. In the trade school, the boys would be instructed in every subject, "which pertained to Swedish culture, economics, commerce, manufacturing, handicrafts, and the arts."[171] Instruction should be given in Swedish, "because Latin is a very difficult and dull language which not everyone can learn." Education should be free, so that everyone could go to school, particularly those who would not have a chance otherwise.

Polhem even wrote about higher education.[172] In one of his manuscripts he wrote about his plan for a special faculty of "economics, manufacturing, and commerce," either within the business schools or in conjunction with the universities. In these schools, instruction would be given in economics and business, and also in mathematics, French, and German, "because," as he said, "students would need to know more than Latin when they traveled through Europe." Latin would not be neglected, but only the most important aspects of the language would be studied. Swedish would be spoken exclusively; even textbooks would be translated into Swedish. The students in "this Swedish school" would learn to write Swedish instead of Latin. "When a twenty-year-old boy has learned to speak and write Swedish, German, and French, and has a knowledge of mathematics, this person has received more of an education than one who knows only Latin and Greek." After the successful completion of the program of study, the boy would live abroad at government expense. The student would send regular reports of the manufacturing and commerce of the country; indicate the source of the raw materials; describe transportation, marketing and selling, costs, buyers, working conditions, the prices and availability of food, the value of money, exchange rates, markets, warehouses, holding companies, the shipping of freight, and so forth. These students or "trade attachés" were also to describe the houses they saw, the factories, machines, farm and garden implements; in addition, they would send plants and other living things which could be grown in Sweden. Their obligations included "everything which is part of the administration of the land and the maintenance of estates." They were "to examine everything which was found in the country they visited, to determine whether or not it could be used in Sweden."[173]

[171] "Om verkskolor i Sverige," *Undervisning.*
[172] *Undervisning.* (KB).
[173] The same point of view is expressed again in "General instruction för all våra konsuler, expeditorer, köpman och betjänte, som på åtskilliga orter kunna vara förordnade och vistande," *Statshushållning.* (KB).

Upon returning home, the students would write a little book relating their experiences to the faculty of the school. After this, they would become lecturers at secondary schools or academies, for a period of no more than three years. Then they would enter what was "to be their permanent profession."

In another article entitled "How to Encourage the Educated to Enter Public Life,"[174] Polhem suggested that a grant be given by the government to enable individuals to live in a foreign country for a period of time. Those who were selected for this program would have to be outstanding, selected from every kind of educational institution, including church schools.

Polhem wrote a number of textbooks for use in the schools. "Wisdom's Second Foundation: for the Adornment of Youth, the Benefit of Manhood, and the Pleasure of Old Age" contained fifty-seven lectures dealing with arithmetic, geometry, symmetry, and algebra. This he termed "the Second Foundation for Wisdom." To read and write, to speak properly and to understand one's own language, as well as other languages, was the first foundation of wisdom. Swedenborg published one of these textbooks, at his own expense, in Uppsala in 1716. Other projected volumes never appeared, however.[175] The second volume was to contain a "higher course" in mathematics, and the third, a study in the principles of mechanics.

Descartes and Leibnitz in the seventeenth century had suggested a universal language. Polhem did too. Polhem wanted to give the world a language which would be easier to learn than Latin, which, he said, "requires a lifetime of study."[176] He wanted to make education more available to everyone, and to save people the difficulties he had faced when he was a child. At the same time, he recognized the necessity of a new mode of expression and communication. The learned, he said, always employ lengthy discourse to get across a simple idea. In this way they show off their erudition. "However, it would seem better to express profound ideas by using simpler language, and in this way educate a greater number of people, reaching many more than one could by using weighty volumes and many notes."[177] Polhem was not very optimistic about his "lingua philosophica." He was convinced that it would never be more than "half" realized. "Every alchemist," he reported in one of his manuscripts,[178] "has lived and died with the hope that one of his plans might be accomplished. I have the same

[174] *Undervisning.* (KB).
[175] *Nat. vet. Allm.* (KB).
[176] "Projekt till ett nytt universalt språk," *Språkvetenskap.* (KB).
[177] "Försök till en ny och kort skriftkonst," *Språkvetenskap.* (KB).
[178] *Nomina rerum naturalium per philosophicam novam, Språkvetenskap.* (KB).

hope, though I, too, like the alchemist, realize that it will never be more than half-realized."

The details of Polhem's universal language were never fully worked out, and there are large gaps in the material he has left us. Nonetheless, what we have is very suggestive. Polhem's alphabet was made up of nine vowels and fourteen consonants, each of which denoted something specific. Everything in nature was designated by a certain letter. For example, s referred to sight (synen); L to hearing (hörseln); N to smell (lukten); M to taste (smaken); and R to feeling (känseln). When these letters were placed in relation to a vowel, "then it could not refer to anything other than what one wanted it to refer to." A vowel before a consonant referred to qualities and quantities. I received the greatest designation, and U the smallest.[179] The noun would always end in N; the adjective in T. The comparative was characterized by F and the superlative by R. All verbs would end in s and all adverbs in L. The case could be designated by adding certain letters: G for genitive, D for dative, E for accusative. The number could be designated by the addition of z. *Si* referred to the present tense, *Se* to the perfect, and *So* to the future. Personal pronouns were as follows: I became *as;* you, *es;* he, *is;* we, *os;* you, *us;* and them, *ys*.[180] Again, it is difficult to determine how original were Polhem's ideas. There is an obvious correspondence between his ideas and those of the British bishop, John Wilkens, who devised his theory of language in the middle of the seventeenth century.[181]

There are a number of literary pieces credited to Polhem, although most of these are extremely fragmentary. The only complete work we have is his "Story of Man," a political fable written in prose form.[182] There are also a number of epigrammatic pieces which reveal Polhem's poetical gifts.

Among Polhem's manuscripts there is even a dramatic piece, though this too is in fragmentary form. Only the third act remains. It appeared that the drama was intended for a university audience.

The plot unfolded somewhat in the following manner: Two students, Olaus and Petrus, meet a simple farm family during their travels. The family consists of Per and Malin, a daughter, Gertrud, and the

---

[179] *Ibid.*
[180] "Projekt till ett nytt universalt språk," *Språkvetenskap.* (KB).
[181] Couturat and Leau, *Histoire de la langue universelle,* 1903, pp. 18–22.
[182] Cf. the conclusion:

> "O frihet ädla skatt! Men hvem vet dig rätt äga
> Du äst det guld så fatt, som alla ej vet väga
> Förgyllning blänker väl i mångens syn och öga
> Men ack att vikten är så ringa eller föga."

servants, Nisse and Sissla. It seemed that Malin was not too happy to see the students. When her husband came home and assured her that they were not soldiers, but scholars, she invited them in. The third act begins in this way:

"FIRST ENTRANCE:
Per and his wife, Malin

Mother! Have you any food for tonight. We can't let these students leave without anything to eat.

Malin

I wished that you would send these students away; they banged on the door so vigorously while you were away, that I thought they wanted to tear the house down. Tell them to go to hell and don't give them anything.

Per

We have to be fair with them. Get a shoulder of mutton and a long piece of sausage.

SECOND ENTRANCE:
Per, Petrus, and Olaus

Here you are – that's all you'll get, now on your way. Next time don't be so insulting, or I will show you something!

Petrus

Your wife is not correct when she says we were insulting. I can tell you who was.

Olaus

If we have been insulting, we haven't made any trouble, not so that both of you had to come home. Be patient, and you shall know who created the disturbance in your house.

Per

I will ask Nisse and Sissla, both of whom were home. They will tell me the truth.

THIRD ENTRANCE:
Per, Nisse, and Sissla

Per

Nisse, did you hear these students acting in an insulting way to my wife, while I was away?

Nisse

No, they were not rude or abusive. It was just the opposite. Your wife was very angry with them.

Per

What do you say, Sissla?

Sissla

They were very good and talked very nicely; just imagine, they gave me a gift of some needles.

Per

For this reason, you may stay with us overnight and are welcome to the fish and bread which we shall eat."

The meal began, and during the meal, Petrus declared that he had received the gift of prophecy and wanted to show them all what he could do. With the permission of the master of the house he "made in a magical way, pancakes, broth, beefsteak, fine ale, and much more." Malin was still not convinced, and urged that they should all "go to hell."

When she and her daughter went to bed later, they prayed that God would save them from the "abominable scholars."

Polhem wrote still another drama, which unfortunately was never completed. In the spring of 1713, he worked on an "historical comedy, in which the heathen gods Sciantirna and Arthificia appear as persons, so that one may learn things which are not in books."[183] His good friend, Pastor Jacob Troilius of the church in Husby, urged him to finish the play. It is possible that this work, of which Polhem said, "it would not be published in my lifetime," dealt with the topic of public administration. In many of Polhem's manuscripts, we find a fictitious person representing one or more points of view. In this manner, Polhem permitted the free flow of ideas.

Among his philosophical studies there is one entitled "A Comedy on the Foibles of People." He divided the manuscript into a number of scenes and acts, and had "Natura, Ars, Mars, Arrogantia" act as persons. A treatise on house construction took the form of a "Conversation Between Miss *Theoria* and Builder *Practicus* on the topic of Housebuilding." Similar "conversations" are found in every phase of Polhem's writings.

[183] Letter to Benzelius, Stjernsund, June 10, 1713. *Codex Bf.31.* Linköpings stiftsbibliotek.

88

Polhem's travels abroad, which were so very profitable, provided him with the idea of a mill which could manufacture iron, tin, and brass products. He was very unhappy when he saw raw materials going from Sweden to other countries. As a result, he said, the economy of these countries flourished. Swedish iron and copper were sold to other countries at a very low price; then later, iron and copper manufactured products came back to Sweden from these countries, but they always had to be purchased at a very high price. Polhem, when he returned to Sweden after his travels, looked again at the mountains, the forests, and the rivers and streams, and envisaged a great industrial future for the land he loved. He had faith in Sweden's potential – a faith which remained with him all his life. "I hope," he said, when he conceived of a canal between Vänern and the Kattegat and the Vänersborg iron-manufacturing works (still to be created) "that this city would be as great a manufacturing city as Bristol in England and Nürnberg in Germany. . . . At least," he continued, "in this way we could be sure of the tariffs." Polhem's immediate dream did not become a reality, but, perhaps, it has been fulfilled in our time.

Polhem's desire to create an industrial Sweden was motivated by his loyalty to his country. He was a Swedish patriot and called for a "Sweden for the Swedish people." He did not want Sweden's raw materials sent to other countries, nor did he appreciate his countrymen's inclination to favor foreigners and their products. "The foreigners," he said, "take us for the worst kind of dunces. They believe that we cannot do anything but put food into their mouths." "Why should useless imported goods be brought into the country?" he asked. "No one receives any benefit from them."[184] "For example," he continued, "no one but the King and his highest ranking attendants should be permitted to wear silk and velvet. If this were so, anyone who imported these materials would do so at great risk to himself. But if everyone is free to wear silk and velvet, it is impossible to forbid its purchase and display. If an attempt is made to save the government money by forbidding it, this too is useless, because people will still find ways to smuggle the material into the country." The greatest threat to his country, he felt, were those foreigners "who were not as faithful to our land as their own," and who might want to control our mines. "In spite of all this," he said, "we work our mines and export and sell our iron. It seems unnecessary to be concerned about material we cannot

[184] Polhem, "Åtskillige allmänne hushålds förslag," p. 5.

use. Yet we must consider those lands which have less of a substantial economy than ours, and consider our wives and children who perhaps are not as daring as we are, and who could so very easily become poor; the unseasonable prosperity and our present pride are two powerful forces which might catch the innocent unaware."[185]

Polhem sought to realize his vision of a national Swedish industry by the creation of the Stjernsund iron mill. He was very fortunate to have as his companion and benefactor, Gabriel Stierncrona. Stierncrona was a very wealthy man, and a nephew of Lars Welt, rector of the church in Ösmo. He became a district judge in Södertörn and was knighted in 1699 with the name of Stierncrona. He later became Sweden's first "attorney general," and later the presiding judge of Svea's Lower Court of Appeal.

In 1699, Polhem and Stierncrona asked the Bureau of Mines for permission to build an iron, brass, and copper mill at the site of the Avesta Falls. This location was considered by many not to be suitable.[186] In March of 1699, Polhem and Stierncrona purchased land from Susanna Danielsdotter in the region around Husby.[187] An agreement was made at the same time with Catharina Sundia, who owned the other half of the land they desired, that she "would not interfere with their work in any way." On the piece of land, which separated Grycken and Sörbo lakes, there was a forge and a small harbor, formed by the stream which flowed between the two lakes. This appeared to be a perfect site for the mill. However, Catharina Sundia wanted to keep the forge for herself. For this reason, Polhem and Stierncrona bought the piece of land located just below this area.

When the "mining engineer" of that area investigated the site, he concluded that the damming of Grycken would not harm the surrounding community. The Bureau of Mines sanctioned "the establishment of a manufacturing mill at Sund." This occurred on May 29, 1700. The owners of the mill were assured that they would be released from taxation for twenty years and would receive the right to use three hundred shippounds of iron and fifty shippounds of steel in their manufacturing.[188] They would also have the right to prepare "brass for their own use." "Whoever it may be," so continued the Bureau of Mines document, "who builds a similar mill or copies their machines

---

[185] Polhem, "Twenne betänkande," 1721 (I), p. 16.

[186] Bergskollegium protokoll, Jan. 5, 1699. (RA).

[187] In 1711, Polhem purchased property in Stjernsund from Reinhold Rüdker, father of his son-in-law, Reinhold Rückersköld, for 1,626 copper daler. The bill of sale is dated May 25, 1711. *Stjernsunds arkiv.*

[188] Shippound is an obsolete measure. 1 shippound equals 20 lispund; 1 lispund equals 8.5 kg. (11 lbs., 12 oz.)

24. *Gabriel Stierncrona (1669–1723), painting, Svea Hofrätt*

or products, will be obligated to give up their goods, and will be fined two hundred silver daler."[189]

Polhem and Stierncrona planned to manufacture a great many different products. These were listed in the charter granted by the Bureau of Mines:

[189] *Rannsakningsinstrumentet*, Sept. 6, 1699. Copy. *Privilegium*, May 29, 1700. Original. *Stjernsunds arkiv*. Stierncrona till bergskollegium, Nov. 20, 1699. *Bref till b:koll.* (RA).

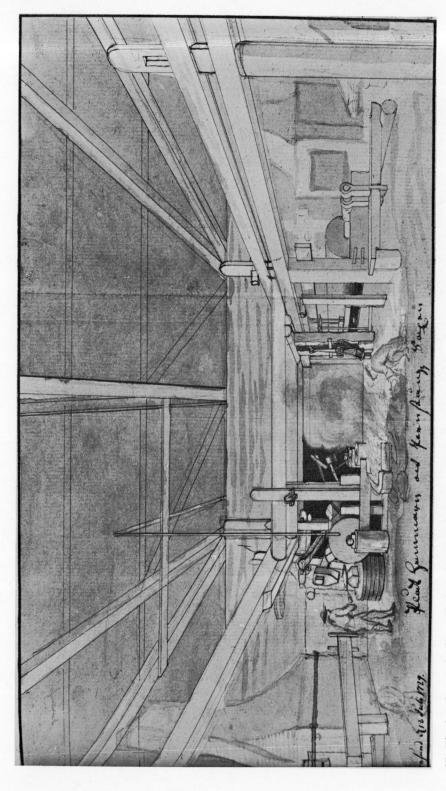

25. *The interior of the large blacksmith's shop at Stjernsund showing a plate hammer and the mechanisms which operated it; drawing by Polhem's pupil, C. J. Cronstedt, 1729; photo from the Tekniska Museet, Stockholm*

"1) Various kitchen utensils such as pots, pans, mortars, and the like, which would be turned on a lathe, tempered and polished.

"2) Hand tools for carpenters, blacksmiths, sculptors, latheworkers, clockmakers, goldsmiths, lacemakers, etc.

"3) Tempered lathe work, such as large and small clock parts, locks and door bolts, plates, bowls, spoons, goblets, etc.

"4) Machines with moving parts, such as steel presses, lifting apparatus, turnspits, presses, clamps, army cots, chairs, and other things.

"5) Long pieces of iron sheeting, with prepared edges, to cover houses, long lengths of iron piping for roof gutters, water troughs that could be plated with lead, iron rods of different shapes (round, cornered, flat, and bent), prepared metals for the locksmith, building materials, blasting equipment, screws and bolts for shipbuilding, and many other things."

There was also "edged and rolled work, with a leaf design, made from brass, pressed into sheets for roofing, to be used also around doors, windows, stoves, fireplaces, mirrors, and pictures; as well as decorated brass rods for lattices and fences, stoves, platforms, alcoves, windows, terraces and the like; also polished and leafed material, pressed and rolled to form different decorations for bureaus, cupboards, and coffins, which could later be painted with a gold finish."

Stjernsund, under Polhem's direction, developed as an industrial settlement. As goods were manufactured and new machines created, it became a very significant part of the growing Swedish economy. The most profitable period for the mill was between the years 1712 and 1722. Karl XII, while at Bender, had exempted Stjernsund from all tariffs and taxes. The workers there were also exempted from paying land taxes.[190] The King had great expectations for Stjernsund. Feif wrote to Polhem and told him about this: "It is His Majesty's wish," he said, "that an abundance of goods shall be produced — iron, copper, and brass products, which Sweden could export to other lands, even as far away as the Mediterranean countries, and that a great profit might be realized from them. . . ." "However," he went on, "if Sweden is to establish a significant trade, salesmen must go abroad with our products. . . . If we cannot produce, for example, sewing needles, it is a shame that we must import them, as we do other goods."[191]

During the period when Stjernsund was exempted from paying taxes, its goods were "bought up quickly." There were so many buyers that the orders could hardly be filled. However, when the tax exemption period was over, the sales diminished drastically, and the mill, as

[190] Karl XII to rådet, March 13, 1713, in: *Historiska Handlingar*, D.9(1874), p. 221.
[191] Feif to Polhem, March 21, 1712. *Biografi P.* (KB).

Polhem said, "lost ground." Thereafter, the goods had to be sold by workers and others who would travel about the country. This system did not work out too well, because, as Polhem reported, there were numerous incidents of dishonesty. Polhem applied repeatedly for a renewal of the tax exemption, both from the government and the Bureau of Mines, but without success. He related that he was not being treated justly, because many other industrial settlements received special tax privileges. "I saw," he wrote in his history of Stjernsund,[192] (written in the middle of the 1730's), "that iron manufacturing was not profitable, particularly when foreign products were duty-free. This mill does not receive the same privileges, and yet we make exactly the same product in a much better way."[193] Undoubtedly, Polhem was disturbed that Stjernsund did not receive any encouragement from the government, particularly when he knew that other mills did. For example, Jonas Alströmer, in his manufacturing plant in Alingsås, received constant governmental assistance. It was Polhem, too, who as a more experienced mill-owner, had advised Alströmer on how he could get his mill started.

Polhem's loom to weave stockings was used in these early days of manufacturing. Carl von Linné said of the loom, "the product brought honor to its master . . . and so much more so because it was simpler than the other machines." The iron mill in Alingsås used two of Polhem's machines, one which drilled holes in iron, the other which made buttons.[194]

In the summer of 1717, Polhem built sheepfolds on the islands of Gotland, Öland, and the Skärgårds, which he believed would "improve the Swedish clothing industry and would make it less dependent upon foreign markets."[195]

Polhem was a pioneer in the transformation of Sweden into an industrial nation. Such a role is a difficult and lonely one, and Polhem very often had obstacles put in his path. Jealous individuals made false charges against him, and said, upon one occasion, that coal was consumed at too rapid a pace, and that the mining industry was being harmed as a result of Polhem's mill.[196] The farmers in the area claimed that the dam in Lake Grycken was going to flood their farm-

[192] "Ödmjuk berättelse om manufakturverket vid Stjernsund." Copy. *Teknologi* (Samlingsband.) (KB).
[193] *Op. cit.*
[194] Linné, *Wästgöta-resa*, 1747, pp. 120–125. Stråle, *Alingsås manufacturverk*, 1884, pp. 41, 261.
[195] "Memorial to Karl xii," June 11, 1717. *Biographica*. (RA).
[196] Elisabeth Funck to Bergskollegium (Jan. 2, 1704). Excerpt from memorial of the authorities of the Falun mine to the commission. May 19, 1722. *Biografi P.* (KB).

lands and make their roads unfit for travel. They also were apprehensive for the future of the forests, and the lands owned by the government.[197] Polhem was always in difficulty with the director of customs, Lorentz Runbohm. The situation got so bad finally that Polhem took Runbohm to court. Feif, in one of his letters, related that Runbohm was disposed of in such a way that he could no longer "harm the mill."[198]

These irritations were minor in comparison to Polhem's major problem, that of getting a qualified work force together. He complained time and time again, that once the workers had been trained to operate the machines, they left the mill, either "to become their own bosses" or because they got "angry and did not cooperate with the management of the mill." In November of 1709 the Bureau of Mines passed a resolution which promised to help Stjernsund "find a way out of its difficulties, and to obtain good craftsmen."[199] As a result of this action by the Bureau of Mines, a worker was forbidden to leave Stjernsund once he had been registered and trained, "without the consent of the management." The worker, pledged to "remain at his work, to be industrious and faithful, as long as he is paid a just wage, based on the kind of work he is doing, his previous experience, and the difficulty of the work; furthermore, he is to instruct his children and his apprentices in his trade, so that they might someday be qualified to do the same kind of work. In this way there would be many more workers in the future, and the manufacturing industry would prosper." If a worker left the factory without a legitimate reason, Polhem and Stierncrona were empowered "to take him back to the mill." If they could not trust him with any kind of work, they could "have him drafted into the military and he would be placed in some isolated district for punishment and as a warning to others." If anyone had a legitimate reason for leaving, he would nonetheless be fined two hundred silver daler and would not be permitted to continue the trade which he had learned in the mill. In this way the government attempted to regulate the behavior of the workers at the larger industrial settlements. Another problem arose when Karl XII recruited large numbers of men for the war against Norway. This robbed Stjernsund of many good workers.[200] Polhem and Stierncrona did not attempt to enforce the Bureau of Mines' resolution with those workers who did

[197] Polhem and Stierncrona to Governor Gripenhielm, Oct. 26, 1706. O. R. Strömfelt to Stierncrona, June 8, 1722. *Biografi P.* (KB).
[198] Polhem to the district court, May 23, 1711. Feif to Polhem, Nov. 4, 1712.
[199] Resolution of Nov. 13, 1709. *Stjernsunds arkiv.*
[200] Polhem to "Välborne hr Secreter," Dec. 19, 1717. *Biographica.* (RA).

26. *The area near Stjernsund, from a lithograph dated approximately 1850*

move away at this time. They were fearful that they "would frighten away many good men who might otherwise come to Stjernsund."

In a memorandum dated from the summer of 1718,[201] Polhem asked Karl XII to give the mine director of each area complete control over his workers. The mine director should also act as an arbiter in all decisions involving "contracts and dismissals," so that both parties might receive fair treatment. In this way he could decide upon conflicts between labor and management.

The ground about Stjernsund was extremely stony and could not be used for farming. "It is difficult," Polhem wrote, "to have people live on rough and stony ground, which could not supply enough food for a goat." The bad terrain about Stjernsund was one of the reasons why good workers could not be obtained easily. Although it was less profitable, the workers had to live away from the mill, so that they could, as Polhem said, "cultivate their gardens of cabbage and turnips." Polhem encouraged his workers to purchase land and build their own homes.

In spite of everything done to improve the conditions of the workers, Stjernsund did not progress as it might have. When Mine Director Göran Wallerius inspected Polhem's mill in December, 1729, he found that discipline there left much to be desired. The workers, he reported, chose the work they wanted to do themselves; they did not obey orders; many of them left the mill and built their own shops. Wallerius commented on these difficulties, and said they were due, in part, to the fact that there were several owners of the mill.[202]

Very often, capable workers contracted to do a specific kind of work at the mill. On February 2, 1706, Hans Andersson Pipare, a blacksmith, agreed to be responsible for all work with "scrap-iron, coal, and slag." For this work he would charge two copper daler, four öre per shippound. This figure included the work of a number of boys, with the stipulation that if there was not enough work for all of them, they would then hammer nails, and Pipare would be responsible for their pay.[203] On November 8, 1716, Zacharias Hoffman signed a contract stating that he would manufacture fifteen dozen sheet iron dishes (tin-plated) every day for the entire year. To do this, he would employ the mill's ironworkers and tinsmiths. With the metal which was not used, he would make other metal items such as candlesticks and strainers.

[201] "Kort memorial på de fel och olägenheter, som synas vilja förstöra Stjernsunds manufaktur, så framt icke höga öfverhetens handräckning emellan kommer, medelst en sådan ordning, som det kan rätta, och på sätt som här bifogad projecteras." (Karlsgraf, Sept. 15, 1718.) *Biographica*. (RA).

[202] "Wallerius memorial," Dec. 10, 1729. *Biografi P.* (KB).

[203] Agreement between Polhem, Stierncrona and Pipare, Feb. 2, 1706. *Biografi P.* (KB).

All that he made over the stipulated amount would be his as a bonus.[204]

In the beginning of the 1730's, there were more than 200 people employed at Stjernsund.[205] Of these, not everyone was an adult worker, because Polhem had the idea that the children of the mill-workers should be employed from the earliest ages possible. To educate the young in the Christian faith, Polhem and Stierncrona requested that a resident priest be assigned to Stjernsund.[206] In November of 1749, a priest was appointed, who came under the jurisdiction of the rector in Husby.[207] Polhem wanted a priest for the mill town because the long and difficult road to the neighboring church had discouraged people from coming to work at the mill. "Instead of pious and godly people, one had to be content with the refuse, who were more concerned with the ale barrel than they were with the church," Polhem related. The wooden church built during Polhem's time was located across from the mill between the roadway and Lake Grycken. It remained there until November 1896, when it was torn down.[208]

A contract had been drawn up between Polhem and Gabriel Stierncrona on September 3, 1701.[209] As stipulated in the contract, Stierncrona was to pay personally[210] for the construction of the mill, "the blacksmith's shop, the sawmill, the furnaces, the granary, the flour-mill, the coalbins, other necessary buildings, and finally, to pay for a fence around the place." Polhem, to fulfill his part of the contract, would use his inventions to make the goods which had been designated. He was assured the rights to one half of the revenues of the mill. When Stierncrona went to advance the money for the purchase of materials, he insisted that he receive two thirds of all of the profits. He did say, however, that when he died, the mill would be divided into two equal shares, one half to his heirs and the other half to Polhem's heirs.

Paragraph VII in this contract read: "When the mill comes into existence, it is to be named after the one who initiated it; nonetheless, I, Christoffer Påhlhammar, have consented to the wishes of Hr. Assessor Stierncrona, that this mill shall be called Stjernesund; this, how-

[204] Contract between Polhem, A. Heyke, and Hoffman, Nov. 8, 1716. *Biografi P.* (KB).
[205] Polhem, "Ödmjuk berättelse om manufakturverket vid Stjernsund." I. Hermansson, *"De praefectura Naesgardensis Dalekarliae,"* 1734, p. 80.
[206] Kungl. bref, Nov. 24, 1749. *Stjernsunds arkiv.*
[207] Polhem, *Memorial*, Sept. 15, 1718.
[208] Carlsson, *Husby socken i Dalarne förr och nu*, 1899, p. 96.
[209] The original belonged to Malin Beijer (nee von Stockenström) Stockholm.
[210] According to Polhem, Stierncrona's share was 18,000 copper daler.

ever, does not give Herr Assessor any more rights than me." Even with this contract, however, there were many battles over the ownership rights of the mill. When Stierncrona died in 1723, his interests in the mill were handled by Auditor Edvard Plaan. Polhem complained at the time that he could have gotten what rightfully belonged to him but that the mill's records had been stolen and were never returned.[211]

The financial records of the mill were kept in order by a bookkeeper. However, when at first the profits were small, Polhem and Stierncrona decided to make him a partner, and in this way give him "an adequate salary." They hoped that, as a partner in the mill, "he might take better care of the mill's interests," which would be "to his own advantage as well as that of the mill." A contract was signed by Stierncrona, Polhem, and the bookkeeper, Abraham Heyke,[212] on February 3, 1711, that guaranteed Heyke ten percent of the profits of the mill, Stierncrona sixty percent, and Polhem thirty percent. There was an additional paragraph to the contract which stated that Polhem would receive the income from all of the ale sold at the mill. This was added because of Polhem's many expenses: "taking care of the sightseers who came to the mill, as well as for expenses he incurred in public service." Heyke was to receive the income from the distillery (there was an added clause which said that no one was permitted to drink more ale and whiskey than his salary would allow). This restriction was included because of Polhem's interest in temperance and is quite unusual for his time. Revenues from the "coalworkers and others" were to go to Stierncrona.[213]

Heyke, in 1721, "leased" Polhem's share of Stjernsund, and held it until 1728. It then went to Polhem's son-in-law, Reinhold Rückersköld,[214] for an annual payment of ten thousand copper daler.

It is known that Polhem moved from Stjernsund sometime after 1730, because of the death of his wife. In 1737 there was a great fire which almost destroyed the mill, and it was a long time before it was rebuilt.[215] Polhem's share in Stjernsund went to his nephew, Anders Polhammar, in June of 1750, for ten thousand copper daler annually, of which two thirds would go to himself and one third to his children.

[211] "Förklaring öfver de 4 kontrakter, som blifvit inrättade angående Stjernsunds manufaktur." *Teknologi*. (KB).

[212] Heyke was appointed in the beginning of 1708.

[213] The original contract was dated Feb. 3, 1711. *Biografi P.* (KB).

[214] The lease dated Dec. 28, 1728. *Biografi P.* (KB).

[215] There is no other direct reference to the damage caused by the fire, except in one manuscript which dealt with the inheritance, in which Polhem speaks of "undan branden räddade möbler och lösören."

After Polhem's death in 1751 this agreement was renewed for another five years.[216] Twenty years earlier, Anders Polhammar had been made a part-owner of the mill, and was in charge of the clockmaking division. About the year 1717, this part of the mill had almost closed down, partly because of the demands for higher wages by the workers, and because Polhem was not present at the time.[217] Polhem returned in 1730 and signed a contract with his nephew to direct the clockmaking division and its manufacturing. He advanced six thousand copper daler to purchase the materials needed to get started. Stierncrona's heirs were invited to become partners, but they declined.[218]

It is difficult to determine whether Stjernsund was a profitable operation for Polhem. He frequently complained that the profits did not come as he had hoped. We must remember, however, that Polhem was extremely careful with his money, and his complaints may not really mean too much. Polhem wrote[219] that the annual "yield" of the mill was between eighteen and twenty thousand copper daler. In January of 1740, he promised to give all of his children eighteen thousand copper daler. It appeared that this was his wife's inheritance he was dividing, rather than his own fortune.[220] Polhem's share of Stjernsund was valued in 1760 at one hundred and eighty thousand copper daler, which was a substantial sum in those days. In addition, many of his private projects paid well. He always demanded substantial payment for his work, and at times people complained that his work was much too expensive.

After Polhem's death, Stjernsund, with all of its privileges, buildings, and surrounding farms, was sold to Reinhold Galle Rückersköld, son of Reinhold Rückersköld and Emerentia Polhem, for one hundred and eighty thousand copper daler. He and his wife, Sophia Lovisa Hacker, arranged that their share in Stjernsund would be held as an estate and that members of the Polhem family would decide

[216] Lease dated June 18, 1750 and June 21, 1755. Copy. *Stjernsunds arkiv.*

[217] In the contract with A. Polhammar on Jan. 15, 1730, Polhem gave the reasons why the clockmakers were not satisfied with their salary. No profits were able to be made on the basis of their salary demands. The work was terminated because no agreement could be reached. In the contract dated March 4, 1738, there was a description of what occurred during Polhem's stay in Karlskrona and Karlsgraf. The water line sprang a leak which was never repaired, and which was permanently destroyed when the ice came. The workers left their jobs and took the tools with them. The machines which were used to make the clocks were also damaged, and the clockmakers left their positions without asking for a leave. The contract may be found in copy in *Stjernsunds arkiv.*

[218] Cf. Sidenbladh, *Om uhr eller uhrvärk af Christoffer Polhem.* 1910, p. 12.

[219] "Förklaring öfver de 4 kontrakterna," *Teknologi.* (KB).

[220] "Öfverenskommelse mellan Polhem och hans barn," Kersö, Jan. 2, 1740. *Biografi P.* (KB).

upon its disposition from generation to generation. Rückerskjöld's nephew, Johan Reinhold Steenman, was the next owner, and then his daughter, Sophia Lovisa, wife of Salomon von Stockenström. It then passed on to their son, Carl Reinhold Polhem von Stockenström, who received governmental permission to sell the estate to the Waern Corporation in 1856. Gabriel Stierncrona's share of the estate was also sold. His grandson, David Stierncrona, received thirty-two thousand "riksdaler" for it in 1816 from Steenman. By virtue of Steenman's purchase, the original shareholders, Polhem and Stierncrona, were united.[221] Stjernsund was purchased in 1872 by the Kloster Corporation, and a thriving iron and steel manufacturing plant began operation soon after.

Polhem had built a home for himself and his family near the mill at Stjernsund. He lived there from 1701 to about 1735. When his wife died, a "tender and faithful wife," as he called her, he was so grieved that he never returned to Stjernsund.[222] She was buried "with great honor," in Jakob's Church on the fifth of December, 1735. In a poem[223] composed by one of the children, she was described as "a Sarah to her husband, a pillar of strength to the poor, and the pride of womanhood."

After his wife's death, Polhem lived with his son-in-law, Carl Gripenstierna on the Kersö estate in Ekerön of Mälaren. He later moved to Stockholm, to his daughter's home near Klara Church. He subsequently purchased a home, No. 113 in the Rosendal section of Maria Parish, on the corner of Björngårdsbrunnsgatan (now "Bellmansgatan") and Hornsgatan. In this house the "Archimedes of the North" died on the 30th of August, 1751. He was buried in Maria Church in Stockholm. Unfortunately, the church burned to the ground in 1759, and nothing remains of Polhem's grave.

Polhem had moved to Stockholm to direct the construction of a canal lock there. In spite of his old age and his annual "fever," his mind was still alert. It was reported later that "he was in full possession of his faculties until the last, and was as lively and cheerful as he was during his youth." When he was eighty years of age, he was still working vigorously. He planned the following projects during this

[221] This history of Stjernsund after Polhem's death has been put together from sales records, wills, and bequests, which are in the possession of Malin Beijer (nee von Stockenström), Stockholm.

[222] Carlen, *op. cit.*, p. 155.

[223] "Ett sorge-ljud från Söder går
    Thet uti Norden möte får
    Då . . . fru Maria Polhem . . . befordrades til sin wälbestälte lägerstad."

101

27. *Posthumous portrait of Christopher Polhem, showing the order of the North Star which is located next to the square and the compass. Polhem received this honor before his death. The portrait was at Stjernsund, but is now privately owned.*

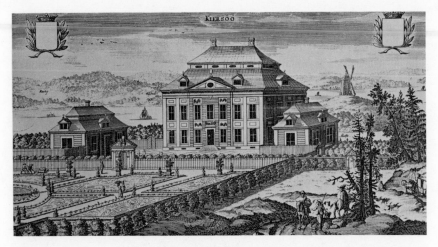

28. *Kersö at the end of the seventeenth century; from* Suecia Antiqua et Hodierna

time: a model for a dock in Karlskrona (1748); a plan for the construction of new fortifications in Landskrona (1748); a plan for the construction of a barricade at Vaxholm.[224]

The lock which he contracted to build in Stockholm in 1744 was not completed during his lifetime. He did live long enough, however, to see the first vessel taken through the lock from Mälaren to the approach to the Baltic.[225] A story is told that when he was elected to membership in the newly-instituted "Order of the North Star" in 1748, the ceremony took place at the lock itself.

Polhem was undoubtedly happy to learn that the government in 1740 had chosen him to determine how a waterway between Lake Vänern and the Kattegat could best be built. It was decided to build such a canal because Polhem had advised earlier that it would be in the best interests of the country.[226] Work on the canal began at Trollhättan in 1749, but had to be abandoned because of lack of funds.

Polhem's great skills and his monumental contributions to the development of Sweden were not fully appreciated while he lived. There were some, of course, who recognized the significance of the "Swedish Archimedes." In 1734, an academic thesis was written by Peter Uggla which dealt with the history of that part of Sweden where Stjernsund was located. In it the following quotation is significant: "What Tubalcain and Bezaleel were to the Hebrew people, because of their love

[224] "Promemoria vid Polhems personalier." *Biografi P.* (KB).

[225] Stockholms *Post-tidningar* 1751: n:r 69 (5–9).

[226] "Trollhättan, dess kanal-och kraftverk," utg. af Kungl. Vattenfallsstyrelsen, 1(1911), pp. 87ff.

29. *St. Maria Magdalena Church in Stockholm. In 1911 a memorial plaque was placed there by the Svenska Teknologföreningen (Swedish Technological Society)*

for wisdom; Zoroaster for the Babylonians, because of his astronomical insights; Mercurius Trismegistus for the Egyptians, because of his learning; Orpheus for the people of Thrace, because of his songs and poems; so the 'Archimedes of the North,' Christopher Polhem, is to us; his inventions and machines and buildings are now seen in almost every part of Sweden."[227]

The members of "The Swedish Association of Engineers and Architects" placed a plaque in 1911 in Polhem's honor in St. Maria Magdalena Church in Stockholm. Polhem's whole life, however, was a monument to greatness, a greatness which can never be destroyed; "As long as ore is obtained from our mines, and water rushes down our rivers, we remember the Swede who, far better than anyone before him, understood that we must treasure and use the riches of our land; a Swede whose whole life was dedicated to the development of his country."[228]

---

[227] Hermansson, *op. cit.*, pp. 76–77.

[228] Fries, *Den svenska odlingens stormän*, 2(1899), p. 26. Cf. "Tankar vid vår oförliknelige Polhems död, som timade den 30 augusti 1751."

> "Haf evig tack för all Din möda
> Du hedersman: om Ditt beröm
> Är hela svenska Norden öm:
> Ditt lof skall Dina foster föda
> Det skall med Dig till höjden gå:
> Så bredt och långt, som vattnet flyter;
> Så djupt, som berg-man malmen bryter,
> Där skall det äfven prägladt stå."

CHAPTER TWO

Polhem's Contributions to Applied Mechanics

BY GUSTAF SELLERGREN

I. Inventions in the Area of Metalworking

A. The Manufacturing Works at Stjernsund

When Polhem returned home from abroad in 1696, he realized Sweden's urgent need to develop an industry, particularly in iron and steel manufacturing. He was able to interest Baron Gabriel Stierncrona in his plans to build a "manufacturing works" in Sund, in the parish of Husby (Dalecarlia). Stierncrona was, as Polhem said, "a little wealthier than me." They began on a very small scale, but in time were able to enlarge the works considerably. The government assisted them at first, and the future of the mill seemed assured.

Polhem had his problems, however, particularly in the hiring of blacksmiths and other skilled workers. At first, he tried to get workers from abroad, but he felt that this did not add to the development of Sweden's indigenous industries. Then, too, he found that "the foreigners were not content in our poor land." His only alternative, therefore, was to teach the trade to the young men of Sweden. Even this plan did not have favorable results, because once a worker became skilled, he left Polhem's mill to work elsewhere, oftentimes because of a better-paying position. Others were encouraged to enter the military service, for war broke out at the same time that Stjernsund was founded. There were other problems as well, among them the extremely high tariff on exported material, and the concentration of Sweden's economy on the war. Polhem's experiences as a manufacturer were not too rewarding. He expressed it this way: "the mill taxed my patience to the limit, and convinced me that I was the biggest fool for establishing the manufacturing works; but now it was too late to regret."

The techniques for refining raw materials were greatly improved at the end of the seventeenth century. Attempts were being made to harness natural sources of power, such as waterfalls and the wind. Hand tools were exchanged for machine-driven tools. This made possible a division of labor in one phase of production, which, in turn, created mass production. Polhem had seen the reform which had taken place in the manufacturing of metals and textiles in England and France. He recognized the great economic significance of a similar reform for Sweden, particularly with Sweden's natural resources, and attempted to reduplicate these foreign methods of production at Stjernsund. He, of course, never really succeeded because, as all men ahead of their time, his genius was not recognized for what it was. In spite of this, he must be credited with being the creator of the Swedish metal industry.

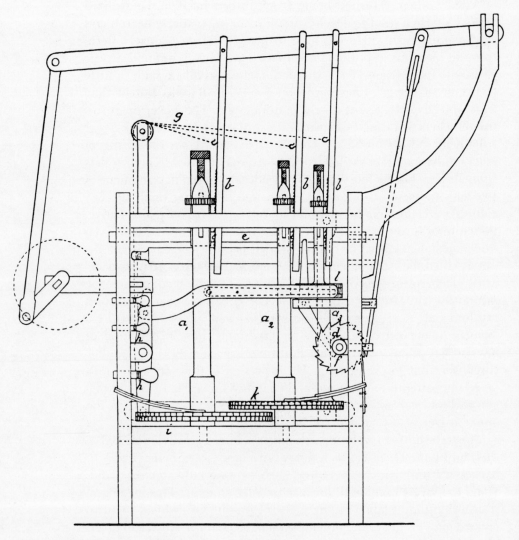

1. *Machine for cutting out cog wheels*

At first, Stjernsund manufactured only different kinds of clocks and locks. Subsequently, they added other metal products such as iron receptacles, files, nails, and similar things. Clockmaking was Polhem's favorite kind of manufacturing, however. He said in one of his papers that "the first thing I could make with any degree of success was a clock." The machines he used to build clocks were operated by water power. All of the gears and wheels on the machine itself were cut by another machine which Polhem constructed. The cogs themselves were cut out by a mill cutter or "file cutter." J. Schröder,[1] who in 1755 was director of the metal industries of Sweden, reported that nine men were employed in Stjernsund's clockworks. Cogwheels and drive-wheels were cut out in the following manner: three, four, or five cogwheel blanks were placed on top of each other in a horizontal position; the cogs were cut out by means of a broach or "file cutter" which moved upward and downward in a sawing motion. By means of horizontally working files, the cogs of the drive-wheels were cut out. It is difficult to determine whether this machine was original with Polhem or whether he learned the technique abroad. The principle behind Polhem's machine is similar to that of the modern broach. For this reason, Polhem's machine is of real historical interest, because it has always been thought that this kind of a broach (that is, one which worked according to the same principle as a file with small cutting teeth) was an American invention. Traditionally, the broach was reported to have been used for the first time in a Springfield gun factory about the year 1820.

A full-size wooden model of Polhem's machine for cutting out cog-wheels may be found in the Tekniska Museet in Stockholm.[2] However, there are a number of significant differences in this machine compared with the one described above. Three cogwheels of different sizes and number of cogs can be cut simultaneously. The blanks, cut from sheet iron, are placed on three vertical spindles, a_1, a_2, a_3 (see Fig. 1). The spindles rotate a part of a turn for every vertical motion of the files, b. In this way, the teeth of the files receive an equal amount of wear. By means of a cam movement, d, the rod, e, is pushed forward and backwards for every rotation of the axle, f, which causes the files in their upward motion to be forced away from the cogs. In the downward motion, they are forced toward the wheels by the ropes, g, and the spring, h. On the spindle a_1 there are two cogwheels, i, with

[1] Manuscript. *Teknologi*. Kungliga Biblioteket (KB).
[2] The inscription reads: "Machin att skära ut flera uhrhjul tillika. Af Comercie Råd, och Comend. af Nordstj. Ord. Chr. Polhem."

2. *A typical clock face of a "pillar clock," made at Stjernsund, with the name of Anders Polhammar on the face. Anders Polhammar was director of the clock factory from 1730–1760; Nordiska Museet, Stockholm*

3. *An eight-day "pillar clock" with a chiming mechanism. It was made at Stjernsund. The name of Mathias Fahlen, who was the director of the clock factory in the beginning of the eighteenth century, is found on the clock; Nordiska Museet, Stockholm*

4. *The mechanism of the clock in Figure 3; Nordiska Museet, Stockholm*

forty-eight and fifty-two cogs; spindle a_2 has two cogwheels, k, with forty and forty-four cogs on spindle a_3 there are three cogwheels, l, with twelve, sixteen, and twenty-four cogs. The cogs on the spindle determine the number of cogs on the wheel being cut. The precision control for the machine was described as a steel gauge (steel rings with cogs inside) through which the finished cogwheel had to pass. This process is very similar to the modern mass production techniques.

A great many floor clocks, as well as clocks for towers and steeples, were made at Stjernsund. The clock face was usually made of brass or sheet iron in the shape of a square, and very often had ornamentation in the corners (see Figs. 2, 3, 4). This kind of craftsmanship spread to other parts of Dalecarlia, particularly to the area about Mora. During the middle of the eighteenth century, in the village of Östnor, which was made up of no more than fifty families, there were at least twenty-five skilled clockmakers. The "Dalecarlian clock," which was usually a wall clock, was made solely by these family clockmakers, even as late as the middle of the nineteenth century. At that time the inexpensive, mass-produced, American clock began to be sold, and it was no longer practical to continue making them.

A catalogue from the year 1711 which listed the different articles made at Stjernsund included a price list for clocks.[3] Schröder's report from the year 1755 indicated that the manufacture of clocks continued after the great fire of 1737, which had destroyed a great many valuable machines, models, manuscripts, and drawings.

Clockmaking was not, however, a profitable operation. It was necessary, therefore, for Polhem to introduce other kinds of manufacturing which would not have to compete with the foreign market. For this reason, he began to "make different kinds of tin-plated cooking utensils, plates, platters, and bowls. . . ." Polhem's factory for making kitchen utensils was complete in every way. Not only did it have the machines to shape the metals, but also to finish and plate them. There was also a forge which could work with sheet iron. Polhem reported that the blacksmith's shop was 80 to 90 alnar long[4] and had seven water-wheels which drove a great number of hammers, among them one rod hammer, one plate hammer, a tilt hammer and six drop hammers, as well as scissors and rollers, and many other things. The dam which was connected to the mill "was built in an unusual way, and was 150 alnar long, and 10 alnar deep."

---

[3] Cf. Sidenbladh, *Om uhr eller uhrvärk af Chr. Polhem,* 1910.
[4] Aln, an obsolete measure, comparable to the British ell.

115

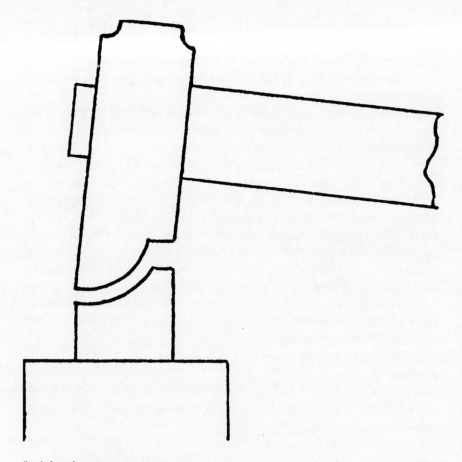

5. *A drop hammer*

In the forge, a kind of drop hammer[5] or "striking ram" (see Fig. 5), as Polhem called it, was used to shape and mold the metal. Iron sheets were heated until they became white-hot, and were then placed on a cast-iron anvil, where they were shaped by several strokes of the hammer (a cast-iron ram or "cube"), which exerted a pressure of more than one thousand pounds. There were different shaped blocks or dies (swages) of different depths for the shaping procedure. Polhem used water power to lift his drop hammer, which could be raised to a height of almost six feet. According to König,[6] this machine could be used

[5] This and the other machines described later may be found in C. H. König's work, "Inledning til mechaniken och bygnings-konsten jämte en beskrifning öfwer åtskillige af framledne Commercerådet och Commendeuren af Kongl. Nordstjerne-Orden Hr. Polhem opfundne machiner." 1752.

[6] König, *op. cit.* Tab. xxv. (The drawings in this work are sometimes incomplete and do not always agree with the description.)

116

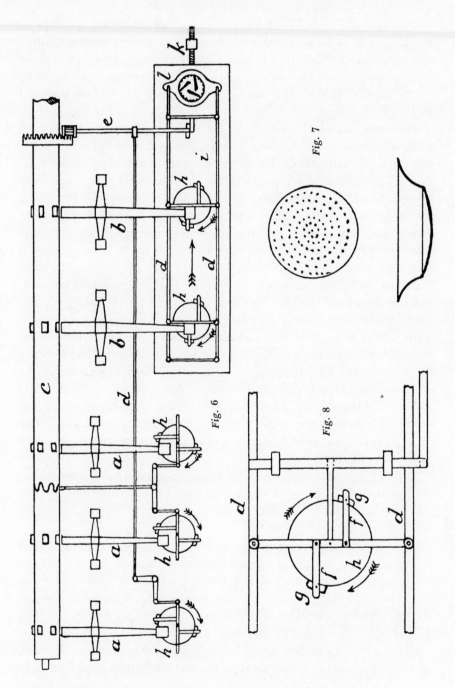

Fig. 6

Fig. 7

Fig. 8

6–8. *Drawing of the "hammer works" used to make plates from sheet metal*

to make many things: "lock plates with designs stamped upon them, various kinds of molded and beaded work, leaf design work on knives and swords, as well as other things." The leaf design process was done by impressing the block or die bearing the design upon the knife or sword handle. It was then casehardened by one of Polhem's special methods.

Polhem's manufacturing works for making plates and platters of sheet iron was almost completely destroyed by fire in 1737. König has given us a description of the way iron utensils were first made, however.[7] The sheet iron was molded by a drop hammer on an anvil and then finished by a mechanical "hammering" machine. This machine was made up of three tail hammers, a (see Fig. 6), which shaped the edge of the utensil, and two hammers, b, which shaped the interior. It was driven by means of a lift cam on a roll, c. This in turn was driven by a water-wheel with "a crown-wheel and a lantern-wheel." The work began in the center of the utensil (see Fig. 7) as it slowly rotated, moving simultaneously toward its sides. The speed of the rotary motion decreased as the radius of the plate increased. This maintained a constant rate of feed. When the center of the utensil was completed, the hammers stopped automatically. The edges were finished by the other set of hammers. Of particular interest was the feed movement of the machine (see Figs. 6 and 8). The rod, d, was moved backward and forward by the axle, e. The arms, f, to which were fastened friction clamps, g, rotated the utensil, h, during the hammering process.[8] The table, i, as well as the utensils, were moved slowly by a screw, k, and a gear-wheel mechanism, l.

Polhem had also designed a machine to make oval-shaped plates and platters. However, he never completed the construction of this machine because, as he said, "nothing is sure at the mill; we are threatened daily with disaster."

Another hammering machine made cups and goblets from sheet iron.[9] This machine is of special interest because it has a universal coupling, or, as it is often called today, a "Polhem joint." The machine had a rapidly-moving hammer which shaped the goblet, a (see Fig. 9), which was held by a chuck with three clamps (see Fig. 10). The goblet was shaped as it moved slowly about a cylindrical anvil. The roller, b, turned a conical roller, c, provided with cogs and a cogwheel, d, and the screw, e, which in turn rotated the goblet and held it in

[7] König, op. cit., p. 164, Tab. xv and xxv.

[8] A similar apparatus was made in Great Britain and called "Worssam's silent feed," and was patented in 1850 by Samuel Worssam.

[9] König, op. cit., p. 174, Tab. xx.

118

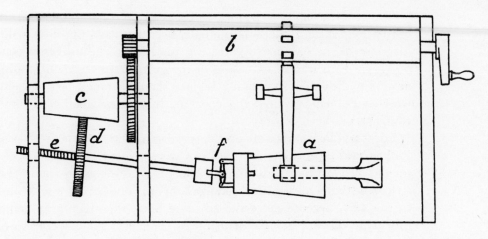

Fig. 9

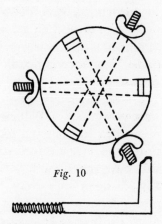

Fig. 10

9, 10. *The hammering machine to make cups and goblets from sheet iron*

position for the hammer. By means of the conical roller, c, the number of rotations of the goblet was gradually decreased, and in this way the diameter of the hammering area was increased. The universal coupling, f, which was an extension of the axle, e, conveyed the rotary motion to the goblet itself as it was being shaped.[10] One does not know whether Polhem invented this coupling himself or whether it came from abroad.

Locks and lock parts were products of Stjernsund in these early days. Polhem was especially interested in the very intricate kind of lock, such as burglarproof padlocks and safety locks. Polhem maintained a strict rule that a locksmith could work on only one part of a lock, and in this way, become more skilled. The work would progress more quickly in this way, too, Polhem argued. The locks which were manufactured at Stjernsund were forerunners of the modern doorlock. They usually consisted of a metal plate with turned edges and had one or more bolts. The locks were fastened to the edges of the door, as Polhem said, "so that when the door was closed, no one could screw the lock off from either the inside or the outside." The lock mechanism, as well as the keys, was usually forged. Polhem's lock (see Fig. 11), which has been used all over the world, never received his name because most of the lock companies were ignorant of its origin. The "Polhem lock," however, was adopted in America, and given the name "Scandinavian padlock." This indicates, however, ignorance of the real origin of this kind of lock.

Among the many unusual locks which Polhem developed, "which were novelties," as Polhem said, and not really useful, the following might be mentioned: a lock from which the key could not be taken unless the door was locked; a key which served as a faucet or a spigot, which regulated the flow of liquid from a barrel; a lock with several keys, made in such a way that the slightest change in any one of them meant the others could not be used. The mechanical principle behind many of these locks has been used again and again in the history of lockmaking. Polhem deserves the credit for much of what is now part of our modern conveniences. Automatic vending machines, for example, employ the principle of Polhem's lock mechanisms. Polhem's "barrel spigot"[11] was so arranged that a key, when turned a number of times, would release the desired amount of liquid. A detailed description of this spigot is found in an article in the journal *Daedalus*

[10] Cf. König, *op. cit.*, "Från patronen gå tvenne armar, emellan dessa armar sitter ett kors af järn på sådant sätt, att tvenne armar af korset gå emellan dessa begge armar, och de tvenne andra armarna af korset gå till armar på den andra patron, hvilken har trenne klor med skrufvar."

[11] König, *op. cit.*, p. 167, Tab. xv and xvi.

120

11. *The Polhem lock made at Stjernsund about the year 1720; Tekniska Museet, Stockholm*

Hyperboreus from the year 1717, and is entitled, "Polhem's Unusual Tap."

In addition to locks, the mill at Stjernsund made files. Finally, however, this operation also had to be discontinued, because Stjernsund could not compete with the British market. Polhem once said that a foreign-made file used to cost at least a karolin, but after he began to manufacture files they cost only "a few pennies." This fact made file manufacturing impossible for Polhem.

We do not know exactly how Polhem's file-cutting machine was constructed. The Tekniska Museet has an ancient model in small scale of a similar machine, but it is doubtful whether Polhem invented this one (see Fig. 12). He never mentioned such a machine, nor do we find any record of one in Gabriel Polhem's description of his father's inventions. This model is made of wood and metal and works by two cutters which move up and down vertically. The materials used for the files are placed under the cutters on a bed of lead on a horizontal table.

Steel knives, forks, scissors, and similar edged utensils were made at

121

12. *A model of Polhem's file-cutting machine; Tekniska Museet, Stockholm*

Stjernsund. Polhem described the operation:[12] a blank of iron and steel was forged out under the tail hammer into the shape of a knife in two heatings; forks in three heatings. The tempering process was done by heating the utensil in a lead bath, then cooling the material to a blue color, shaping, grinding, and polishing. The grinding was done with sandstone and the polishing on wooden disks coated with emery and cottonseed oil. Polhem reported that two workmen could make twenty to thirty dozen of these knives per day.

Polhem also made use of a "nailsmith" at the Stjernsund mill. The nail was made from strips of sheet iron. The machine invented by Polhem for this purpose was still in use in 1752. The strip or sheet of iron was cut lengthwise into three narrow strips by a cutter which consisted of a movable part, a, and two stationary parts, b (see Fig. 13). The motion of a was caused by the cams, c, on the axletree.[13]

At about this time, countries outside of Sweden were beginning to use rolling mills when working with metals. It is believed that Polhem brought the rolling mill to Sweden. His work, "The Use of Rolling Mills in Manufacturing"[14] demonstrated the superiority of the roll over the hammer. He said that "a rolling mill can do ten to twenty times the work of a hammer," with the result that production could be increased tremendously. He showed how iron could be worked into all kinds of shapes on a rolling mill and he devised ways to use the rolling mill for the production of metal products. For example, he showed how two pieces of metal, back to back, could be rolled and then cut. Polhem talked about his rolling mill and said: "a length of one aln could be drawn out to seven alnar five or six times, and all at one heating; I have seen this myself at my mill."

The greatest difficulty when rolls were first introduced was, of course, the lack of the necessary machine tools. James Watt, for example, related that it was almost impossible for him to find a machine which could be used to bore the cylinders in his steam engine. How ironic this is, for Watt did not know what Stjernsund had introduced into technology one hundred years earlier. For this reason, students of the history of engineering might want to investigate Polhem's manuscript "Rolling Mills and Their Construction," which reveals how he made different kinds of rolls from cast iron and forged iron.

The wrought-iron roll was turned on a lathe or "turning-bench" which was driven by a water-wheel, and was mounted by means of a screw clamp. The feeder screw was made in the following way: first a

[12] Polhem, *Patriotiska testamente*. 1761, pp. 78–89.
[13] König, *op. cit.*, p. 167. Tab. xxiv and xxvi.
[14] Polhem, *op. cit.*, pp. 57–58.

123

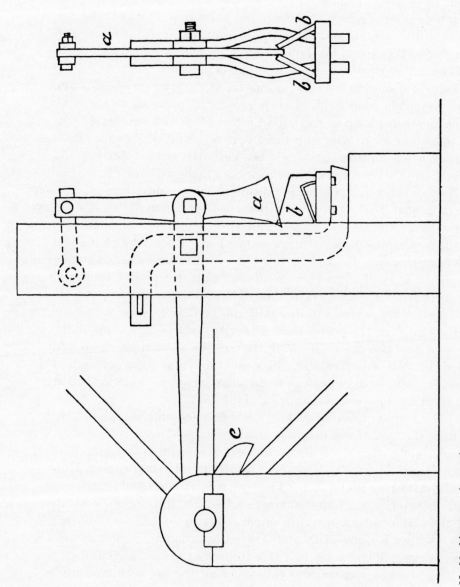

13. *Machine to cut iron strips*

hard wood spindle (or feed-worm) one aln long and two and one half tum[15] in diameter was turned on a lathe. Parallel lines were drawn on a paper, with the distances between them corresponding to the desired diameter (for example, one quarter of a tum). Then the paper was wound around the spindle so that the lines that were drawn formed a thread or screw track which could be reduplicated on the spindle itself by pressing a knife against it. The thread was then cut out from the spindle. This wooden screw was joined by means of a square chuck or coupling to the iron rod which was to be threaded. The two spindles were put in place in the lathe and set in motion by a hand crank. A long iron rod with a bent end, which had been worked to a thin blade, was inserted into the threads of the wooden spindle. At the same time, a cutting instrument (a chisel) was attached to the other end of the iron rod. When the crank was turned, the iron rod was fed forward and threads were cut in the spindle.

All of this complicated work only produced a feed-worm. The lathe work, of course, was not too precise. What a difference there is between Polhem's machine and those which are used today!

After the lathe work was completed, the surface of the roll was filed smooth and then tempered by placing it in running water or in oil or in melted tallow (which had been placed in a receptacle in running water). Rolls of forged iron were casehardened or steel-plated. After the tempering process, the roll was ground, if necessary, by a special process that Polhem had developed, which is very similar to present-day methods of grinding. Polhem said that this process was used by his son Gabriel in the mint at Cassel in the year 1737.

Polhem found that "large rolls are less effective than the smaller ones," and on the basis of this principle he gave directions for the construction of his rolling mill at Stjernsund. Sheet metal was pressed into band iron by the insertion of two smaller forged iron rolls, B, between the larger cast iron rolls, A (see Fig. 14). The larger rolls were designed to "hold the smaller rolls together correctly, so they would not become crooked."

From this description of the mill, it is obvious, even from a modern standpoint, that Stjernsund was an outstanding industrial settlement. From a technical point of view, the products manufactured there met the highest standards of the period. Furthermore, Stjernsund was of major significance to the development of an industrial Sweden. However, as has occurred too often in the pioneer days of industry, economic difficulties terminated the operation.

In his work, "A Short History of the Present State of Manufacturing

[15] Tum, an obsolete measure; 1 tum equals 1 inch.

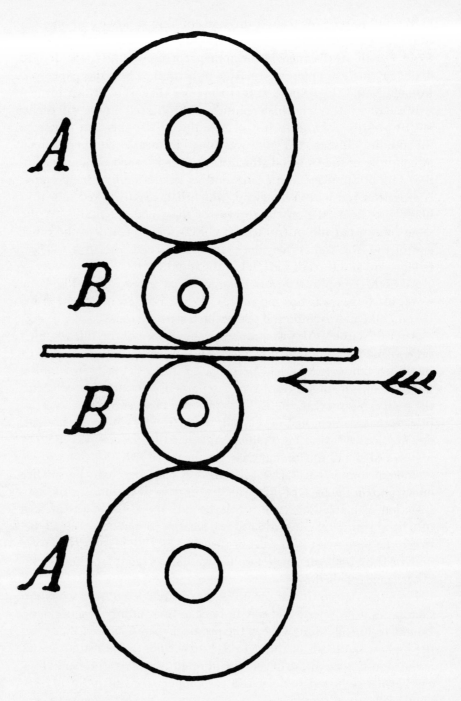

14. *Polhem's rolling mill*

at Stjernsund,"[16] which is dated 1730, Polhem complained about the grave economic situation of the mill. He feared that it was "on the point of ruin." This was unavoidable, he said, in "a country where the entire population hates domestic manufacturing." Furthermore, Polhem recognized that iron ore became inferior when there were too many mines. "If such a bad situation could be overcome, it would be very desirous," he said, "otherwise we must perish along with many others." Stjernsund continued long after Polhem's death manufacturing and exporting iron and steel products. His complaint about the iron ore was certainly justified, however. It was a long time before techniques in metallurgy could contribute to the newer mechanical methods.

Schröder's *Journal*, which described his visit to Stjernsund in 1755, is of special interest to our study. His visit was made only four years after Polhem's death and fifty-five years after the establishment of Stjernsund. Schröder wrote that Polhem's mill was made up of the following:

1) A large blacksmith's shop or forge, with two open hearths in "German style," one rod-iron hammer, one "annealing furnace," one plate hammer, as well as a plate-finishing hammer. In the same shop there were also one trip hammer, one pinch hammer, anvils, sheet-metal shears, and other tools, as well as a mill cutter (with furnace) "to cut nails and rod-iron blanks from bars of iron." All these machines were driven from an axletree connected to a water-wheel. There was also a little open hearth to make tools.

Beside this large forge, and in the same building, there was an old rolling mill with two water-wheels, which had not been used for a long time because of a lack of usable rolls.

2) Two nailworks with a hearth and two nail hammers; four nail-workers and four helpers in each, with a change of shift every six hours. All sizes of nails were made, from two and one half to six tum.

3) A lockworks with five locksmiths and assistants or helpers. "They made a large padlock using Hr. Christopher Polhem's design, and in addition to this there were two other kinds of padlocks, one which used a key, and also the usual kind." There were also several kinds of anvils and swages to make the bolts on the locks. A swage hammer was also used to stamp and edge plates and dishes.

4) The "steelyard" works, which was operated only occasionally, and then by the locksmith, "because the man who had been employed there previously had lost his eyesight."

5) A clockworks, with nine workmen.

[16] From a manuscript in KB, *Teknologi*.

6) A tin-plating works, which produced "casseroles," cooking pots, pans, scoops, lanterns, window frames, and other things from forged sheet iron. The tin-plating operation was criticized for not bringing about a satisfactory finished product.

In 1754, the "utensil machine" was rebuilt, after it had been destroyed in the fire of 1737. Soon after, however, even this kind of manufacturing was discontinued.

Schröder also reported in his *Journal* that one half of the mill at Stjernsund was owned by the heirs of Polhem, with the exception of the clockworks, which according to the contract, was divided up in the following manner: two thirds to his heirs and one third to the manager of the mill, Polhammar, as a compensation for his many inventions. There were two managers of the mill, Polhammar and Hilleström, who were put in these positions to watch over the interests of the two principal parties. Schröder said that this dual management was detrimental to an orderly and profitable business. It appeared, Schröder reported, that the mill employed about sixty workers.

Harald Finch who, in the early part of this century was the director of the Kloster Corporation, reported that there was an ancient "Polhem cottage" still in existence. A number of models and machines from the time of Polhem have been collected, but most of them are in very poor condition.

The Kloster mill did very fine work in iron and steel manufacturing and for a number of years made the "Stjernsund clock."

B. Polhem's Inventions in Foundry Techniques

Polhem worked to develop the foundry and its techniques and often wrote about this subject. During his time, the quality of cast iron was not good, largely because the cupola or cope furnace had not yet been invented and, furthermore, a material which resembled pig iron was usually used.

Polhem described how rolls were made. The material used for the molds was either clay, sand, or metal. The rolls were cast hollow and the cores were turned in such a way that a shaft was placed in the bearings on a bench and provided with a crank. A straw rope was wound around the spindle, over which soft clay and mold clay was applied. This was then turned and dried. The cracks were filled in, and then a more careful turning followed, and French clay and fresh milk were applied, followed by fine sand and lime water. It was then dried, and finally it received a layer of goat fat, and was then carefully rounded and smoothed. The core, with its layer of insulation, was prepared in this way. Finely powdered graphite and a powdered "tobacco pipe"

128

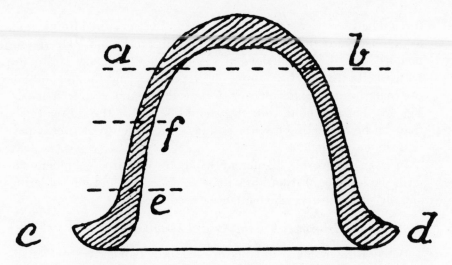

15. *Diagram of the cast-iron church bell which Polhem had constructed*

compound mixed with curdled milk, egg white, and ale was applied on top of this. After this mixture dried, a layer of clay, sand, and manure, which had been mixed into a paste, was spread on. It was dried and the paste applied five or six times. The roll was reinforced with four iron rods placed lengthwise alongside of it. These rods were bent at the bottom with eyelets at the top. On top of this, steel wire was wound and clay applied and dried. Thus the mantle was formed. The rope was pulled out to leave room for the gases to escape. The mold was dried and then baked in a potter's kiln. The layer of loose clay between the cope and the core was taken away by hand from the ends of the mold, and then the core was taken out. The mantle and the core were placed in sand and packed in such a way that it could not be broken by the gases at the time of the casting. When the roll was reddish-brown after the casting, it was tempered, after which it was rotated for even cooling. Polhem gave instructions to watch very carefully for blisters. These, as he said, "could be smoothed out with a material composed of steel filings, vinegar, and egg white."

Polhem also devised a technique to cast bronze church bells.[17] He pointed out that the bells used in Swedish churches were cast much more crudely than those in foreign lands. Furthermore, he noticed that the clappers were twice as heavy, and the bell itself appreciably heavier than foreign ones. From this he drew the conclusion that foreign bells were constructed for the sound produced, but that Swedish bells were produced for their strength. He questioned whether or not

[17] Polhem, *op. cit.*, pp. 101–108.

foreign bells "were not more melodious and better suited for playing, as one may hear in the German Church in Stockholm." He recommended that the proportions of the bell should be similar to the Dutch bells, that is, ab=7 units, ac=10, cd=14, and the thickness of the material at a=one quarter, f=one third, and e=one half (see Fig. 15). For the mold, thin clay should be used ("the thinnest clay that can be found"). The bronze should be made up of twenty percent tin, he asserted.

In a special work[18] "Different Kinds of Soldering," Polhem described a number of techniques to be used for hard and soft soldering and the lead mixtures which might be used in each.

C. Additional Discoveries in the Area of Metalworking

When King Fredrik and his brother, the Landgrave of Hessen-Cassel, visited Stjernsund in 1732, they were so impressed by the mill that they asked Polhem to construct a coining mill or mint in Cassel. Gabriel Polhem built a model of a mint on the basis of his father's design. This was received "with great appreciation" in 1738, and a mint was built in Mässinghoff near Cassel.

The coining mill[19] was completely new at that time. It was operated by water power, and consisted of two rolling mills (see Fig. 16), a large roll, *a*, and a smaller roll, *b*, to make the coin, a metal cutter, *c*, two stamping machines or punches, *d*, three minting stamps, *e*, a stamp, *f*, "for rough and special coins," a shearing mill, *g*, to cut metal strips or rods, as well as a "cleaning pan," *h*, for copper and silver blanks. The machines were powered by a breast-wheel, fifteen feet[20] in diameter, and the gear system consisted of bevel gears ("crown-wheels") of metal with the cogs "placed obliquely" so that "the pressure on the cogs was the same whether it was near the center of the wheel or at the outer edge." The rolls in the larger rolling mill (see Fig. 17) were three and one half tum in diameter, and could be adjusted accurately by means of a regulator screw. The smaller rolling mill had smaller rolls, which rotated a greater number of times. The smaller rolls had as their function to adjust the thickness of the coin. The cutting mill was made up of two rotating rolls with circular cutters which cut the metal sheet into narrow strips ("fillets" or "planches") from which the coin blanks were made and stamped. The stamping operation for "thicker and special coins" had two punches, four tum squares, each one with a particular die. The punch was moved by a lever and a lifting cam. Af-

[18] *Ibid.,* pp. 96–101.
[19] König, *op. cit.,* p. 169, Tab. xvii, xviii, xix.
[20] The measure, foot, is used as it is in the United States.

130

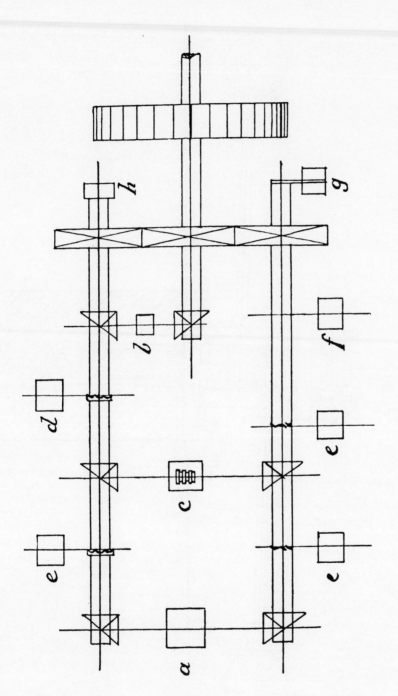

16. Diagram of the coining works in Cassel

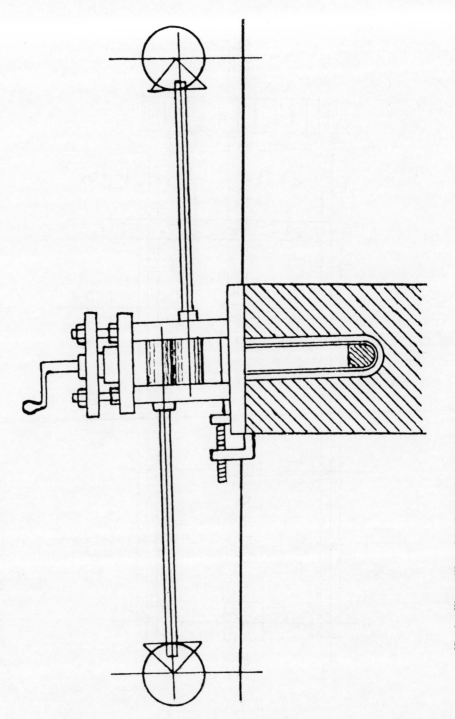

17. *A rolling mill used in the coining works in Cassel*

ter each stamping, material for another coin was fed in, and after it was stamped, the coin was ejected automatically. There were two stamping units for smaller coins. Another machine made ridges on the edges of the larger coins, as well as designs and inscriptions. It was reported by König that with these machines, four or five boys and a supervisor could do more daily than twenty to twenty-four persons using the old-fashioned machines.

Polhem's first, and what was probably his most significant, mechanical accomplishment was the work of repairing the astronomical clock in the Uppsala Cathedral. He said about this clock that it had been standing for one hundred years and had never worked properly. He was only twenty-seven years of age at the time he began to work on the clock, and was still a student at the university. This is a clear indication of the precocious character of Polhem's greatness. He was able to repair the clock "by the labor of his own hands," as he reported. It took him two years to complete the work, but when he was finished, he received "a year's scholarship of sixty copper daler."

This remarkable clock, which unfortunately was destroyed during the fire of 1702, was thought to have been the work of a monk from Vadstena, Petrus Astronomus. Polhem described in detail the different parts and mechanisms of the clock. These were quite complicated because, as he said, "it was so constructed that it did much more than what is usually required of a clock." It showed the entire *calendarium* with its *computus ecclesiasticus,* the motion of the sun and moon in their orbits, and the phases of the moon. It was supposed to show also the hours of the day, and the location of the planets as determined by "the worthless superstitions of the astrologers." The frame of the clock was of wood, ten or twelve alnar high. There was an *astrolabium catholicum* on the front of the clock, four or five alnar in diameter, which showed the location of the sun and the moon in relation to the earth, with the earth in the center and the moon a short distance away revolving around the earth, and the sun farther away in the zodiac. Below the *astrolabium* a large calendar for the three hundred and sixty-five days of the year could be seen. A number of maxims of the peasants were also found on the clock. Polhem, as he reconstructed the clock mechanism, put a pendulum into the clock instead of a balance wheel. He devised a way so that the weight had to be raised only once a month instead of every day, as it had been done previously, and also made some of the movements automatic. The work was done by Polhem with the greatest degree of industry. But he was prompted to say upon one occasion that "if I had known that the

133

clock would be destroyed by fire so soon after I finished repairing it, I would not have spent so much time on the difficult thing, because it did not attract people's attention at all."

When Polhem visited Paris during his student days, the scholarly world was concerned with the problem of how a clock could be constructed which would indicate the time in Turkey or Palestine, in Babylonia, in Italy, as well as the time in Paris. "Envoy Cronström" encouraged Polhem to make a model of such a clock, which was later shown to the well-known mathematician, Perrault. Polhem did not complete the clock, however, but it was finished soon after he left France by a Parisian clockmaker.

After his return to Sweden in 1696, he had many new ideas and hoped that he could use these ideas to further the mechanical and scientific understanding of his country. He began soon after to plan his *laboratorium mechanicum,* in which he hoped he could make "machines and other apparatus when called upon." His project attracted the attention of the authorities, and some financial aid was given. The war, of course, prevented any further expansion of this unique institution. The name *laboratorium mechanicum* suggested that experimental work in a laboratory should be related to mechanical principles. However, after Polhem's death, the *laboratorium mechanicum* limited itself to collecting models of his machines and other things he had made. These were brought subsequently to the "Royal Model Chamber." A catalogue, published in 1759 by Gabriel Polhem as an appendix to his father's "patriotic testament" listed twenty-one apparatus, models, and machines which had been collected. Examples of these are:

"1) An experimental machine to determine the effect of water on water-wheels, in relation to various falls and inclinations . . .

"2) An experimental machine to show the trajectory of a cannon ball in flight.

"3) An experimental machine to determine the different characteristics of balls of different weights and materials, while rising and falling . . .

"4) An experimental machine to demonstrate the influence of motion upon other motion."[21]

Among Polhem's discoveries in the area of metalworking is his technique to determine the size of the hole in a drawplate.[22] Two trial holes were made and were measured by a beveled punch. The other

[21] See the later section on Polhem's scientific work.
[22] Polhem, *op. cit.,* pp. 73–77 (Chap. 17: "Om dragverk").

holes were then made in diminishing proportion to the first.[23] Polhem added that "the size of the holes may not be according to these extensions or distances, which run *in ratione simplici,* but according to their radius *in ratione duplicata*" (i.e., the square of the radius) "as the wire extends alike to each hole, for example, to 1/2, 2/3, 3/4, etc., to the extent that the iron is softer and more tensile." Polhem also described how raw material for making thread was prepared in the tanning process.

In Gabriel Polhem's catalogue, other machines are listed:

a) A machine to raise and aim a cannon which was to be used for bombardments, flatboats and batteries.[24]

b) Rigging for factories where muskets were made, and powder mills with a sifting machine.

c) An apparatus to produce shells and cannon balls, powered by a water-wheel, which was to be made for the "Royal Naval and Defence Stations." A description of the "rigging" has not been found. Polhem told that it had been used by "Hr. Capitaine Elfwing to improve the operations of the factory." It was considered especially useful by the War Department.

II. Inventions in the Textile Industry

It is not well known that Polhem invented a number of important machines for the textile industry, particularly for knitted goods. A number of his ideas for these machines were undoubtedly received from abroad. However, many of these are not copies but are his own inventions. This is still another indication of the great diversity of his mechanical skills.

When Polhem created machines for the textile industry, he was motivated to do away with hand-operated apparatus. Jonas Alströmer, "the father of the textile industry," was at that time working to make more raw materials available, particularly domestic wool. It is sad to relate that neither of these great men, Polhem nor Alströmer, had his dream fulfilled. Alströmer's special merino breed of sheep, which was to supply the raw material for all of Sweden's wool industry, and Polhem's machines for a domestic wool industry, were never successful.

[23] Polhem added that "efter dessa utteckningar eller distancer, som löpa *in ratione simplici* får storleken på hålen intet vara, utan efter deras *radius in ratione duplicata*," (d.v.s. kvadraten på radien), "då tråden sträcker sig allt lika efter hvart hål, såsom vid pass till 1/2, 2/3, 3/4, etc., allt som järnet är blötare och segare."

[24] A number of these were in the Royal Model Chamber, 1761.

Many of Polhem's textile machines have been lost. On the basis of his descriptions and drawings, however, it is quite obvious that some of the basic principles of his machines were later used in the textile industry of Great Britain.[25]

Polhem related how he had improved the common loom so that it could manufacture hosiery; "a loom which was only one sixth the size of the original." These looms, which required nonetheless a degree of manual operation, were again improved by Polhem, and the resultant machine was, as he said, "undoubtedly the most perfect that can be made." The loom was not very large, and as Polhem said, "could be put in the trouser pocket." Usually it was attached to a table or a window sill by means of screws. It did not have pedals, but "when silk thread or yarn is placed on the loom, only one motion of the hand simultaneously performs all of the operations which before needed many operations." He went on to say that in order "to facilitate the manufacture of wool," a machine had to be made, powered by water, "to wash, break, comb, card, and spin the wool, and work so quickly that eighteen to twenty people could accomplish as much as five hundred in the ordinary method of spinning." He built a machine to spin wool which was so designed "that the thread could never break," and it was "so strong and intricate that the machine could regulate itself and yet produce thread which was as even as brass clavichord string." The drawing frame consisted of "a countless number of small steel needles, which all had to be exactly even and placed accurately." Undoubtedly Polhem was referring to an early version of a carding loom, which, however, could not be constructed for lack of competent workers.

The spinning machine must be constructed in such a way, said Polhem, "that of the thousands of spindles which operate at once, each one should be able to be taken out separately when it has completed its operation, that is, the spindles should be spun full without anyone touching them, causing one thread to lay alongside the other, the spindle tapering a little toward either end. I have also built a twisting machine," continued Polhem, "which can turn many spindles at one time, which one would think had been powered by hand."

A particularly interesting machine is a shearing machine for woven cloth (see Figs. 18 and 19).[26] There is a model of this machine,[27] but it is slightly different from Polhem's original, particularly in its mov-

[25] Cf. Polhem, "Kort berättelse om de förnämsta mechaniska inventioner." 1729.

[26] Described in König, *op. cit.*, p. 180. Tab. xxiv.

[27] This model carries the following inscription "Modell på öfverskärningsmaskin, i anledning af Commersierådet Polhems, men i många mål förändrad af Commissarien Norberg."

136

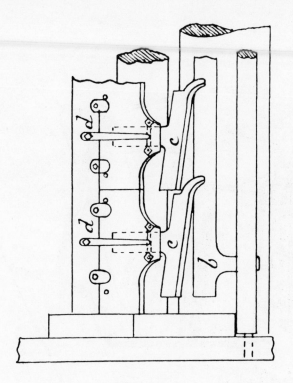
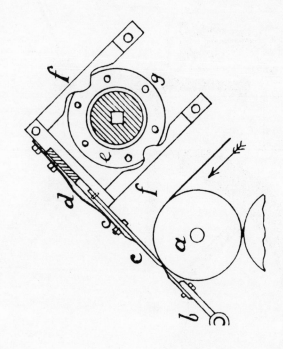

18. *Polhem's shearing machine*

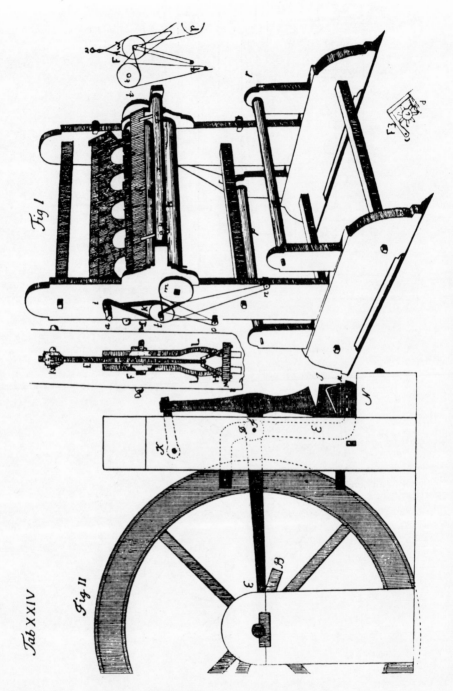

19. *A shearing machine (on the right in the diagram); from König, Inledning til Mechaniken*

ing parts, i.e., cogwheels are used instead of belt and rope transmissions. The fabric to be cut was passed over the roller, a, and was then fed slowly by means of a gear operated by ropes and weights. The strands of the woven fabric were cut by a stationary knife, whose edge stretched horizontally across the whole loom. Other shorter knives (six in the drawing), moving in a vertical direction, c, made an angle of eight degrees with the underlying straight edge. These movable knives were held tight to the frame by springs, d, and were moved by the rotary disk, e, with bolts, g, which pushed up and down the projecting arms, f. Because of the cutting motion of the machine, the edges of the cloth were still a little uneven. Later, the knives were changed to spiral-shaped knives, placed on a rotating axle, which gave an even, as well as a continuous cut.

Polhem's machine to make ribbons and bands consisted of a loom which wove six bands at one time and had a mechanism to arrange the warp as it wove a single band. Polhem said that this "band-loom is much better than the Dutch model, because the warp moves by itself; on the regular loom, however, the weaver had to constantly move every weight which held the warp." The loom (see Fig. 20) was powered by a hand-crank and had six harnesses and six shuttles, which moved automatically forward and backward by a number of angle arms. In order for the thread in the shuttle to receive sufficient friction-resistance, a small spool with a spring was included. The warp, a, was strung in the regular way with a ratchet and pawl, b. Resistance came about by means of a weight, c, supplied with an iron rod, d, which knocked against the pawl, b, and released the warp-beam. The weight descended until the next tooth in the ratchet was engaged. It was said about this procedure, "that this is a strange machine, not at all like the usual band-looms." In the machine (see Fig. 20), we see two harnesses which transmit their motion by means of the rods, e, and the four lifting cams or projecting arms, f, and the roller, g. The shuttle also was moved by these arms and the spring, h, and the line, i. The bar, k, was turned by the crank from the wheel, l, which rotated four times for every rotation of the roller, g.

Polhem had invented a special warp machine which could operate six warp systems.[28] Six warps were wound simultaneously onto the beam (see Fig. 21). The threads were reeled from the spool, a, and directed over two or more hooks, b, in order to obtain the necessary friction-resistance. They then passed through the guide holes, c, in the rod, d. This was moved forward and backward by means of the lever, f,

[28] Found in full scale in the collection of the Tekniska Museet; cf. also, König, op. cit., p. 178, Tab. XXIII and XXIV.

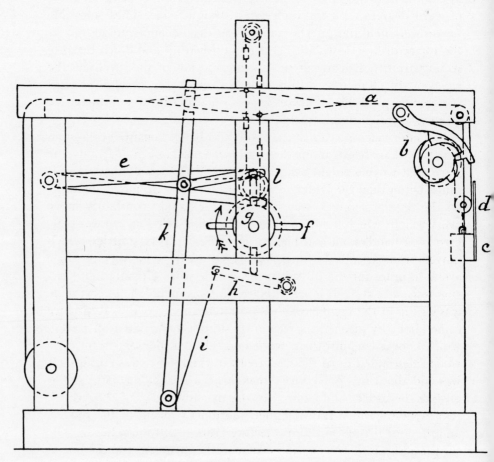

20. *A band-loom for six bands or ribbons*

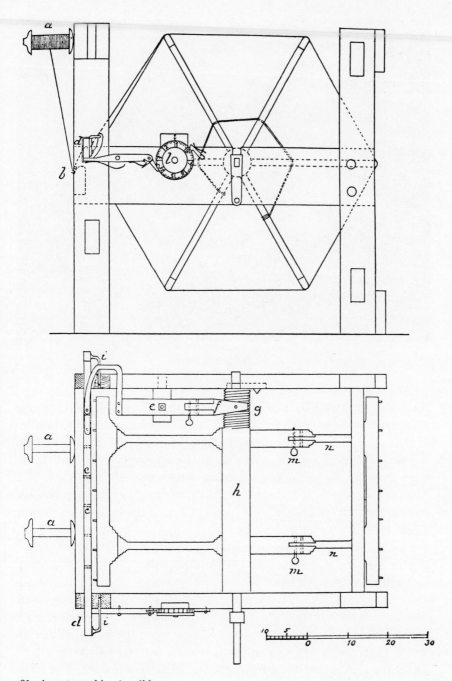

21. *A warp machine for ribbons*

22. *Polhem's ribbon loom; Tekniska Museet, Stockholm*

pivoting on the peg, *e,* the lever having a pin at one end to engage the thread, *g,* on the axle of the beam, *h.* When this had rotated a number of times in relation to the desired length of the warp, the motion was stopped by a pin, *i.* It then moved in the opposite direction, laying warp threads around the pin, *k,* on top of the warp. This reciprocating motion continued until there was the proper number of warp threads in each row. Their number was indicated on the disk, *l,* which turned a gear 1/32 of a turn for every new warp. After the beam was lifted off, the warps were taken from the warp crown by pulling out the cotter pin, *m,* so that the arms, *n,* could be bent inwards.

Another interesting band-loom which was made of wood, is a hand-driven loom (see Figs. 22, 23, and 24).[29] The remarkable thing about this loom is the unusual mechanism which moves the harnesses, that is, the lateral motion of the handle, *b,* located on the bar, *a,* which by means of the angle-arms, *c,* and the rods, *d,* with the two harnesses to which the heddles are fixed by threading them to two wires. The warp is wound on the beam, *f,* and the proper tension is achieved by means

[29] In the collection of the Tekniska Museet, and presumably an original. The inscription reads: "Ny invention af liten bandstol, inventor commercedrådet och commend. af Nordst. ord. Chr. Polhem."

142

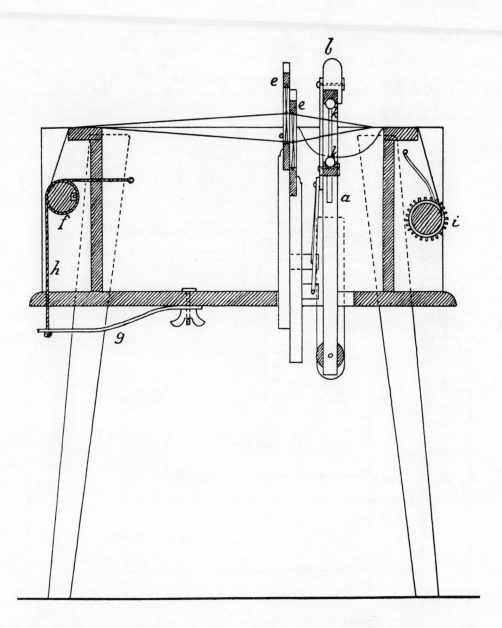

23. *A smaller ribbon loom*

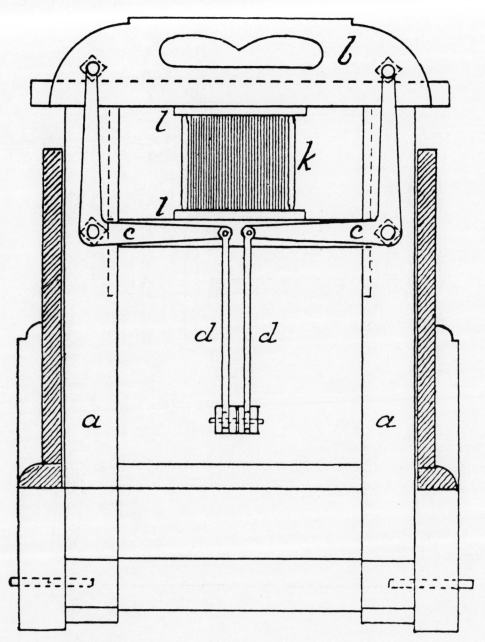

24. *A smaller ribbon loom*

of the spring, *g*, and the line, *h*. The woven ribbon is wound onto the beam, *i*, which has a ratchet and a pawl. The "weaver's reed," *k*, is made up of thin slivers of wood placed between the split sticks, *l*, ten per centimeter.

Probably the most complicated of Polhem's machines is his stocking loom (see Fig. 25). Gabriel Polhem referred to this machine in his catalogue.[30] Although there are a number of new techniques in this machine, it did not function properly, undoubtedly because a number of its parts were missing. The needle-holders were situated horizontally, and were made of flattened brass thread (75 mm. long with a cross section of 2.5 and 2.25 mm.). Their ends were sharpened and were located between two knife-edges which worked against each other. The needles could be raised and lowered by side handles and were moved backward and forward by a treadle. The machine had two additional treadles which raised and lowered the frame.

Polhem also constructed a machine to wash wool.[31] The wool was soaked in a vat of lye and pulled through a roller to press out the water. The roller was turned by a crank which could be connected by a rope to a board, and loaded with weights or pressed down with the foot. The washing roller was covered with netting and twine to make it easier to take the wool out of the water.

Another machine which was catalogued by Gabriel Polhem bore this description: "An invention and a model of an unusual shearing machine, as well as a mangle, which can be controlled by a treadle on the floor, and which is driven by a little water-wheel with a shelter over it." He added, "this invention His Royal Highness, the Crown Prince[32] had examined twelve years earlier." There are notes in the same reference to the following inventions:

"A loom to weave chenille."

"A clothespress made of wood, without screws, which is driven by a treadmill."

"A machine to make ropes and twine which is not larger than three or four alnar."

"A carding machine run by a treadle."

All these were kept in the Royal Model Chamber.

Finally:

"A mangle with a wooden roller."

Polhem's clothespress (see Fig. 26) is described in a paper which he

[30] Found in full scale in the collection of the Tekniska Museet.

[31] Also in the collection of the Tekniska Museet, probably one third of scale, not an original.

[32] Who later became King Gustaf III.

145

25. *Stocking loom; Tekniska Museet, Stockholm*

Tab.VII.

26. *Polhem's clothespress; from* Proceedings of the Royal Academy of Science, *1746*

wrote for the Royal Academy of Science in 1746. The treadmill had two rolls on which the lines from the pulley were wound. When maximum pressure was reached, wedges were used to maintain the pressure. In this way, the clothes could be pressed. A model of this press may be found in the Tekniska Museet.

III. OTHER MECHANICAL INVENTIONS

It is easy to understand why Polhem would direct his attention to one of Sweden's most important raw materials, wood. Immediately after his return from the continent, which included a visit to Holland, "the land of the windmills," he saw the great need of developing the sawmill industry in Sweden. His idea was to apply wind and water power directly to the sawmill, in which he wanted to have many saws operating at one time. He said himself about his first "multi-bladed" sawmill that "it was often criticized, even though the mill was so well-made that no one could do it any better." The difficulty lay with the workers of the area who were not used to this kind of apparatus.

Polhem wrote that his windmills "would always go at a constant rate of speed, even if the wind blew moderately or if there was a violent storm," and, "that with water-wheels one could grind flour and saw wood at one time; also, the instant the wood was sawed, it was planed and shaped in any way one desired." So convinced was he of the value of his mills, that he said: "one can see in the mill how many

147

barrels of flour were milled, even after fifty or more years, so that the miller cannot deceive anyone, even if no one is watching him and he is dishonest."

Polhem wrote about his mill in a paper read to the Academy of Science in 1741, which was entitled: "A description of a mill, which shows how much a mill can grind in a year." This mill consisted of a series of cogwheels, operated by a screw thread from the mill axle.

Among the models in the Royal Model Chamber which were listed by Gabriel Polhem was a "windmill which could grind and make bricks, and from which the canvas could be slackened and drawn in at any time. This mill was intended for Landskrona." There was also a model of another windmill that "would not turn faster in a storm than in normal weather, but which could use the strong wind more effectively. A model of this mill was sent to Leipzig, and another to Harz in Hannover." There is also "a windmill with horizontal arms."

In the collection of the Tekniska Museet, there is a machine, probably not an original, of a vertical frame-saw with a self-feeding mechanism which was driven by a windmill. Polhem's "sawmill" was made completely of wood, and was probably one twentieth of the original size (see Fig. 27). The horizontal axle of the wind-wheel is located in a special shelter with a roof which moves around a vertical axle, so that the windmill itself can always be directed toward the wind. The wheel axle is a double crankshaft and serves directly as the crankshaft for the frame-saw. The model shows a single saw blade with the wedge facing upwards. By means of a ratchet mechanism the wood is fed forward and carried along onto the slide or board with straight-lined tracks. The ratchet wheel is connected to a roller to which a line is fastened which connects to the end of the slide. This unwinds itself and carries the log or the plank with it. This feeding mechanism had been in use long before Polhem's time. In 1860 it was replaced by friction feeding, which is named for its inventor, "Worssam's silent feed." Polhem, we have seen, used a similar arrangement in his utensil manufacturing work.

Gabriel Polhem mentioned several other inventions: "a sawmill with planing and grooving operations"; "machines and tools to make boxes and containers which also punch out box bottoms, which had been shown to the Government's Manufacturing Bureau"; "a model of a sawmill, a stamping mill, a lathe, and a planer, all driven by a water-wheel."[33]

Even in the area of agriculture, Polhem suggested things which were of value, although it took a long time before his ideas could be

[33] Found in the Royal Model Chamber, 1761.

27. *Sawmill with a wind-wheel*

realized in any concrete way. Among the most important of his inventions in this area was his threshing machine (see Fig. 28). He said that it was constructed[34] so "that the grain was beaten and separated from the husks in such a careful way that no grain was lost. The husks were spread out by a man and then by means of rollers brought forward under the pounders of the stamping machine. The grain was then separated from the chaff and cleaned. It then fell into a large room, for which only the farmer had a key, and he could be assured in this way that none of the threshed grain would be lost. This machine could be powered by water, a windmill, or by horses, and only one man was needed, who laid the husks in the machine and bound them together, while the threshing progressed; the machine worked very quickly, and it was large enough to thresh ten or twelve barrels of grain a day." This machine was exhibited in Stockholm,[35] and Polhem made a duplicate of it, "which," as he said, "was made for my own use on my little estate." The threshing machine at Stjernsund was driven by a water-wheel.

From this description, it appears that Polhem's threshing machines used a "stamper," which was an imitation of the manually operated pounders. In König's book, there is a drawing of Polhem's threshing machine. It seemed to be similar to the old-fashioned stampers which had a cam or gear to lift the press, which would then fall by its own weight. König added in his description that "Polhem suggested that the stampers ought to hang on rods fixed with springs, so that the stampers may be suspended a little above the floor and in this way the husks could be crushed more easily."

After reading a paper entitled "The Reasons for the Increase of the Grain Crop," by Christopher Wolff, Polhem conceived of a seeding machine[36] which sowed seeds in straight rows. He described the machine in this way:

"1. The seed can be planted at any distance from another, according to the kind of soil and the field.

"2. The seed can be planted as deep or as shallow as is necessary.

"3. The machine would cover the seeds and make the soil even.

"4. A horse or an ox, if he pulls this machine (which is not heavier than a bushel of seed) at a width of four alnar, can sow one quarter of a mile in an hour, and plant eighteen thousand square alnar in an hour, and fifteen acres in twelve hours.

[34] König, *op. cit.*, p. 175. Tab. xxi.
[35] This model was found in 1761 in the Royal Model Chamber "of the new Royal Palace."
[36] "En maskin att plantera säden på åkern," in the Royal Model Chamber, 1761.

150

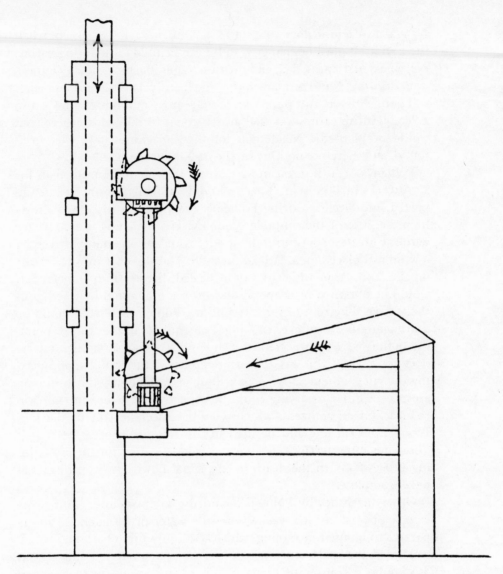

28. *Threshing machine*

"5. The machine does not require too much attention, except when the seed itself must be changed, and it can be used for planting barley, rye, wheat, oats, peas, flax, and turnips." This machine, of which there is no drawing, could be made rather inexpensively, Polhem claimed.

There is also a "tuft plow which can remove mounds of grass"; also a "conveyor to carry away the largest stones in the fields, where seed would be planted." No designs for these machines have ever been found, and therefore nothing can be said about them.

Polhem's great interest in agriculture is evident from his plan for a saltworks in Bohuslän. There was only a small amount of salt imported into Sweden during Polhem's time, and its price was always high, because of the unstable economy. His plan was to take water with the greatest concentration of salt, by means of a pump driven by a windmill placed on a flatboat or barge, and direct it into reservoirs on the land, from which it would be led directly into boilers. Salt would be obtained by evaporation in the summer and by freezing in the winter. The result of this technique, Polhem believed, would be a stronger salt for quicker cooking. Polhem tells us that the evaporating boilers were constructed in such a way as to conserve fuel, but he does not tell how this was done. In reference to the problem of purifying the salt, Polhem said: "As salt liquefies quickly when it is heated, a process similar to drying could be carried out (before the salt was refined and crystallized), which would reduce the cost of the salt. Blood from cattle could be used in the refining process because it draws out imperfections. Rain water could be used for the crystallizing process." With the death of the King, however, his project was never completed.

Other machines by Polhem included: "a straw-cutter with many compartments," which was powered by water or by hand;[37] "an apparatus to be used in roofing, which used only birch-bark and which concealed the nails, (such a roof can be seen in Kersö and also in Stockholm"; "a machine to make grooved iron sheets for roofing, and which can be seen on the same roof in Kersö"; "a way to cover grain and haystacks, so that the roof can be raised or lowered"; "a new way to draw dried malt without disturbing it"; as well as "a machine to make watertight straw mats for roofs."

Polhem constructed a model of a machine[38] which could make bricks (see Fig. 29). It was powered by a water-wheel. The clay was put into a mixer, in which there was an extension of the axletree rotating. There were four rows of slanted iron knives on the axle, which

[37] Found in the Royal Model Chamber, 1761.
[38] In the collection of the Tekniska Museet.

152

29. *Brickmaking machine; Tekniska Museet, Stockholm*

worked against a similar row of knives fastened to the wall of the mixer. The clay was forced to the far end of the mixer where an opening in the bottom was just large enough to form the brick. The clay was pressed down by means of a spring located on the axle. The form when filled was forced through the opening by an arm, which moved also by means of the water-wheel which had a rod extended from it. This machine, which is described in König's work[39] under the title of "A New Way to Make Bricks," was used at Stjernsund and later in Finland by Colonel Ehrensvärd in the construction of a fortification system.

Of great interest is Polhem's "machine to saw, grind, and polish marble and plate glass, which is operated by water power."[40] König said that "this machine was not very large," and that it was built for the marble works at Kolmården. According to the design and description of the machine,[41] the sawing was done by means of two horizontal frames placed lengthwise, into which was inserted the cutting blade, which had no teeth. Sand and water were used for the cutting itself. The cutting instruments could be placed at different distances from one another. The grinding took place by laying two marble slabs on

[39] König, *op. cit.*, p. 183; Tab. XXVII, XXVIII.
[40] In Gabriel Polhem's listing.

153

top of each other; one was stationary, the other moved backward and forward and was turned slowly by means of a ratchet and pawl. The polishing was done with a "polishing board" laid on a marble slab held tight to the surface by a spring, which was lined with felt. The usual polishing powders were used, as well as oil. The principle of the machine is repeated in our modern stonecutting machines.

One of Polhem's inventions, the pile driver or rammer, made in 1744 and used in the building of the canal lock in Stockholm, was also described by König.[42] The ram itself was lifted by a treadmill, so arranged that the "men worked the treadmill from the outside." It was constructed with a lock which hooked onto the ram, and by means of a rope released the ram at the proper time. The rammer was eighteen alnar high and the treadmill was three alnar in diameter.

There are other machines and apparatus which should be mentioned in conclusion:[43]

"A control to be used at mills and canals to determine how many ships passed through and how many barrels of grain had been milled."[44]

"A dredging machine, for clear or muddy channels, which had no logs or beams."

"A device to ring large and heavy bells in an easy way."

"A lifting jack with an adjusting screw."

"A bed which could be unfolded easily and which fitted into a closet in the chamber."

"A smaller lathe to make medallions, which was powered by a mechanism which employed weights."

"A brass logarithmic table."

"A mining drill which could bore perpendicularly overhead."

"An inexpensive vertical printing press."

Finally there was a device to prevent horses from bolting and running away, which consisted of a brake on the back wheel of the coach and which could be operated by the coachman.[45]

IV. POLHEM'S THEORETICAL WRITINGS

Polhem wrote a great deal, and as we read his many manuscripts and papers, we find that he had a very practical mind. Nevertheless, he

[41] König, *op. cit.*, p. 176; Tab. XXII.
[42] *Ibid.*, p. 181, Tab. XXVI.
[43] Cf. Gabriel Polhem's listing.
[44] Found in the Royal Model Chamber, 1761.
[45] Found in the Tekniska Museet.

154

emphasized that the theoretical and the practical belonged together.[46] He said: "the theoretical and the practical have been separated from one another, so that no one today is bold enough to write a book dealing with both of them . . . separately they are fully discussed, especially the theoretical, by the learned professors." Polhem pointed out how important it was for the young student to occupy himself with practical work rather than with games and sports. "If I were permitted to speak my mind," he wrote, "I would urge students to spend their time doing carpentrywork, lathework, handicrafts, and other similar activities, instead of playing games, throwing balls and bowling, and other things which consume a lot of time and stimulate the blood, but have no real value."

To find solutions to the problems which his experiments and investigations brought to light, Polhem often employed a question-and-answer technique. In many instances he used a dialogue to clarify his ideas to his audience. This may be seen most clearly in his "A Conversation between Miss *Theoria* and Builder *Practicus* on the topic of Housebuilding."[47] He always presented his ideas in a concrete manner, and avoided glittering generalities. His ideas were always original, at times unsophisticated, but always motivated by the desire to instruct and clarify. He readily used Latin words in his writings, because this was the custom of his time.

His theoretical writings dealt primarily with mechanical problems. In a paper entitled, "Mechanical Questions and Resolutions"[48] he dealt with the topic of geostatics. Some of the other problems which interested him were the determination of the laws governing the balance of concrete bodies, the center of gravity of solid bodies, and similar problems. A clear illustration of Polhem's theoretical mind can be seen in the following problem (see Fig. 30):

"*The Problem:* If a rod, log, or beam AB was to be weighed, but because of its size it could not be put on a scale or a steelyard, the question is, how then could it be weighed?

"*Requisita:* 1. The bar, log, or beam is to be placed on a triangular piece of wood and balanced. The point of balance is indicated as C.

"2. A weight, P, is placed at end, B, whose weight is known, such as one half or one shippound.

"3. Then the log or bar is moved to another point of balance at D,

[46] "Theoriens och praktikens förenande i mekaniken" in the papers of the Royal Academy of Science, 1741 and 1742.

[47] Manuscript in KB. *Teknologi*.

[48] *Ibid*.

155

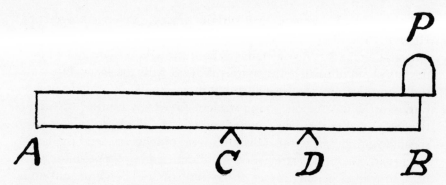

30. *Polhem's solution to the theoretical problems of determining the weight of a log*

so that distances *CD* and *DB* are proportional, or their distance is known; the weight is determined in this way.

"*Resolutio:* As *CD* is to *DB,* so *P* is to the weight of the log, even if it is regular or irregular."

Polhem dealt rather extensively in his writings with the subject of solid bodies and liquids. Most of these can be found in the *Transactions of the Royal Academy of Science* for the years 1739–1746. Emanuel Swedenborg published a journal called *Daedalus Hyperboreus* in 1716 and 1717 and several of Polhem's studies in applied physics are found there. His primary concern was with the topics of falling bodies and wind resistance.[49]

He also dealt with the problem of the trajectory of a cannon ball. It is reported in *Daedalus Hyperboreus* that Polhem set up an experiment "for the Royal Bureau of Mines . . . and one can see it demonstrated there even today. Major General Carl Cronstedt, who has elevated the art of shooting to the highest plane, has highly praised it." Polhem said that a natural trajectory is a parabola. However, when one sees it, it appears quite different, that is, as he said, "when a cannon is fired, the ball seems to travel more directly down-field than up." Polhem's experimental apparatus consisted of a "shooting cylinder" which could be placed at different inclinations in a frame in which parabolas of different heights had been drawn. In the experiment itself, small slips of paper were used, which were placed along different points on the parabolas. In this way, every parabola would be

[49] A number of these were, "Om vädrets resistance mot fallande tyngder," "om de tyngre och lättare kroppars åtskillnad i fall," and "om *ratione duplicata,* som förmenas vara i fallen." "He demonstrated that wind resistance is proportional to the horizontal cross section of the body," and added, "en kropp, som faller lodrätt, ökar sin fart hvarje moment i proportion som en *area trianguli,* när tiderna göra dess *latera;* det är, *in ratione duplicata tempp.* eller som *quadrata* hafva sig till *radices.*"

hit by the ball. The experiment showed that "the ball follows the line of the parabola."

In another paper entitled "Remarks on the Use of Curved Lines in Mechanics,"[50] Polhem demonstrated how curved lines could be used in construction; for example, the parabola for arches and spouts for water-wheels; the catenary for suspension bridges; as well as the hyperbola, cycloids, and spirals for other kinds of construction.

"Polhem's Mechanical Alphabet" is also of theoretical interest, and may also be found in the Tekniska Museet (see Fig. 31). The models display different ways to transmit motion and change its direction, as well as different kinds of gear systems, gear constructions, ratchet mechanisms, windmills, pulleys, universal couplings, eccentric motion, driving shafts, power machines, and so forth. Many of these, of course, are of greater interest as novelties than they are of real technical value.

There were experiments in the areas of hydrostatics and hydrodynamics, as well.[51] Polhem demonstrated, for example, the theoretical principles for the stabilization of a floating vessel. He showed how the weight of a vessel could be calculated and how the difference between *"centrum aequilibrii* and *centrum gravitatis"* could be determined.[52]

Polhem constructed many different kinds of water-wheels which were used for a great many of his machines. He wrote a number of papers dealing with the water-wheel and the principles of its construction. As well, he demonstrated the effect of pressure, weight, and shock upon water. In addition, he described different kinds of water-wheels and their use in different kinds of streams and rivers (the overshot wheel, the undershot, breast, and horizontal wheels), how their power could best be conveyed to the machine, and so forth. In a paper entitled "Waterworks," he described how the height and quantity of a waterfall could be measured. In another entitled "Refriction and Attrition," Polhem described ways to measure friction. Another, which was entitled "Momentum Motus and Momentum Refrictionis," told how force and resistance could be employed for practical purposes.

Still another paper[53] described an "apparatus which would bring ale and wine from the cellar, which was so constructed that one did not have to go into the cellar." He called this his "hydrostatic technique."

[50] *Transactions of the Royal Academy of Science,* 1742.
[51] *Transactions of the Royal Academy of Science,* 1741, 1742; manuscript (KB).
[52] Cf. the paper, "Nytt sätt att pröfva lasten i ett skepp till lagom styfhet och rankning."
[53] *Transactions of the Royal Academy of Science,* 1743.

157

31. *A number of models belonging to Polhem's "Mechanical Alphabet"; Tekniska Museet, Stockholm*

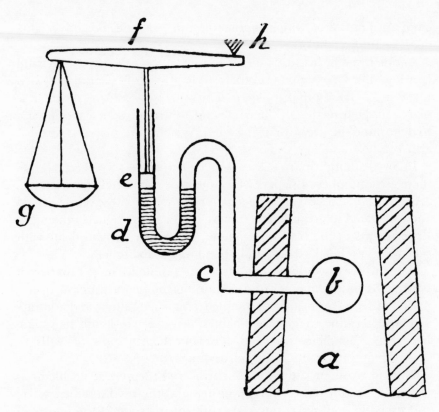

32. *Polhem's instrument to measure the temperature in an oven*

It consisted of a reservoir located above the wine cellar, which was connected by a pipe to the wine or ale cask. The liquid rose, by hydrostatic pressure, to the reservoir, where it could be tapped.

One of Polhem's theoretical papers in the area of physics dealt with "the elementary powers and forces in mechanics,"[54] in which he commented on the nature of heat. He attempted to deal with the problem of fire and heat, and by so doing reveals that he was a product of his time. He said, "fire is compressed or concentrated air, which suddenly breaks through its *elastique natur* or form." He attempted to demonstrate how "fire and heat could be measured." He constructed an apparatus to determine gradations of heat (see Fig. 32). In the oven, *a*, a hollow copper ball, *b*, is placed; the ball is connected to a tube, *c*, which is joined to a U-shaped tube, *d*, filled with mercury, "which comes into contact with the gases which are created by the heat." When the gases in the ball, *b*, expand, the level of mercury is raised. Pressure is applied by means of the plunger, *e*, upon the mer-

[54] *Transactions of the Royal Academy of Science*, 1739.

cury, until the bar, *f*, which has the fulcrum, *h*, at one end and weights on the scale, *g*, at the other, is level.

Another one of his instruments measured the velocity of the wind (see Fig. 33). On a tripod, *a*, there rests a horizontal arm, *c*, which turns on a vertical pin or pivot, *b*. The arm, *c*, has a plate, *d*, which is placed in the direction of the wind, and a thin rod, *e*, of a specific size to determine the pressure of the wind. Weights are placed on *f* until arm, *c*, is level.

In Swedenborg's journal *Daedalus Hyperboreus* for the year 1716, there are a number of papers which deal with acoustics; for example, "Assessor Polhem's ear tube, made up of two spherical parts, described and calculated in great detail." There is also a paper on "Polheimer's Experiments in the Nature of Sound," in which Polhem dealt with such topics as the speed of sound, sound waves, and echoes.

Polhem discussed some mathematical problems in a number of papers; "A simple manner of determining compound interest over a period of years, by means of a simple triangle";[55] "a new and accurate way to determine weight on a hand-scale" (i.e., to divide its weighing arm); "mathematical and mechanical principles of bells";[56] "watches or watch parts,"[57] as well as others.

Polhem wrote on almost all scientific and theoretical problems as they related to metalworking, farming, and the textile industry. He concerned himself for a long time with the question of the nature of the tempering process. He summarized his findings in a little paper entitled "General Tempering,"[58] which reflected the technical knowledge of his time. "The reason why heated steel becomes hard in cold water," he said, "is that as the iron expands when it is heated, it becomes blue. The tempering process is similar to what happens to glass as it is submerged into water. A hard shell is formed on the heated glass and all the *poros* are closed, and no air can get in and fill the *vacuum* within the glass particles. When the shell is broken, air rushes in with the result that the glass breaks into small pieces and only a fine glass powder remains. The steel particles would act in the same way, if the cooling process took place evenly and all at once. However, it occurs slowly on one side, so that the air which tries to enter when the steel cools does not have the same effect. In this way we see that when white-hot steel is tempered in water, it does so more slowly than when it is red-hot. The steel particles are separated from

[55] *Daedalus Hyperboreus*, 1716.
[56] Manuscript (KB).
[57] *Ibid.*
[58] Polhem, *Patriotiska testamente*, pp. 47–51.

160

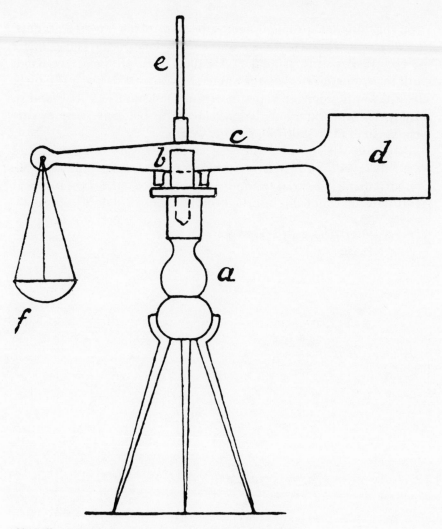

33. *Polhem's instrument to measure the velocity of the wind*

each other, and therefore the tempering effect is decreased. The steel
is not as brittle when the cooling process is gradual, for then more of
the steel particles come into contact with one another than before."
The tempering process occurred in the following way: "The *sal
volatile,* which is in the powdered material that is placed in the iron
container with the iron which is to be tempered, absorbs so much
of it that most of the pores on the outside become stopped up and
consequently get hard as steel when quickly cooled." Polhem also explored the nature of the annealing process and the resultant colors,
which were dependent, as he said, upon the concentration of oxides.

161

In conclusion, some mention must be made of his experiments dealing with rope. He related these to the work done on the same subject by Nils Wallerius in Uppsala.[59] He dealt with problems associated with the strength of ropes, the angle of twist used to make the rope, the different tensions in ropes, how yarn is made from fiber, and so forth. All of this experimentation had a great influence upon the development of the textile industry in Sweden.

Polhem has been called the "Father of Swedish Mechanics," and richly deserves the title. He was a pioneer in Swedish technology. He initiated many industrial techniques and methods in our country and for this reason could also be called the "Father of Swedish Industry."

[59] *Transactions of the Royal Academy of Science,* 1739.

CHAPTER THREE

Polhem, The Mining Engineer

BY HERMAN SUNDHOLM

When we use the term "mining engineer" (Swedish: *konstmästare*) in this chapter, we refer to the individual who was responsible for building the machines and apparatus which pumped the water and raised the ore from the mines during the early period of Sweden's industrial history. This was usually done by a mechanism which conveyed power from a water-wheel to the hoisting machine itself. Polhem was this kind of "engineer" (German: *kunstmeister*) at the Falun mine during the years 1700 to 1716. In addition, he was what could be called the "technical director" of the mine.

Polhem had begun very early in his career to concern himself with the problems of how ore could be raised from the mine. He described the first machine he built for a mine as a "novelty." Most of the machines and apparatus he constructed for the Swedish mining industry were made during the time he was at Falun. We only know how a few of these operated, because Polhem did not make diagrams of his machines, but rather built models of them. Often when Polhem wrote about one of his "inventions," he said that it was "very difficult to describe how it functioned," or that "the machine speaks for itself." There would never be more than a few brief sentences of explanation as to how the machine worked.

In the following pages, an attempt will be made to list some of Polhem's contributions to the field of mining.

I. The Hoisting Machine at Blankstöten in the Falun Mine

After repairing the ancient astronomical clock in the Uppsala Cathedral, Polhem began immediately to build a model of a conveying and hoisting machine which, he said, could be used at the Salberg silver mine.[1] The Royal Bureau of Mines in Stockholm asked him to demonstrate the model, with the result that, as he said, "they were very pleased with the invention."[2] The Bureau offered him twice the amount of scholarship which he had previously received at Uppsala. We can understand a little more clearly the economic situation of his time when we read that Polhem said of the scholarship, "I actually received it!"[3]

Polhem's machine was shown to King Karl xi and, as Polhem him-

[1] Polhem, *Kort berättelse om de förnämsta mechaniska inventioner,* 1729, p. 10.
[2] *Ibid.*
[3] *Ibid.,* p. 11.

165

self related: "he examined it for three hours and was very much pleased." Polhem was then asked to build a similar apparatus for the Falun mine. He suggested that for this mine wooden rods or poles might be used in the construction, instead of ropes.[4]

Polhem's "hoisting machine" was thought to be extremely useful, "but more of a curiosity and a novelty,"[5] than anything else. His idea was to construct a machine which could hoist buckets loaded with ore from the mining area to the surface, to convey the buckets to the place of dumping, to dump them, and then return them to the mine. All of these operations were to be done automatically.

Polhem said this about his invention:[6] "A number of innovations were included in this machine:

"1. The buckets could not move until they were filled with the proper amount of ore.

"2. The movement of the buckets to the hoist was performed quickly.

"3. A new way to hook the buckets to the lines in the pit or shaft was used.

"4. A new technique to control the movement of the buckets up the hoist was devised.

"5. A new way to unhook the buckets from the lines or poles when they arrived on the surface was employed.

"6. The movement of the buckets was done in an entirely different manner than had been done previously.

"7. An automatic way to empty the buckets by means of an opening in the bottom of the bucket was added.

"8. A new way to close the bottoms of the buckets was employed. Previously, it was this which had prevented the buckets from returning to the shaft.

"9. A technique to transfer the buckets from one pole to another was put into operation, as there were many buckets which followed after each other.

"10. Finally, a way to unhook the buckets and to return them into the mine was devised. The whole operation was automatic and did not need the help of anyone."

Polhem had difficulty introducing his hoisting machine into the Falun mine. The mine engineer, Olof Henriksson Trygg, "who al-

---

[4] The lines were made of leather in the Falun mine. One line was made from about 180 ox hides (skins). A line of leather did not last more than 2 or 3 years, and for this reason, was extremely costly.

[5] Polhem, *op. cit.,* p. 11.

[6] *Ibid.,* pp. 10ff.

1. *The hoisting mechanism at Blankstöten. Polhem's first machine at the Falun mine, completed in 1694. Engraving by Jan van Vianen in Amsterdam, from a drawing by Samuel Buschenfelt*

ready had the reputation for having built the most complete unit," was very suspicious of Polhem and his novel ideas. Trygg attempted to influence others at the mine to think as he did. His primary objection to Polhem's "invention" was that the water supply which was to drive the water-wheel for the hoisting apparatus was inadequate. Nevertheless, Polhem completed his hoisting machine in 1694. A contest was devised soon after which was to test Polhem's machine in order to compare it with the older one. Of the contest Polhem wrote: "It turned out much better than I and the others had expected; sixteen buckets of ore were brought up in an hour by using the old machine, whereas with my machine, twenty-two buckets were brought up in the same period of time. When a bucket was brought up by Trygg's machine, my machine brought up two, one right after the other; when three buckets were used, the machine operated so fast that the workers could not unload a bucket before another one was upon them. Furthermore, not as much water was used as had been used in the past."[7]

Polhem's hoisting machine consisted of a horizontal pole or rod powered by a water-wheel. The rod was joined to two pairs of hooks furnished with vertical poles suspended into the pit. The buckets were hooked onto the poles at the lowest level, and then lifted vertically to a higher pair of hooks by the alternate motion of the pairs of poles. This motion continued until the bucket was raised up to the surface. The vertical poles were one hundred alnar long (59.4 meters) and had fifteen pairs of hooks.

The buckets were emptied by means of an iron chain which hooked onto the bottom of the bucket. The ore was emptied onto a platform and then loaded into carts, which carried it to the place where it could be processed. This was located on a higher level than the platform. For this reason, a smaller platform, which could be raised and lowered, was constructed. This was also powered by the water-wheel. The worker and the cart were lifted onto this platform.

The buckets were lifted off the vertical poles by the machine, so that they could be processed directly without any unloading.

The buckets were then returned to the mine by means of an iron chain which had thirty spheres, identical in size, wired to it at regular intervals. The empty buckets were fastened to them. Just below the pulley which operated the chain, two iron bolts were placed which stopped the chain. In this way the empty buckets could not descend too rapidly into the mine.

[7] *Ibid.*, p. 12.

2. *Polhem's hoisting apparatus at the Karl XII shaft at the Falun mine, built in 1701; by Samuel Sohlberg in 1731; Kommerskollegium*

This apparatus, which was completed in 1694, was still being used as late as 1731. It had been reported that the apparatus "had not received excessive wear or damage, and certainly would be able to be used for fifty or sixty years more; the wooden parts of the apparatus do not decay easily at Falun because of the smoke from the furnace, which gives off sulphur and vitriol."[8]

II. The Force Pump at the Hällestad Iron Ore Mine

Polhem wrote: "My first practical test was to construct a force pump which would drive the water out of the Hällestad iron ore mine."[9] It appears that he finished the pump before the hoisting apparatus was constructed at Blankstöten.

The Hällestad iron ore mine, which was located near the Finspong's gun foundry, was so sloped that the workers and the horses could easily go up and down the paths. At the bottom of the mine, where there was an accumulation of water, Polhem constructed a force pump, which was to be driven by four horses. The wood used in the pump was oak, which had been banded with iron. From Polhem's description it is apparent that it was very substantially built. The cylinders were made of brass and were five or six quarters high (seventy-five to ninety cm.) and seven or eight tum in diameter (seventeen or twenty cm.).

Polhem wanted to make the pipes of cast iron and have the work done at the Finspong foundry. However, the mine owners did not want to do the work nor pay for it. For this reason, Polhem was forced to make the pipes from hollowed-out logs.

Even while the pumpworks was being built, the ore in the mine began to diminish. As a result, no one was anxious to see Polhem continue his work, nor to pay him for his time. Instead, they wanted Polhem to compensate them! Polhem said, "But after the project was finished, I was ordered to pay them. However, the Royal Bureau of Mines, who best understood what I was doing, adjudged otherwise."[10]

III. Other Machines at the Falun Mine

Having completed the hoisting machine at Blankstöten, Polhem set off on his first trip abroad (1694–96), and traveled to Holland, England, France, and Germany. Shortly after his return he was commis-

[8] *Ibid.*
[9] *Ibid.*, p. 40.
[10] *Ibid.*, p. 42.

3. *Model of the hoisting apparatus at the Karl xi shaft; the model belonged to the laboratorium mechanicum, and is now in the Tekniska Museet, Stockholm*

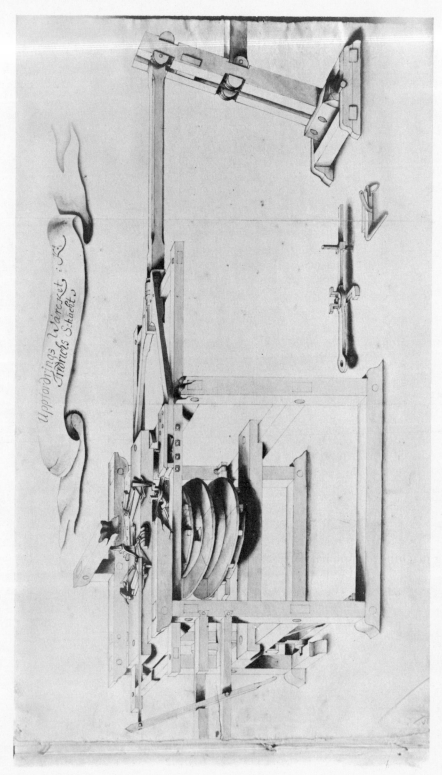

4. *The hoisting machine at King Fredrik's shaft at the Falun mine*

sioned to build a hoisting machine for the Karl XI shaft at the Falun mine. This was so "because," as he related, "the old machine could not be used any more owing to the depth of the mine and to its proximity to three other mines."[11]

He completed this machine in 1701, which indicated the remarkable rate of speed with which he worked. In this machine he used two rope drums for raising the ore barrels. The rotation of the rope drums was brought about by means of a complicated wooden rod transmission from a reversible water-wheel with one crankshaft.

The hoisting machine at the King Fredrik shaft was called a "mangle machine" because of a reciprocating lever, operated by a transmission rod, which affected a pawl mechanism atop two rope drums. This alternately rotated the rope drums which raised the barrels of ore. The rotation could also be reversed.

This machine, as well as some of the other inventions of Polhem, was nothing short of revolutionary. As a rule, however, Polhem's machines were extremely complicated and fragile. A further difficulty was the fact that Polhem's approach to problems was unconventional. The men with whom he worked, of course, were convinced that "the old way was the best."

IV. The Hoisting Machine at Humboberget

While the machine at the King Karl XI shaft was under construction, another hoisting machine was built for the Humboberg mine located in the parish of Norrbärke near Smedjebacken. This machine consisted of two sets of poles with hooks attached. One set brought the loaded carriers to the surface (carriers were used instead of barrels), the other brought the empty carriers down into the mine. This hoisting machine, completed in 1698, was in operation until 1717 when it was destroyed in a cave-in.[12]

[11] *Ibid.*, p. 17.
[12] Cf. Hülper, *Dagbok öfver en resa igenom de under Stora Kopparbergs höfdinge-döme lydande län och Dalarne år 1757–1762*, p. 810, in which he described Polhem's machine:

"Hjulet af 21 alns diameter, stång-gången 1,932 alr. lång med 10 brott, det yttersta brottet vid grufvan skjuter och drager en triangulair lutande vändvall, hvarvid en skjut-stång är häftad med 39 tänder, som kringdrifver 3 små trille-hjul af 23 trill-valar hvardera, hvilka upp-och neder-fordrings verket sin rörelse gifva: berörde triangulaire vänd-vall skjuter äfvenledes vatn-konsten, som neder i grufvan med en vändare balanceras, att därmed hålla konsten å bägge sidor i gång, hvilken, tillika med uppfordrings-verket på 48 graders sluttning, efter malm-gångens fallande, är nedsänkt. Grufvans djup i donläge var då 115 famnar. Omkostnaden till detta konstverk har bestigit öfver 60,000 Dlr."

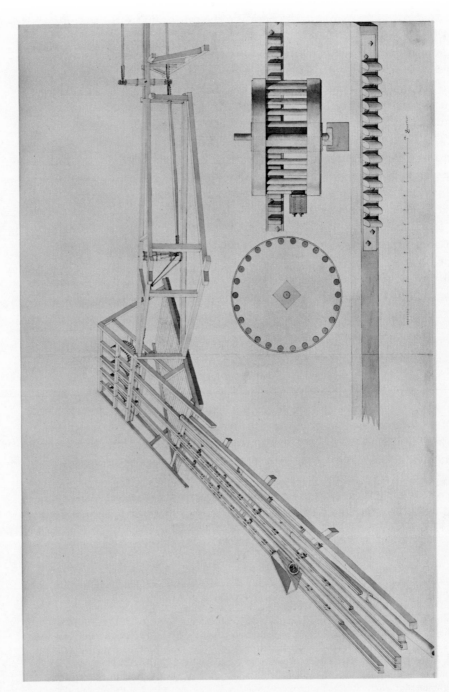

5. *Hoisting machine with rods at Humboberg's mine. Drawing by C. J. Cronstedt, 1729*

In association with the Humboberg hoisting machine, Polhem built a pumping machine for the Bispberg mine. The distance from the water-wheel to the mine measured 2,500 meters. Power was transmitted over this distance by means of wooden rods, which connected directly to the pump pistons. Some improvements had been made in this device which, as Polhem claimed, were "better than the older method."[13] Other pumping machines were constructed at Ulfshyttan in the parish of Silfberg, Kopparberg, Nyhyttan, Riddarhyttan in the parish of Skinnskatteberg, Västmanland, and other places, "which functioned well and would serve their purpose as long as the mines provided ore."

VI. The Pumping Machinery at the King Karl xi Shaft at the Falun Mine

In 1707, while Polhem was in the Harz mine, the hoisting mechanism at the Karl xi shaft in the Falun mine burned down. Polhem was called home to construct a new one. He added a number of "improvements which made the older machines obsolete." What these improvements were, which Polhem called the greatest of his inventions, no one will ever know. No sketch or description of them has ever been found.

Every hoisting mechanism which Polhem built had to have a great number of buildings and other equipment, as well as a source of water power. Too often, however, an excessive number of buildings were constructed and there was a tremendous waste of water power as well as an over-all inadequate mining operation. Polhem referred frequently to the less than satisfactory conditions in the mining communities.[14]

Polhem's major improvements over the previous mechanism consisted of introducing two cranks, one at either end of the wheel stock. In this way the arms which conveyed the motion to the shaft itself could be increased in number, and the whole operation improved. He demonstrated that his apparatus could control a number of other devices, and that the power from the water-wheel could be conducted over long stretches of land. Before Polhem's machine there had been

[13] Polhem, *Kort berättelse om de förnämsta mechaniska inventioner,* p. 19.
[14] Polhem, *op. cit.,* p. 60.

175

6. *Water-wheel and the transmitting rods; c.1690; from Löhneyss, Bericht vom Bergwerck, wie man dieselben bawen und in guten Wol- stande bringen soll. 1690*

7. *Water-powered hoisting mechanism; c.1690; from Löhneyss,* Bericht vom Bergwerck, . . . , *1690*

8. *The transmitting rods on Polhem's machine extended for great distances over the land. This photograph, taken in 1922, shows the rods at the Bispberg mine; photo, Tekniska Museet, Stockholm*

no success in this kind of system.[15] The hoisting mechanism Polhem built for Blankstöten was finished in the year 1694 and had only one crank for its operation. At the King Karl xi shaft, which was finished in 1697 or 1698, there were two cranks on the water-wheel stock.

The older mechanisms transmitted motion vertically to the pumps at the different levels of the mine. Polhem radically changed this procedure by putting the wooden rods of his apparatus directly into the mine shaft. On the larger rods, he placed metal arms, to which smaller rods were attached. When the machine was put into operation, with

---

[15] Klingenstierna, *Åminnelsetal*, 1753, p. 18; "Det är ganska naturligt att tro, att om en ström skall draga en maskin, måste antingen vattnet ledas till maskinen, eller maskinen sättas vid vattnet, och det är svårt att föreställa sig, att en ström, som löper en fjärdedels mil ifrån en grufva, kan där göra någon tjänst. Icke desto mindre hade våra konstmästare försökt att genom stång-gångar uträtta en så oväntad och otrolig sak. Utgången hade likväl ej på långt när svarat emot deras föresats, i brist af nödig kunskap om vänd-axlarnas och vinkel-armarnas rätta ställning, hvarpå alltsammans beror. Det var Polhammar förbehållit, att på ett noga och geometriskt sätt öfvervinna den svårigheten hvarigenom han var i stånd att utan förminskning af kraften fortsätta den samma till en otrolig distance."

178

the two smaller rods connected to two larger rods, the result was a very smooth operation.

The water-raising mechanism which Polhem developed was far superior to the older ones. The mechanism used wooden rods to transmit motion. Polhem said that this method "was twelve to sixteen times better than the older method."[16] Among other things, it did not cost as much as the older models "because one wheel served several shafts."[17] Polhem indicated that water, as well as manpower, was saved with his mechanism. However, the greatest contribution, he felt, was the fact that the water-wheel did not have to be located at the edge of the mine shaft. Water would fall into the mine itself and fill it. Furthermore, during the winter months, the ice would break the walls of the mine, with the result that the machine itself would have to be moved. If there were a cave-in, there was always the danger that the mine would be flooded.

VII. The Wooden Chain

At the Nyhyttan copper mine, which was owned by Baron Nils Gripenhielm,[18] Polhem designed a wooden chain to replace the expensive and impractical hemp lines. His wooden chain "was made almost like a watch chain."[19] It was made to go around a hexagonal roller, which was placed in the center of the shaft. When Harald Lybecker[20] learned of Polhem's invention, he wanted to use it at the Falun mine. A chain was built, "but when it was about to be used in the King Karl XI shaft, the workers did not want to try this new and dangerous method to bring the ore from the mine, and decided to leave if the chain were used." To convince the workers of the chain's strength, Polhem tested it. But it broke when one hundred and forty shippounds were applied, "which might not have occurred," as Polhem said, "if there had not been a fault in one of the links of the chain." Needless to say, as a result, the wooden chain was never used at the Falun mine.

[16] Polhem, *op. cit.*, p. 24.

[17] *Ibid.*, p. 25.

[18] Nils Gripenhielm was born in 1653, became governor of Stora Kopparberg in 1692, land marshal in 1697, member of the King's Council and president of the Bureau of Mines in 1706, but died before he assumed his office.

[19] Polhem, *op. cit.*, p. 29.

[20] Harald Lybecker was born in 1649, became mine engineer at Stora Kopparberg in 1691, assessor in the Bureau of Mines in 1692, remained in Falun, became a member of the Mining Council in 1713, died in 1714.

VIII. Carriers for Transporting Ore

During a depression year at the beginning of the eighteenth century, Falun was overwhelmed by poor and needy people. Lybecker wanted to employ the able-bodied among them by putting them to work moving ore. Horses had been used for this operation in the past, but the horses "ate all the hay and the people were deprived of both milk and butter."[21] Polhem devised an ore carrier which a man could operate manually while seated. He was not encouraged nor aided in the construction of the carrier, and it took him a whole year to finish it. Polhem tells us of the outcome of this project: "By the grace of God, good times have come once again, and all the beggars have disappeared; it was unnecessary to bring in workers to the mine to work the carriers. Furthermore, it was not advisable, because experience has shown that any mechanized device is met with strong opposition by the workers, who have an aversion for the new and unusual; the workers from Salberg had to be ordered to use the carrier at Falun."[22]

IX. A Proposed Hoisting Machine
for Cave-ins at the Falun Mine

In 1687 there occurred a huge cave-in at the Falun mine, which could be cleared only with great difficulty. Harald Lybecker suggested that Polhem construct a hoisting machine which could bring the earth and rocks from the mine to the surface. Polhem believed that he could do it, but it was a difficult task, "because," as he said, "I could not conceive of a place to deposit the earth after it had been brought up from the mine; furthermore, there was no river which I could use to power my machine. This was the most difficult task I had ever undertaken."[23]

Lybecker was persistent and suggested a number of other reasons why the machine was necessary, among them that the future of the mine was dependent upon it. Polhem thought about the machine for two years, and, as he said: "as soon as I determined how I would construct the machine (one must remember that I had no model to follow) without making it complicated, I was convinced that it would be able to take up hundreds of barrels of dirt and rocks in a day. It was decided that a model of the machine should be built." The materials were purchased for the machine, but, as Polhem related: "just

[21] Polhem, *op. cit.*, p. 30.
[22] *Ibid.*, p. 31.
[23] *Ibid.*, p. 42.

180

9. *A model of the water-wheel used for Polhem's machine to lift rock and debris from the Falun mine. The model is from 1704; Tekniska Museet, Stockholm*

as I was about to build it, and there was nothing to stand in the way of its completion, the project was forgotten."[24] The project was abandoned, and it was said that the dirt and the rocks in the mine should remain where they were to keep the walls of the mine steady, an idea which Polhem, of course, did not believe. This hoisting mechanism was no doubt to be similar to his first model, which was intended for use at the Sala silver mine. The barrels would be carried horizontally on the bottom of the pit, then brought up the side of the pit and then carried horizontally again to the unloading area, where the barrels would empty automatically. They would then return to the bottom

[24] *Ibid.*, p. 43.

181

of the pit. The barrels could not be moved until they were fully loaded. Water power was to be used instead of power from a windmill or from horses.

X. POLHEM'S OTHER DEVICES FOR THE MINING INDUSTRY

During his visit to the mines at Harz, Polhem suggested the use of wooden pistons in the mine-pumping operation. He showed his idea to the authorities there and stated that it had been used in Sweden with good results.[25]

A great many other devices were built during this period, but it is very difficult to determine Polhem's contribution to them. Then, too, so many of Polhem's innovations were so far ahead of his time that the general impression one gets from the period is that there was almost universal resistance to his work.

XI. CONCLUSION

Dr. Torsten Althin, of the Tekniska Museet in Stockholm, writes that since this chapter by Herman Sundholm was written 50 years ago, there has been a tremendous "breakthrough" in the understanding of the construction of the hoisting apparatus and machines at the Swedish mines. Furthermore, the impression that one receives that Polhem was a man who was not fully appreciated by his time, because of the novelty of the ideas, is clearly substantiated. Dr. Althin reports, too, that a monograph by Professor Sten Lindroth, entitled *Christopher Polhem och Stora Kopparberget,* published in Uppsala in 1951, is the best contemporary source of information for this period of Polhem's life. Lindroth indicates that Polhem was motivated throughout by the desire to make Sweden an industrial land. He was impressed by what he had seen in other lands, and by what he had read in the technological and scientific literature, and he tried to make all of this applicable to the Swedish scene. Therefore, Stora Kopparberget (The Great Copper Mountain) and the Falun mine were symbols for Polhem of what could be realized in Sweden. They provided him with more than a site for the construction of pumping and hoisting machines – they meant that in Sweden a great industrial nation could be born!

[25] Polhem's memorandum, Braunschweig, Nov. 16, 1707, and Albert von dem Busch's report, Clausthal, Sept. 28, 1707. *Biografi P.* (KB).

CHAPTER FOUR

Polhem's Contribution to the
Art of Building

BY NILS CRONSTEDT

Polhem's greatest contribution in the area of water transportation was his idea of a waterway or canal which would stretch from the eastern to the western shores of Sweden, from the Baltic Sea to the Kattegat. His design for this waterway and his understanding of its significance for a developing Sweden are among the few great contributions in the entire history of our nation.

The idea of a navigable waterway through Sweden was an ancient one. In terms of the possibilities of greater avenues of transportation both within the country, as well as the new trade routes such a waterway would open up, it was absolutely necessary that a canal be built. However, political conditions at different times in Sweden's history made the need for such a waterway even more important. Time and time again, plans were made for its construction, but nothing concrete ever resulted. For example, during the time of Gustaf Vasa, Sweden wanted to free herself from the domination of Lübeck. In order to increase the avenues of trade with the west (and with Holland in particular), a plan was devised to use the Göta River as a departure point for ships traveling west. This same plan was brought up again during the reign of Erik xiv. In addition, there was always the fear that Denmark would blockade the Baltic. The thought had also been expressed from time to time that the inhabitants of Reval could ship their goods through Mälaren to Arboga, through Hjälmaren and to Örebro, and then by land to Vänern, and finally to Älfsborg. Different routes for the canal had been suggested, but the principal one seemed to be as follows: In the west, the route from Vänern to the Kattegat would go through Trollhättan and Uddevalla; in the east from Vänern to the Baltic, through Slätbaken or Bråviken, or through Hjälmaren and Mälaren.

Polhem's friend and assistant, Emanuel Swedenborg, received a letter from his brother-in-law, Eric Benzelius, the Bishop of Linköping, in which Bishop Brask's plan for a similar canal was given. The war with Denmark and the troubled political scene at the beginning of the eighteenth century made Sweden more and more of an isolated country. Because of this situation, Polhem and Swedenborg began to devise ways to make a canal through Sweden a reality. Swedenborg convinced King Karl xii that such a waterway would protect the country from military attacks and economic blockades. Karl xii, who was greatly interested in the political administration of his country, was a sovereign who initiated many improvements in Sweden. He listened attentively to Swedenborg. During the years of 1716 and

185

1717, when the King was in Skåne, he held meetings and worked vigorously to bring the canal into being.

Polhem, who had already become a public figure, and whose genius had already been employed by the military strategists of his country, was asked to design the plans for the canal. During the winter of 1717, Karl XII and Polhem had discussed the nature of the proposed canal. Prior to this time, Polhem had presented a diagram to the King of a canal which would connect Göteborg and Vänern. The lower part of the Göta River had been made navigable during Karl XI's reign. More than 100 years earlier, the first canal lock at "Lilla Edet" had been opened for traffic. This project was begun by Swedish workers and completed by a Dutch builder. Polhem suggested that to overcome the difference in height between the water in Vänern and the water below Trollhättan, a canal lock had to be built at Karlsgraf, and three more at Trollhättan. The locks were to be made of wood and covered with stone which could be gotten from Kinnekulle. The enormous height of $55\frac{1}{2}$ alnar (33 meters) had to be overcome at this point, which meant that the locks could not be constructed entirely open, but had to have an arch over the opening. This "tunnel lock," as it was called, was a technique which Polhem probably had learned during his stay in France. In a short paper dealing with the construction of the lock, he estimated that each one would cost 10,000 to 20,000 silver daler, based upon the materials used and the salaries of the workers.

The Göta River between Trollhättan and Vänersborg had to be cleared before it was navigable. Polhem thought that this work could be carried out by Russian prisoners of war or by soldiers. In this way, he believed, the cost of the project would be kept down. In addition to this, repairs had to be made on the old lock at Edet. He estimated that the total cost for the entire canal, from Vänern to Göteborg, would be approximately 100,000 silver daler.

Polhem was not simply involved with the technical problems of building a canal, but, as he later wrote, he believed that the canal would be of great significance to the development of an industrial Sweden. He told about the various mills which had been built at Trollhättan. Vänersborg, too, he believed, could become an industrial city, as soon as ships began to pass through the canal. At Vänersborg, he visualized an iron mill, a saltworks, and other manufacturing works. In addition, steel, brass, and other metals could be worked there, he said, and knives, locks, clocks and other things might be manufactured. Water power could be obtained inexpensively. To make this "industrial center" more appealing, Polhem suggested that the workers who

186

settled in Vänersborg should be freed from all taxes for twenty to thirty years. He believed that similar industrial sites, which would come into being because of the canal, would have tremendous economic value for the future of Sweden. In this way, the canal would soon pay for itself. Goods could be transported from the east to the west by this waterway, instead of the costly, time-consuming sea route around Sweden. The cost of shipping goods from Vänersborg to Göteborg would cost about one half of what it had before. In addition to all of these advantages, Polhem noted that the property which was used for the land route, "Edsvägen to Göteborg," was not valuable. "The farmer," Polhem said, "makes a grazing meadow out of his farmland, and exchanges all his cattle for horses."

Polhem, as well as designing the canal, suggested ways to raise the money needed for its construction. He wanted to form a special shareholding company with one thousand shares of stock which would cost 100 silver daler each. To make such a stock attractive, he suggested that stockholders receive a substantial dividend for their shares. He felt that as a just compensation for his work, a number of shares should be issued in his name. This plan could not be immediately realized, however, and it is doubtful if a real attempt was ever made to bring it into being.

In 1717, Polhem continued designing the plans for the canal, and suggested that a more realistic project would be to build a lock at Karlsgraf, and that the state should pay for its construction. Polhem believed that a smaller project at first would convince the authorities that a canal system could be built, by Swedish workers and with Swedish materials, and that bricks, cement and canalbuilders did not have to be brought from Holland to complete the work. In addition, he felt that many other cities in Sweden would want a share in this project; for example, those cities which lay between Lake Vättern and Norrköping, as well as Halmstad, Kristianstad, and other cities. Polhem wrote in his letter to the King, "If no one in these difficult times can conceive of such a project, it can nonetheless be of great significance for the future, for who knows when there will be a Swedish mechanical engineer who is familiar with four different areas of knowledge; that is, of theoretical matters, of the practical application of theory, of physical laws and invention, and even resolution, which is not the least of all of these."

The canal lock, which Polhem proposed for Karlsgraf, in addition to a dam in the river and the necessary clearing of the river, was estimated to cost 6,000 silver daler. The lock itself would be 30 alnar high and 18 alnar wide (17 8/10 by 10 7/10 meters). Polhem requested

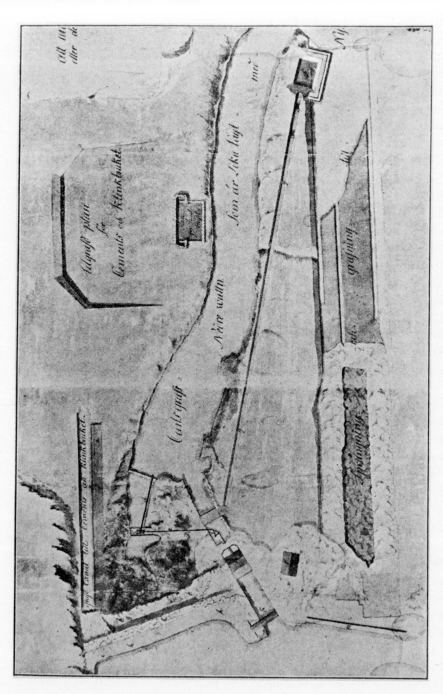

1. *Diagram of Polhem's plan for a canal lock at Karlsgraf (1763); Riksarkiv (Royal Archives)*

that he be permitted to do the work and that the lock be freed from taxes, and that the Polhem family be given permanent possession of it. In return, Polhem would be responsible for the maintenance of the lock, but he would also have the right to collect duty from the boats passing through. Because of the political and economic situation of the times, this proposal was satisfactory to the State. The government at that time tried in every way to support private ventures in the hopes that this would promote a better economy. Polhem had great faith in the future of Sweden, particularly as an industrial land, and he added tremendously to the realization of this ideal. This confidence in Sweden and its potential had already been expressed in his dream of Vänersborg as a manufacturing city.

When the contract was finally signed for the construction of the canal, a further suggestion was made that the canal be built through the heart of Sweden from the Kattegat to the Baltic Sea. Polhem was undoubtedly behind this proposal, for in 1718 he met Karl XII and probably at that time recommended the construction of such a canal. Some of the details of this meeting are known from the report of "His Royal Majesty's approval of Christopher Polhem's proposal to build a waterway between Göteborg and Norrköping." The King was convinced that such a waterway would be of great value for the commerce of Sweden. Although the financial situation in Sweden at that time was not good, Polhem was assured that nothing would hinder its successful completion. Karl was undoubtedly impressed with Polhem's thought that all of the work could be done by Swedish men, with Swedish materials, and with no help from abroad. This was to be the beginning of a new age in Sweden; a time of greatness for the country, industrially, scientifically, and intellectually!

Polhem thought the canal should pass through Trollhättan, and could then join the Uddevalla canal which stretched to the Kattegat. There were many reasons for this connection; the distance was a great deal shorter; the water was calmer than in the Göta River; navigation would therefore be easier and a fewer number of locks would have to be built. It was necessary, he said, for Göteborg to be the starting point for the canal, but also that the canal must connect Vänersborg and Trollhättan.

The plan to improve Karlsgraf and construct a lock at Brunkebergskulle began in the spring of 1718. The government had approved the plan, timber had been set aside, taxes from the neighboring lands had been collected, and in every way an attempt was made to further the work. King Karl visited the area on his way to Norway, and demonstrated that he was greatly concerned with the undertaking.

189

From the outset, however, there were a great number of problems: workers were hard to find, especially the skilled and the responsible; it was difficult to transport materials; economic conditions were unfavorable; war with Norway was an imminent possibility. Polhem directed the work himself, aided by his friend, Emanuel Swedenborg. Supervisors were chosen and, as well, additional men were hired so that they could gain knowledge and experience in this kind of work. The work at Karlsgraf moved along rapidly, and as soon as it was completed, the construction of the lock began. Polhem suggested that the lock be made of wood, in the form of a "tunnel lock." The height of the entire lock was to be 8 or 9 alnar (approximately 5 meters), and the clearance for the ships (which were to have folding masts in the future), would be 4 1/2 alnar (2 7/10 meters). Polhem pointed out the advantages of a single high lock instead of several lower ones. The wooden lock, he said, could be repaired and even rebuilt if necessary. He added that additional parts might be made available in case there was need of repair. In order to pump out the water from the area where the work was progressing, Polhem built a small mill with a water-wheel. In addition to this, Polhem planned to open and close the lock by the water-wheel. However, the lock was never completed, and the reason is not entirely known. Whether it was due to the death of King Karl, or the foreign pressures which resulted, one can never be sure. Polhem was deeply disappointed, because the work had already cost 22,075 silver daler. When he asked for more money to complete the work, his request was turned down. The entire project was disbanded at this point, although attempts were made later to continue the construction of the lock.

In the meantime, however, Polhem had designed a waterway to connect the Baltic Sea with the Kattegat. He gave a detailed report of what he called the "Svea Canal" to the government in the year 1720. The connection between Stockholm and Göteborg would take the shortest route over the lakes which included Mälaren, Hjälmaren, Toften, Skagern, and Vänern in central Sweden. Although the plan was extremely feasible, the government was not interested in it. However, in the period which followed, which was a period of peace in Sweden, the government began to think in terms of developing the natural resources of the nation. Because of this, Polhem's project was kept alive, and the work which Polhem had instituted in his time later received the name of the "Trollhättan Canal." Other individuals became interested in the project, but Polhem remained the spirit behind the proposed canal between the Baltic Sea and the Kattegat.

Finally, in 1740, it was decided that a canal should be built between Lake Vänern and the sea. However, no specific directions were given as to how this was to be done. The work was offered to contractors, but again, nothing happened. Conversations were held with Christopher Polhem, with the result that Gabriel, his son, and Major B. V. Carlberg received a commission from the government to investigate the entire matter. Several plans for the canal were considered, but finally Polhem's design was adjudged to be the most satisfactory. His proposed route was the shortest and it was the most practical. Another advantage was that the canal was to be built through the rock in the area. Carlberg's plan differed from Polhem's, and had many more locks, and the canal itself was much longer.

In October, 1747, Carl Gustaf Tessin and Claes Ekeblad, members of the Council, were chosen to manage the construction of the waterway at Trollhättan. They decided to seek Polhem's help. Polhem was, however, occupied at that time with the Stockholm lock. He was asked to improve upon the present plans and to design a canal, for the least possible cost, from Karlsgraf to Trollhättan. It was decided that the canal should be built in such a way that it could be used for ships transporting food and materials, as well as for warships. In this way the canal could serve the nation's commercial interests as well as its defense system. It was soon realized, however, that such a canal would cost too much money. As there was no additional income for the increased expenses, it was decided to build the Trollhättan Canal solely for the transportation of goods. The original plan of Polhem for a narrower waterway and fewer locks, to be used solely by smaller crafts with folding masts, was the most practical plan, and it was readily accepted by Tessin and Ekeblad.

When one thinks of the difficulties that were encountered with huge construction projects such as this one during Polhem's lifetime, and compares it with present-day techniques, Polhem's canal must be considered a work of engineering genius. The canal, he said, had to be blasted out of the rock and be as short as possible. Dams were constructed in the river so that the navigable passage around the Trollhättan Falls was divided into two parts. A lock was built between them, so that ships could travel up the river. By the falls in the Kafle stream, between the island of Malg and the shore, a dam was built which eliminated the "Prästskede Falls," and a basin was formed. A canal was blasted through the island of Malg and a lock was built which was 23½ feet (7 meters) deep. South of Malg Island, at Öjebro, another dam was constructed which held back the water to Håkans-

2. *Polhem's waterfall at Trollhättan. Engraving by J. A. Cordier, about 1800*

hamn. At Håkanshamn another lock was constructed with a depth of 56½ feet (16 8/10 meters), and the canal continued to Hajum's "warp." Across the river, at the lower falls in the Flottberg stream, another dam was built, which held back the waters of Olidehålan, so that Helvet's Falls, 28 feet (8 3/10 meters) high, disappeared. The result of all this was that ships could travel from Hajum's "warp" to the Göta River. By the Flottberg Dam, a lock was constructed which had a depth of 34½ feet (10 3/10 meters). The locks were built according to a French pattern (the "tunnel lock") which Polhem had used before. A canal was blasted out of the rock, which was followed by the lock itself. It then continued to a tunnel which had been blasted directly through the rock. The main reason for building the locks in this way must have been that the sides of the locks would be strengthened. Then, too, the construction of the lock was simplified, particularly when a great height was required.

The folding masts on the ships added to the ease of passage. The dimensions of the lock were to be 66 feet in length, 18 feet in width, and 8 feet in depth (19 6/10 meters, by 5 4/10 meters, by 2 4/10 meters). Other measurements had been given, one of which was a width of 19 feet (5 6/10 meters) and a depth of 6 feet (1 8/10 meters). The clearance in the tunnel was 7 feet (2 1/10 meters). For the higher locks, Polhem designed special lock gates.

Polhem was not discouraged by the tremendous amount of blasting which was required. Because of his work in the mines previous to this time, he knew how to handle explosives. The mass of rock which had to be blasted was calculated to be made up of at least 2,000 cubic fathoms (about 11,300 meters) and would cost 85,000 copper daler. Polhem designed a complete plan of operation with detailed instructions and directions, which included the size of the work crew and the specific way in which the work was to progress. The plans were presented to the King in May, 1748, and Polhem informed him of the importance the canal would have in the future of Sweden.

The dams, especially in the Kafle and Flottberg streams, were extremely difficult to construct. Polhem finally suggested that the Göta River be dammed up for a period of six weeks (or a maximum of two months), so that the dams could be built on dry ground. Two temporary dams were to be constructed in the upper part of the river for that purpose. A wooden foundation was to be constructed and then placed in the river, and stone walls added to it at a later time. The damming of the river, which naturally could only be done when the water was at its lowest point, was to be completed in two years. The smaller dams between the islands of Malg and Gref, and also at Håkans-

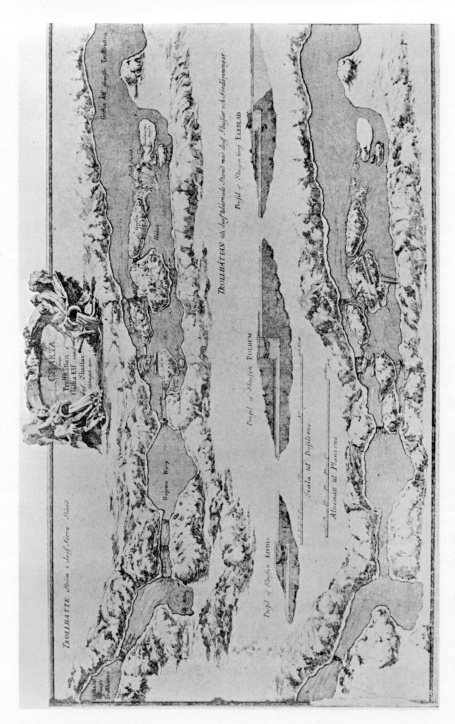

3. I. Rehn's map of Polhem's plan for the canal at Trollhättan

hamn, were to be constructed when the water was dammed up. Polhem did not fully appreciate the problems which such a plan presented. The lack of modern construction methods and machines were the real reasons why his ingenious plan could never be completed. In addition to the technical problems involved, Polhem was at that time too old to travel to Trollhättan, and was dependent for his information about the canal on the reports of others. Per Elvius, the Secretary of the Academy of Science, was asked to assist with the project. The result was that Polhem's plan of operation was better appreciated. During the year 1749 Polhem worked to complete the models for the dams and locks which were later to be constructed.

The financial arrangements for the project were on an unsteady foundation. Some believed that not enough money could be raised to build the canal. In addition, costs had to be kept low. The prospect was that no income could be collected until the entire work was finished. Individual persons were uncertain about the canal and were reluctant to contribute to it. No public funds were available, and the powerful East India Company would not advance any money. Finally, however, funds were made available by the government and some contributions were made by private persons. Stocks were sold. Before these contributions were received, however, an attempt was made to calculate the cost of the project. In March of 1748, an engineer from the Sala silver mine, Gustaf Adolf Wiman, made an estimate of 550,000 copper daler, which was more than the 300,000 copper daler Polhem had estimated. Even so, Polhem's plan was accepted, with few minor exceptions, and on September 11, 1749, Gustaf Adolf Wiman and Lars Moëll, an artillery officer, signed "a contract to construct the waterway from Lake Vänern to Göteborg through Trollhättan over the falls in the Göta River and finally to Karlsgraf." It was to take three years to complete the work, and during that time Wiman and Moëll were to be responsible for the blasting, damming, and the clearing of the river, the construction of the locks, and all that was necessary to make the canal operable. The cost for this work was estimated at 610,155 copper daler, and was divided up as follows:

	Copper Daler
The dam at Vänern	40,000
The lock at Karlsgraf	78,350
Clearing of Karlsgraf, above and below the lock	41,385
The lock at Malg Island	85,980

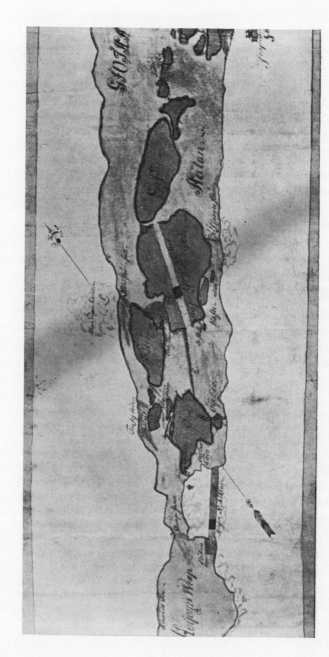

4. Drawing of Polhem's plan for the Göta River; from Kungl. Biblioteket (Royal Library)

	Copper Daler
The Kafle stream dam, also the damming of "Prästskede Falls"	24,000
The lock at Håkanshamn	161,730
The dam at Öjebro	6,000
The lock at Flottberg	71,210
The dam at Flottberg	40,000
Additional work	31,500
Commissions and travel costs	30,000

The government had promised to help. Wood from the government's forests would be supplied, powder from the Åker powderworks would be reduced in cost, workers from the army would be at the disposal of Wiman and Moëll, and skilled handlers of explosives from the mining areas or the artillery would be made available.

Commissioner Karl Hårleman, who had been appointed by the government to supervise the handling of supplies, as well as to direct the builders, was now assigned to take charge of the entire operation. The work began immediately. Houses, storerooms, blacksmith's shops, and warehouses were built. Details of the working plan were confirmed. Orders went out to the Provincial Governor, the Bureau of Mines, the Department of War, and other agencies. District Judge Thure Ollonberg was appointed to see that all aspects of the work were kept under control. The workers were cared for in many ways; their education was provided for and all of the necessities of life supplied during the period of their employment. During the year of 1750 the working force grew to 350 men, and in 1751 to 700, of which 500 were soldiers and 200 workingmen from the neighboring areas. The main office was established in Vänersborg. All accounts were settled there, and the necessary drawings worked out. As well, the materials which were needed were purchased through the office located there. Progress reports were to be given every week, and an annual report made to the Commission at the conclusion of each year. On December 2, 1749, the blasting work for the lock in Håkanshamn began (the same lock which later was to be called "Polhem's Lock"). As the work progressed, additional requests were made, especially from the Department of Navigation and the military, to build the canal in such a way that larger vessels could go through. Yet all these requests could not be granted. A few changes were made in the plans, but on the whole, Polhem's original plan was followed.

Polhem left the construction of the work to other hands. He had

197

seen the project started, but was spared the disappointment of knowing that his plan was later rejected by the government. The reason for this rejection must be understood in terms of the fact that Polhem's theories and techniques were ahead of his time. They are just now beginning to be appreciated!

The dam at Vänern, which was to hold back the water in the Göta River so that work could be done on dry ground, presented insurmountable difficulties. The Trollhättan Dam, too, was difficult to construct. The temporary dam in the Kafle stream was destroyed. Various techniques which Polhem had worked out for dam construction were tried but often they were not successful. The large dam in the Flottberg stream presented many grave problems. The dam was to be built above the narrowest section of the river and was to be made of blocks and trestles, which were to be anchored on both sides of the river by means of large stone foundations. Time and time again these were washed away by the stream. After five years' work, they had advanced to a point where the dam was almost completely finished. An accident occurred, however, when some lumber which was being floated to a sawmill located near the dam broke through the dam. Lack of money, a lack of interest in continuing the works, and a realization that the techniques of construction were inadequate caused the project to be discontinued.

Nonetheless, a number of Polhem's proposals were carried out. The river at Karlsgraf had been cleared and a lock was built, even though it was not placed exactly where Polhem had specified. It was opened for traffic in the autumn of 1752 and was named for Count Karl Gustaf Tessin. The lock at Malg Island was opened in August of 1754, and received the name of "Count Claes Ekeblad Lock." The lock at the Flottberg stream, which was never completed, was named for Per Elvius. The lock at Håkanshamn bore Polhem's name. The "Polhem Lock" stands today as a memorial to the great engineer and pioneer of Sweden's inland waterways. It is an achievement which has been admired by engineers of every generation. It is a great Swedish accomplishment!

Because of this initial work, the land transport route between Lake Vänern and Göteborg had been shortened. There remained only the short distance past the Trollhättan Falls. Christopher Polhem's design for the canal had gone as far as the technical knowledge and methods of his time permitted. A half-century later, the Trollhättan Canal was completed. The canal had been rebuilt once, and the third Trollhättan Canal was opened for traffic in the year 1916.

The ancient route from Värmland and Västergötland always passed through Lake Hjälmaren. This was then joined to a land route which passed through Hyndevad and Torshälla, and finally to Stockholm and Södertälje. As early as the year 1603, a waterway between Hjälmaren and Mälaren had been planned. A few years earlier, work had started on a canal which would by-pass the Torshälla Falls. This canal, however, was never used extensively, for an alternate route between the Arboga River and Hjälmaren was proposed in its place. During this time King Gustaf Adolf II and his daughter Kristina were patrons of the Swedish waterway system, and the literature of the period spoke eloquently of this fact.

The work on the Hjälmaren Lock began in 1629, but it progressed very slowly. Interest in the project was lacking and workmen were not available. There were other problems, including a lack of sufficient funds. Innumerable attempts were made to stimulate interest in the project. However, it was not until Axel Oxenstjerna addressed the Council in October, 1633, and told about the great significance of the canal, that work began in earnest. Before the project was completed, it was necessary to repair a number of locks which had been built elsewhere. They were made of wood, which had been covered with stone. To repair them, cement and a Dutch type of brick was used. The dimensions of these locks were: 8 feet in depth at the threshold; 24 feet in width at the lock gates; 80 feet, the minimum length of the lock basin (2 4/10 by 7 1/10 by 23 8/10 meters).

It seemed that this canal was never completely satisfactory for the needs of the time. Already by the 1720's and 30's, complaints were heard of its bad condition. The walls of the lock had begun to sink. Interested persons got together and offered to manage and repair the canal. At last, the whole matter was brought to the attention of the government. The result was that Polhem was instructed to examine the canal and the locks and try to solve the problems associated with them. Whether he accepted this proposal or not cannot be known with certainty. In the manuscripts left by Polhem, no mention is made of the Hjälmaren Lock. Nonetheless, the incident reveals the great reputation Polhem had at that time in engineering circles, particularly in the area of waterways and inland navigation. One can maintain, quite correctly, that Polhem was the first and foremost of Sweden's "consulting engineers."

In the latter part of the seventeenth century, Finland began to believe that inland canals would be of value to the growth of her nation.
The first canal which was planned was between Lake Saima and the
Baltic Sea. It is known that this project had been attempted earlier, but
was unsuccessful because technical knowledge was limited and funds
were not forthcoming. Water transportation was made possible in Finland by the use of long shallow boats which could be rowed or hauled
up the rivers. Ropes had to be used to pull the boats up the more turbu-
lent rivers. However, the boats could go down the rivers and streams
as fast as the current could carry them. In order to make navigation
easier, it was decided that the waterways had to be cleared of debris
and obstructions.

Judge L. J. Ehrenmalm brought up the subject of a canal for Finland at the beginning of the seventeenth century. Polhem mentioned
in his papers that he was contacted and asked to determine the feasi-
bility of such a canal system for Finland. The projected canal was discussed in reference to a number of construction developments on the
coast of Finland. Polhem felt that it was possible to transport timber
to Björneborg if the streams were cleared. For ships to transport goods
it would necessarily mean that a system of canal locks would have to
be constructed. The difference in the height of the water between the
Gulf of Bothnia and the inland waterways was very great. For example, Polhem noted that between Björneborg and Pajana alone, fifty
or sixty locks would be required. He was convinced that wooden locks
should be built because of the proximity of the forests in Finland.
Under no circumstances, he insisted, were locks of the Dutch type
(using cement and bricks) to be built. Dams were to be built in the
rivers to aid in the canalbuilding process. Polhem would not estimate
the exact cost of the canal before he had a chance to examine the extent of the work in great detail. However, he thought that the costs for
this canal system would be much too high and that a sufficient profit
could not be made. Furthermore, he predicted that when duty was
charged, people would choose the older means of transportation, and
not use the canal. In one of his writings, Polhem referred to a waterway north from Tammerfors to Ruovesi and Ruojärvi, and suggested
that it might be a continuation of the canal to Björneborg. He pointed
out that even if a canal could not be completed according to his
specifications, nonetheless, it would be extremely beneficial to Fin-

land if a number of locks were built. These he believed would greatly improve the inland water routes. A number of the locks and canal routes which Polhem suggested have been completed. Daniel Thunberg worked for a number of years to make the rivers navigable, but it was not until the middle of the nineteenth century that Finland's inland waterway system was completed.

IV. THE KARLSKRONA DOCKS

In August, 1680, Karl XI had granted a charter to the city of Karlskrona and had given special privileges for the construction of the city. Free powder was offered, as well as the use of the government's blasting equipment. Prisoners of war were at the disposal of the city officials to be used in any way they wanted. The political situation of the time had made it essential that Karlskrona become the new headquarters of the Swedish fleet.

It became necessary almost immediately for the ships of the Swedish fleet to have docks in which they could anchor. A design had been made by "Master Shipbuilder" Charles Sheldon which was shown to Karl XII. When the King returned to Sweden in 1716, he indicated an interest in these plans for the docks. Remembering Christopher Polhem's good work in the past, he asked the Department of the Navy in Karlskrona to consult Polhem regarding the work to be done. In 1694, the Department of the Navy had been asked to consider the advisability of building mills at Lyckeby to be used to supplement the Navy's food supplies. After lengthy negotiations, a single mill was purchased. A dam, too, was constructed during the years of 1710 to 1712. The dam was located so that other mills could be added later; mills which could saw wood, cut and stamp metals, and manufacture different kinds of goods. Polhem's plans were used in the construction of this dam, which was built as an "arched" dam with a facing of wood.

Polhem also negotiated with the Department of the Navy to begin constructing the docks at Karlskrona. When Karl XII was in Lund, Polhem visited him to discuss the matter. Emanuel Swedenborg was Polhem's assistant at this time. The work on the Karlskrona docks was divided among a number of individuals. The superintendent of construction was Admiral C. H. Wachtmeister, who was assisted by the captain of fortifications, G. O. Lindblad, Charles Sheldon, and Christopher Polhem himself.

201

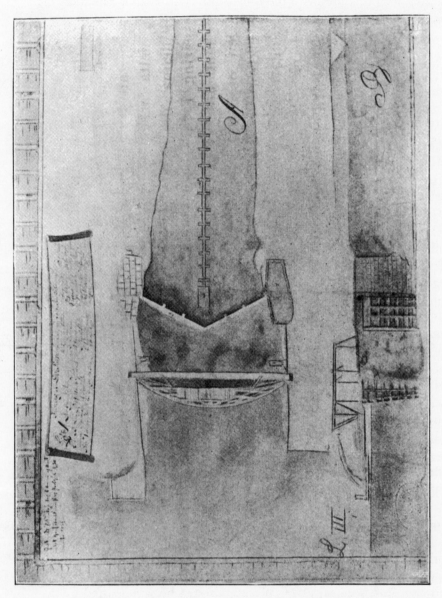

5. *Charles Sheldon's plan for the dock in Karlskrona; from a drawing in Stationsingeniörens Arkiv*

The docks were to be blasted from the rock on the island of Lindholm. The blasting work could take place only on dry ground, and the problem arose as to how a dam could be constructed which would permit the work to proceed. The bottom of the harbor was examined by Swedenborg and a wooden "catch dam" was built to prevent water from passing through. It was built according to Polhem's specifications, in the shape of a parabola. Such a dam was extremely difficult to construct at that period, especially because so much water had to be removed. As a result, there were constant leaks in the dam. The pumping operation took a great deal of time and manpower. As many as seventy men were needed. It appeared that Polhem could see that the dam was not going to be successfully built, for just one year after the work began, he left the project. Perhaps the reason for this was that not all of his work methods and machines had been used. He tells us (not without some bitterness) that time and money would have been saved if his advice had been taken in the first place.

On September 8, 1724, the first dock in Karlskrona was finished and the ship "King Karl" anchored. The ship, which was built in 1694 using Charles Sheldon's design, was 180 feet (53 5/10 meters) long, 47 feet (14 meters) wide, and had 108 cannons mounted on it. It was the largest ship in the Swedish Navy. The dock, which was called "Polhem's Dock," was a remarkable piece of work. Foreign visitors termed it the "eighth wonder of the world."

Polhem suggested other things for Karlskrona. He proposed building another series of docks between Söderstjärna and Lindholm. In the year 1729, these plans were presented to the government.

The size of Polhem's dock soon was too small, and in the year 1746 the dock was rebuilt and enlarged. This dock at Karlskrona was called "incomparable" as late as the beginning of the nineteenth century. A model of the dock shows a lifting device made of two flat-bottomed boats which were joined together. The device was powered by a waterwheel. The boats were lifted to the dock and held in place there.

The originality of Polhem's ideas was not always fully appreciated, and his contributions not always seen for what they were. He once wrote, "Nothing can be rejected without at least one reason given for its rejection."

Karlskrona's first water supply system can also be credited to Polhem, although the incidents surrounding its construction are not known. There is a notation from the year 1750 which informs us that a "water skiff" would bring water from Lyckeby to the inhabitants of Karlskrona. There would be a fixed rate for the water, which would be so adjusted that the Crown would not be involved.

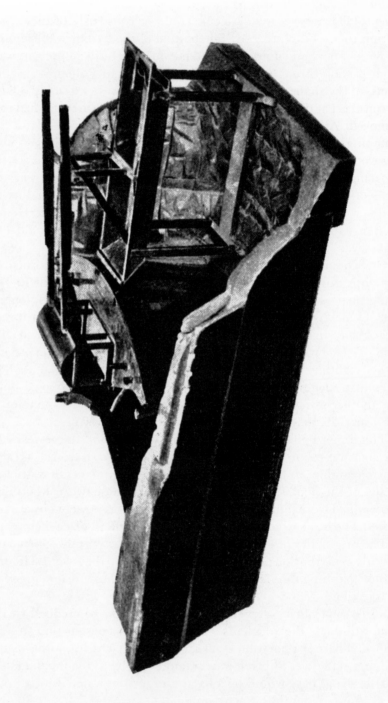

6. *A model of a part of the dry dock in Karlskrona, showing the elevating mechanism*

Polhem contributed a great deal to the creation of Sweden's defense system. He was considered an authority in this field. During the first half of the eighteenth century the defense of Stockholm's coast was considered to be of the utmost importance. The main line of defense had been concentrated about Vaxholm. A narrow channel in the area had been blockaded by wooden logs which were held together by iron chains. This was not a satisfactory arrangement, however, because the metal rusted, and the logs were loosened by the motion of the water. Polhem was called to rebuild the blockade. In 1748 four channels were barricaded with logs and the total length of the barricades was 536 alnar (318 meters). Polhem's idea was to build the barricades as strongly as possible, but to make them flexible as well. He did not use any metal in the barricades, but made them completely of wood. Pine logs, 12 tum square (3/10 by 3/10 meters), and 4 alnar long (2 4/10 meters) were joined by sidepieces and movable bolts. There is a similarity in this construction to what came to be called "the Polhem joint."

Polhem was also commissioned to rebuild and enlarge the fortress at Landskrona. This work was one of the most important contributions to the fortification and defense system of Sweden. He also constructed a scaffold under water upon which emplacements in the harbor could be located. Polhem's disciple, Daniel Thunberg, took a number of his teacher's inventions to Count Augustin Ehrensvärd in Finland where they were used in the construction of the fortresses near Helsingfors.

In addition to the docks in Karlskrona, Polhem was occupied with building a "repair slip" or dry dock to be used at the harbor in Stockholm. A model of this was completed in 1738. It consisted of a slip which rested upon a great number of wheels. It was so constructed that a number of men could operate it. Polhem told of the advantages of this apparatus: repairing costs would be lessened, work could proceed much faster, and several ships could be hauled onto dry ground at one time. By changing the gear system, heavier ships could be lifted onto the shore to be repaired.

Most of his ideas were resisted, however, by "Master Shipbuilder" S. Falk. Polhem apparently was offended by this rejection, and regarded most of Falk's suggestions as irrelevant. He said upon one occasion, "If I were to say something to the shipbuilder, he would think that I considered myself to have more knowledge than he; how-

205

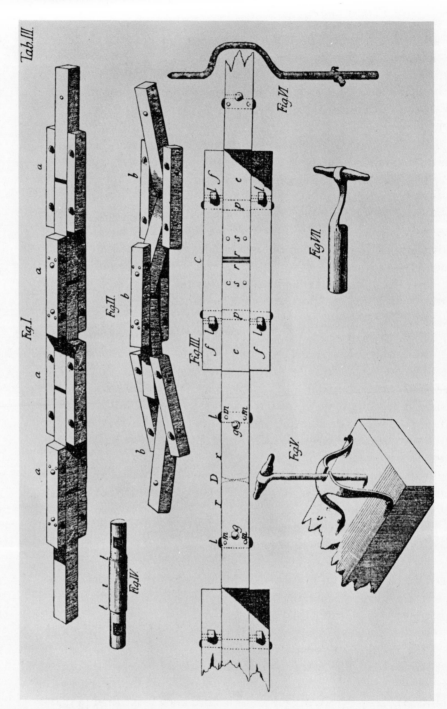

7. Polhem's wooden barricade; from Proceedings of the Royal Academy of Science, 1753

ever, if he asks me something, I will answer him in a straightforward way." Polhem was anxious to contribute to the work, even though he was an old man by this time. He did say, however, that "it was not advisable to permit a decrepit old man like me to take part in such an expensive and imposing construction." He did make suggestions, however, as to how the work might proceed, and believed that there should be a division of labor which would make the best use of the experience of the different men on the job. He wrote: "However, remember that there must be two masters, one responsible for the work of the men, the other responsible for the time and costs of the construction; the work of one consists of a careful examination of each piece before it is used, as an imperfection can go unnoticed for some time; the work of the other consists of choosing and measuring the timber and dividing the tasks among the workers according to the specifications of the work."

VI. The "Floating Bridge"

In the *Proceedings of the Royal Academy of Science* for the year 1742 there is a manuscript by Polhem called "Notes on the Use of Curved Lines in Mechanics." He wrote about the following kinds of lines: the circle, the parabola, the catenary, the hyperbola, and the spiral. He also listed their uses, among them, the construction of vaults and arches, water troughs, gutters, and bridges. He described the use of the catenary in the construction of hanging bridges and designed such a bridge for the Dal River at Uppbo and Husby. He also described a kind of "floating bridge" for the Dal River at Alfkarleby, which was located at one of the widest points of the river. It was to be built in the shape of a parabola with the convex side upstream.

Göran Wallerius, in 1743, described in great detail the construction of a bridge over the Dal River which employed Polhem's designs. A number of bridges over the Dal River near Hedemora had been built before with the use of stone foundation blocks to which the span was attached. They had been built so that they could be raised and lowered. However, these bridges were exposed to the very great variations in the water level of the river. The stone blocks became icebound in the winter, and the damage to them was very great. During a great flood in 1727 and 1728, the bridge at Husby was washed away.

Polhem's "floating bridge" was constructed in the following way. Two large parabolas were sketched on the ice and upon these, timber

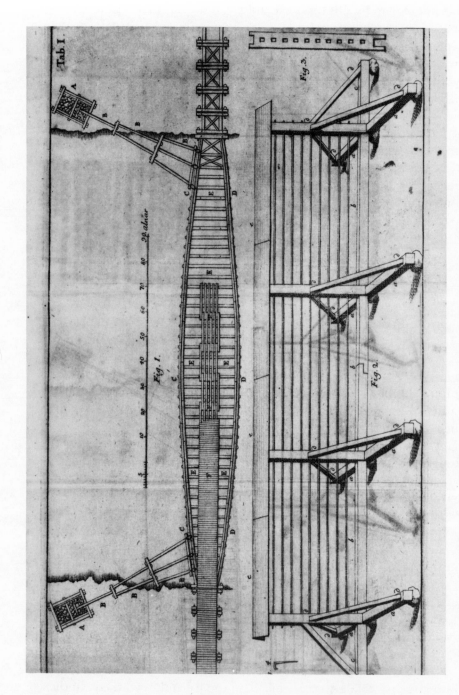

8. *Polhem's bridge with the parabolic arch; engraving from Proceedings of the Royal Academy of Science, 1743*

lengths were laid out and connected. Crossbeams were fitted to these, bearing the roadway of the bridge. To avoid building in the river itself, stone blocks were placed on the shore upstream. The anchoring of the bridge was done in such a way that the bridge could still be raised and lowered in relation to the surface of the water. The bridge was very strong and secure, and, in addition, it did not cost as much as previous bridge constructions. The use of stone blocks on the shore was the greatest innovation, for they could easily be maintained and repaired. The bridge itself was built without any iron parts and was much lighter as a result. The bridge could not overturn, either, because of the way it had been erected. The planks which were used were placed on a slant, which protected the bridge from the ravages of the ice and the strong currents.

VII. The Laboratory for Water-wheels and Water Power

The primary means for obtaining power for industry in Polhem's time was water. Industrial sites were built near waterfalls because there was a ready source of power. In the *laboratorium mechanicum*, which was initiated and directed by Polhem, a special water laboratory was built, which was undoubtedly the first of its kind in Sweden.

In Polhem's "water laboratory" (which is described in detail in Triewald's "Lectures on the New Natural Sciences," 1728–1729), a number of experiments were devised which tested water-wheels and water systems. In addition to this, methods to determine the weight and load of different machines were discussed, as well as the problem of how much power was necessary to operate the various kinds of machines. Polhem wrote about many of the experiments he performed and enumerated, in great detail, the advantages and disadvantages of one water system over another. In a series of papers from the years 1739 and 1742, Polhem related that some of his conclusions based upon experiments at the water laboratory, particularly those which were made before 1702, were incorrect. His conclusions were based solely upon theory, but, as he said, other factors had to be considered which influenced the results. Polhem also described how water-wheels were constructed, the size and weight of the wheels, the width of the paddles, the distance between the various parts, as well as many other things. He spoke of the different kinds of water-pipes and the importance of relating the curve of the pipe to the flow of the water. One of his most important papers was called "The Unity of

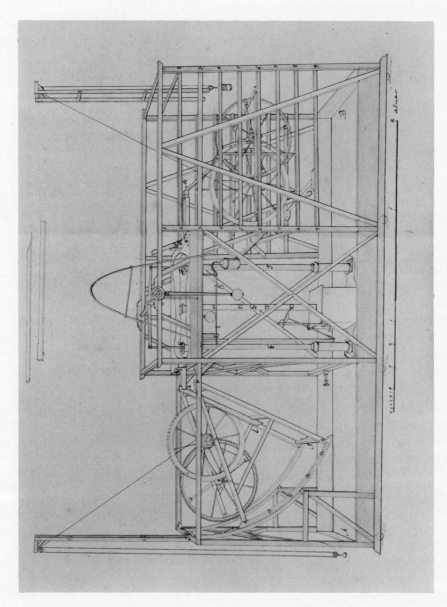

9. *Polhem's laboratory for measuring the efficiency of water-wheels. Drawing by C. J. Cronstedt, 1730; Tekniska Museet, Stockholm*

Theory and Practice in Mechanics; particularly in Waterwork Construction" which dealt with problems in the area of hydrography. "When a waterwork is to be built," he wrote, "the waterfall and the amount of water it turns must first be measured, in order to determine if it is sufficient to bring about the desired result. If it happens that there is more than is needed, then two or three more works can be built, and then the one will be used much more effectively."

Polhem also worked with problems in the area of the measurement of the speed and quantity of water. Per Elvius continued Polhem's theoretical work in this subject.

VIII. BUILDING AND BUILDING MATERIALS

Builders in Polhem's time, whether they were architects or engineers, were decidedly different from the present-day "specialists." They had to work with every kind of technical problem in wide and diversified areas. Christopher Polhem, who involved himself in a great many fields, demonstrated again and again the breadth of his abilities. The subject of building and construction seemed to be of special interest to him. The most detailed and comprehensive of his writings in this area was entitled "Mechanica Practica" or "The Fundamentals of Building," which was, however, not completely finished. According to his own notes, it was to consist of two parts. It was probably a handbook of instruction for those involved in "the art of building houses," and was directed to engineers, architects, contractors, and even builders themselves.

The first part dealt with dwellings and the second with church buildings. He had intended to go into more detail in this second part, which dealt with the larger kind of building, but unfortunately never finished it. From Polhem's writings on this subject we get a good picture of the conception of building of his time. He spoke first of the choice of land for the house. Next, he described the foundation of the house and the masonwork. A description of the main part of the house itself and its over-all construction followed. He concerned himself with the problem of building roofs and the way to make walls perfectly straight. He discussed how to heat a room. There were special instructions for carpenters in their work with windows, doors, and panels. He even gave advice on how to get rid of bedbugs, fleas, and other vermin. Other sections dealt with the houses adjacent to the main

211

building, cellars, toilets, the brewing-house, the washhouse, the black-smith's shop, boathouses, the granary, food stores, a house for animals, and barns. In the same section of his projected book, a number of sections discussed reservoirs, flourmills, bridges, and even flatboats and ships. This, he felt, would be of interest to those homeowners who were situated near the water.

The second part, which dealt with various kinds of churches, described foundations, masonwork, materials, roofs, bells, church decorations, organs, church doors, locks, and was to conclude with a section on church grounds and cemeteries. In Polhem's work "A Conversation Between Miss *Theoria* and Builder *Practicus*," he dealt with many of the same subjects. There was already in his time a conflict between theoretical and practical approaches to mechanical problems. Christopher Polhem was one who wanted to deal with practical problems, but to do so on the basis of theoretical principles.

Polhem dealt at great length with the topic of the construction of cellars. Once when asked to say something about this subject, he answered that knowledge of that kind was readily available. When this statement was refuted, he wrote a paper which began: "Although old and experienced housekeepers know all about it, it does not follow that all young housekeepers are as familiar with the subject," an utterance typical of Polhem's thoughts on technical problems and the professional practitioners of his time. Polhem pointed out the importance of building the cellar below the surface of the ground, so that the danger of frost would be lessened, and in this way the temperature in the winter and the summer would be the same. He also pointed out the importance of not building a cellar too small, especially as this would present a problem of ventilation. The masonwork was to be done in gray stone, but care was to be taken that the stones were not gotten from the ocean, because this kind of stone held the dampness. The arch should be built in the shape of a parabola and made of bricks. On top of these another layer of bricks could be placed. Only lime and brook sand should be used for the mortar. Draining and the ventilation of the cellar had also to be considered. If the cellar was built under the house, he said, it could be ventilated by means of the chimney. If it was built away from the house, an artificial ventilating system had to be constructed. This could be done by placing air vents on the north and south sides of the cellar. For compactness, putty composed of pitch and brickpowder was to be used, which, when heated, strengthened the structure. Cement could also be used. He described a process for making cement which he said he had learned from a Dutch builder. The lime on the island of Gotland, he added, was much better than the Dutch "shell lime." His description of the reasons for whitewashing cellars was very amusing. He asked whether the cellar was whitewashed solely to cover the mold. He talked of cellars which were blasted out of rock and stressed the importance of dividing the cellar to preserve wine, ale, and garden produce.

Polhem gathered a great deal of information during his trip to Germany, Holland, England, and France during the years 1694 to 1696. When he returned to Sweden, he attempted to put many of these ideas into practice. In a number of shorter papers and memoranda, he told of his experiences. He believed that the technical methods he had learned abroad would be useful for the development of his own country.

In a number of papers, he wrote about raw materials and how they could be used in construction. There are two papers in particular, one dealing with clay as a material for building, and the other with the principles of masonwork. In the first, he divided clay into different categories, blue clay, sand clay, white clay, slate clay, red clay, and presented the different uses to which these clays could be put: for bricklaying, for tightening of walls, for various kinds of masonwork, for burning ovens, kilns, and crucibles. He also asked if other clays could not be found in Sweden and whether Swedish clay could not be used to make a brick similar to the Dutch type. He found, too, that different colors could be mixed to make various kinds of bricks.

In the second paper dealing with masonwork, he talked primarily about the different composition of bricks and pointed out how the composition of the brick influenced its firmness. The costs, too, varied with the component parts. He described how lime could be used in the mixing of cement and mentioned different mortars, using iron filings and sawdust. He wrote about the nature of brick manufacturing and referred to the Dutch process and in particular to their ovens for burning bricks. The clays that are to be found in Sweden, he said, are especially good for bricks. He advocated the Dutch type of kiln to be built. A number were subsequently built in Falun, Västerås, and in Roslagen.

The finished bricks were classified in the following manner:

1. The light brick, which must have one more burning.

2. The medium or red brick which is useful for the wider walls under the roof.

3. The reddish-brown colored brick which could withstand water and fire.

4. The dark-glazed brick which is the best, but which sometimes

213

becomes smaller in the burning and shrinks, with the result that it cannot be mixed with the red.

In addition, he mentioned the different results which can be achieved by the different mixtures. Sawdust made the brick lighter and more durable, he said. There are directions for the testing of a brick in terms of the proper weight and sound of a brick (when tapped). He designed what he believed to be the normal size for a brick, 1/2 of an aln long, 1/4 of an aln wide, and 2/3 of an aln high. Brick flooring should be made up of 1/2 aln squares.

He wrote about cement in another paper, and told of the cement-works which he had seen in Holland and Western Germany. He described the methods for making cement there. He also told about certain kinds of materials, which when mixed with lime and sand, could be used to make the highest grade cement. Mention is made of a non-porous cement which was made of pitch, sawdust, and brickpowder. Lastly, he pointed out that Sweden had materials which could be used to make cement and urged Swedish industrialists to attempt to find new uses for the raw materials and do research on how they could best be employed.

On the fifth of May, 1714, there is a notation in his diary entitled "A Memorandum on Swedish Cities." He reported the well-known fact that fires had devastated many cities in Sweden and that safety measures had to be taken to reduce the possibility of their occurrence. In reference to the development of the building trade in London and Holland, he presented ideas which were significant for the growth of Swedish cities in the future. He said that brick houses were safer than wooden houses. They can be built with thin siding and strengthened by means of iron cramps. He believed that Sweden could build whole blocks of houses as had been done in London. A large part of this work is concerned with roof construction. He spoke of the disadvantages of the old wooden roofs. A roof covered with cast-iron plating was very difficult to make, he said. There were too many seams and it could not be made watertight. He referred to the rounded Dutch tiles and said that the reason they were constructed in this way was because of the need to gather water in the summertime, although they appeared useless for this purpose. A rounded tile required more material and was heavier than the flat one. The more uneven a roof was, he said, the greater was the damage caused by a storm and there was a greater possibility for moss, dirt, and soot to become lodged in it. The most preferable roofing material is a grooved, glazed, brick-type covering, which is burned in the Dutch way. The roofs should be made as simple as possible, too, he added.

214

10. *Stockholm, 1650; from an engraving by Wolfgang Hartman*

Polhem did not lack the ability to be critical. He was fond of criticizing specific conditions, as he did once in reference to the Bureau of Construction in Stockholm which, he said, should have communicated with him about "the important matters of construction." The mistakes of the past would have been avoided in this way, Polhem asserted. Many improvements would come about in the Swedish building trade "if old habits and self-sufficiency did not rule." "The durability of a building," he wrote, "is the most important consideration and depends upon two facts: (1) good construction; (2) high quality materials." This observation appears to be so obvious, but nonetheless has often been forgotten by builders of later generations.

One might think that nothing of contemporary interest has been found in Polhem's papers. They give us, however, as complete a picture as is possible of the situation in the art of building in the beginning of the eighteenth century. They show, furthermore, the ever-present conflict between experience and new ideas. All of this is seen within the context of Polhem's efforts to improve the methods of building and to make greater use of Swedish materials, thereby bringing about an industrial Sweden. Polhem, the master technician, the architect and building engineer, speaks through these manuscripts and reveals the contemporaneity of his ideas!

IX. The Construction of the Stockholm Lock

The waterway between the Baltic and Mälaren during the Middle Ages had passed through Söderström. However, the ships which used this route had to be hauled by means of lines and ropes and had to go through the waterway only when the current was not too strong. In the charter, which Sten Sture and the Senate wrote in 1470, Söderström was designated "as a passageway for ships and boats." One can assume that a specified route was established soon after. To make it easier to haul the ships, iron chains were used. These were costly to maintain and often were destroyed by mischievous persons. There was a great deal of sea traffic and the city received a considerable sum of money from the duties levied. However, the route was only open from the middle of April to the end of November.

Traffic increased a great deal by the beginning of the seventeenth century, and it became apparent that another method of bringing

216

ships through the waterway would have to be devised. It was believed that a canal lock should be constructed. During the last years of Gustaf II Adolf's reign, a few designs were made for a lock in Söderström, and the first lock was, in fact, planned. In 1634 a water route between the sea and Mälaren was opened for traffic. The first lock was built of wood and was probably five feet deep and twenty feet wide. In the west wall a plaque was placed "to commemorate the work carried out during the administration of Flemming and while Grundel was Mayor of Stockholm." This wooden lock soon needed a major repair job, however. Dutch workers were brought in and Dutch materials were used to repair the lock during the years of 1639 to 1642. Brick and sandstone were used. The ordinances and regulations for the lock were established. The lock was to be open four times daily, "in the morning at 6 and 9, at 12 noon, and in the afternoon at 3." A mill and a number of other buildings were constructed. In the year 1661, the question again arose of a canal at Södertälje. Eric Dahlberg was given the task of determining whether such a canal was feasible. Work was started, but never finished. It was not until the nineteenth century that the Södertälje Canal was completed.

"Queen Kristina's Lock" in Söderström served as the primary point of entrance into the channel for a great many years. However, by the beginning of the eighteenth century it was defective and its dimensions too small for ships to pass through. It had to be rebuilt. The King wrote a number of times to the Governor of Stockholm, pointing out that a new lock was necessary so that navigation would not be hindered for too great a period of time. In the beginning of 1724, work on the lock began, and it was recognized that the canal had to be deepened to 8 or 10 feet (2 4/10 or 3 meters). With the enlarging of the canal, building materials could be transported to the fortification outside of Stockholm. Through the Bureau of Construction, a very comprehensive examination of the lock took place, and it was decided that nothing could be done to repair it. The stones were crumbling, the filling between the piles had washed away, and the wood was rotten. Captain Johan Eberhard Carlberg, the City Architect, suggested that a new lock be built which would be much larger than the old one.

The city magistrates next turned to Christopher Polhem. In a letter to Polhem dated February, 1712, M. Lundström, the City Contractor, complained that he had not been asked to do the work. He thought this strange, as he had gotten his position on the basis of Polhem's recommendation.

Negotiations continued between the city and the Crown and many

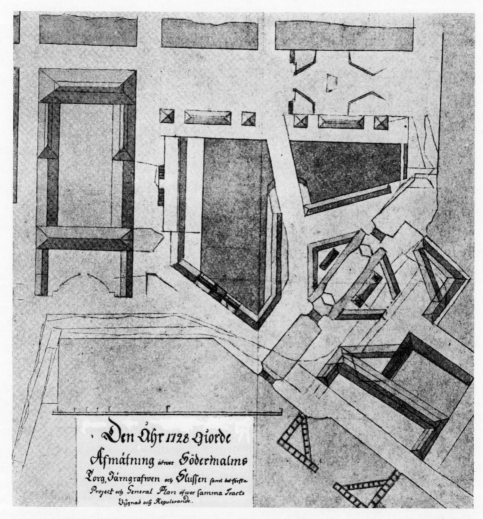

11. *The Plan for the Queen Kristina Lock, including the area about the lock; from J. E. Carlberg's map in Stockholms Stads Arkiv (Stockholm's City Archives)*

of the problems associated with the site and dimensions of the lock were discussed. The matter of who was to do the work was also questioned. Finally the decision was left to the King, the Office of Fortifications, the Secretary of the Treasury, and other informed people, including Christopher Polhem.

Public opinion was in favor of Polhem's doing the work. The two most relevant proposals for the project were those of Mayor Adlercrantz, who said that the lock should be constructed on the old site, and City Architect Carlberg, who wanted the lock located between Järngraven and the old lock. In a letter to Polhem in May of 1729, Carl Cronstedt estimated (on the basis of the information of Major General Axel Löwen) that the lock would cost 119,000 silver daler. Cronstedt proposed that a contractor should do the work for 100,000 silver daler. In a very flattering letter to Polhem in 1730, the magistrates of the city stated that they were anxious to contact Polhem about the construction of the lock. The letter also expressed the fear that his age and poor health might be a hindrance to the completion of the project. Polhem wrote back on July 8, and said that a wooden lock could very easily be constructed and offered to do the work himself.

Baron Gustaf Adam Taube, in a letter to the King, suggested that the lock be built of stone on the old site. There was a lack of money at that time and the necessary materials could not be purchased immediately. The magistrates, on July 13, 1730, decided that nothing could be accomplished and thanked Polhem for his suggestions.

Eleven years passed, during which time the great inconvenience of the absence of a lock between Mälaren and the sea made itself felt. Finally in 1741, the government was forced to take action to rebuild the lock. The King rushed a letter to the Governor's office in February of that year which urged that the previous arrangements for a lock be carried out. Polhem, although nearly eighty years of age, was commissioned to design a plan for the new lock. In February, 1744, a contract was drawn up between Christopher Polhem and the City of Stockholm, that he and his son would build the lock. After a great deal of discussion, the plans were approved and Polhem began his work.

In 1745, the "Queen Kristina Lock" was torn down and a new lock was built on the same site. This lock was to serve trade and navigation for one hundred years. The construction of the new lock began immediately. On the same day, Polhem wrote a work plan, or memorandum, on how the lock was to be built. Polhem's plan was followed as far as was possible. There had to be a number of changes, however,

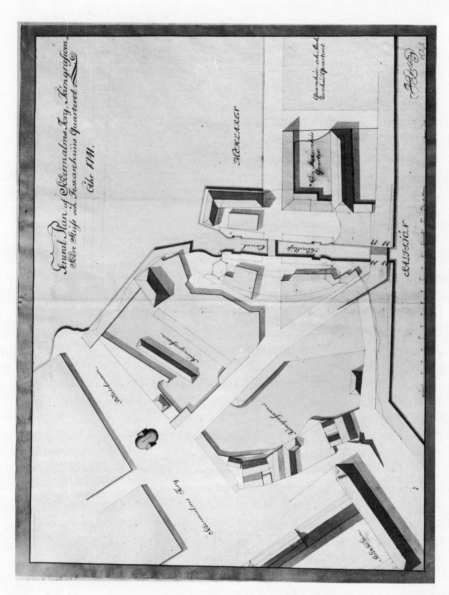

12. *J. E. Carlberg's drawing of the new lock; from his map (1741). Stockholms Stads Arkiv*

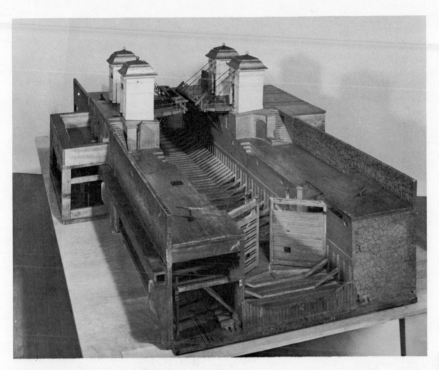

13. *A model of the lock Polhem planned for the city of Stockholm, including a draw-bridge for road traffic; Tekniska Museet, Stockholm*

as the work progressed. It was found that the bottom was filled with gravel and rough stones, and for that reason great difficulties were encountered, particularly in reference to holding back the water from the working area. Many extensive pumping arrangements were made, and according to reports, the pump machines, in spite of the 200 buckets of water they pumped out per minute, could not reduce the level to less than 7 1/2 feet (2 2/10 meters) below the original level. When the work called for a shaft built to a depth of 16 feet (4 8/10 meters) it was necessary to dredge out the rest of the canal. By so doing, Polhem's plan had to be revised. The work for the undersiding was completed on land, and a large "lock caisson" 200 feet long, 32 feet wide, and 9 feet high (59 4/10 by 9 5/10 by 2 7/10 meters) was sunk in the proper place. The caisson was fastened together by screw bolts and the holes in the wood were strengthened by steel casing. The builder did not believe that these materials would last forever and recognized that replacements would eventually have to be made. The bottom of the lock chamber was made of sandstone blocks 7½ tum (2/10 of a meter) wide and 2 feet (6/10 of a meter) long, bedded down

221

14. *Röda slussen (the red lock) in Stockholm, built according to Polhem's design; painting by Anders Holm, 1780. Stockholms Stadsmuseum (Stockholm's City Museum)*

in a kind of cement to prevent water from seeping in. The sidewalls were made of gray stone, and the greatest part of the masonwork was done under water, after the caisson was lowered into place. It only sank a little at first, it was reported, but came into place after 22 hours, to its clay bed, which had been constructed on the bottom to tighten the lock. The top of the caisson was 2 feet (6/10 of a meter) under the low water level, and lay in a horizontal position. Later, an arrangement was made so that the lock basin could be pumped out very easily. To prevent the water from getting under the west and east sides of the lock, a threefold grooved piling was constructed. The lock gate rested on the bottom on special cases. Grease was applied to the metal parts to prevent corrosion and reduce friction. The south side of the lock was arranged so that it could be repaired easily and also pumped dry. Here two basins were built with an overflow culvert, and in each of these 4 metal pumps of 14 tums ($3\frac{1}{2}$ tenths meters) in diameter were placed, and arranged so that water could be brought in from the bottom of the lock. Polhem had devised a way to dam up a small part of the lock itself and keep it dry by using these pumps. When the lock was repaired in 1840, Polhem's pumping mechanism was taken away.

Christopher Polhem did not live to see his work concluded. His son Gabriel finished the lock in the year 1755. The entire project had cost 315,656 silver daler. The cost was divided up according to the annual expenditure:

Year	Silver Daler
1744	15,800
1745	34,100
1746	43,600
1747	20,100
1748	17,400
1749	39,100
1750	64,000
1751	20,500
1752	3,700
1753	28,700
1754	25,400
1755	3,100

In the records of the city of Stockholm there is another figure which is given that is 70,000 silver daler higher. This probably included the cost of bridges and approaches to the lock. The time needed to com-

15. *Polhem's crane, used in building of the locks. Original from 1740. Tekniska Museet, Stockholm*

plete the work had also been extended. On May 2, 1755, the "Polhem Lock" was opened for sea traffic.

The lock was the primary reason why navigation increased between Mälaren and the sea. Larger ships could now go through the lock. The depth of the lock was increased from 10 to 12 feet (3 to 3 6/10 meters) when it was rebuilt by Nils Ericsson in 1850. The fact that it only had to be deepened 2 feet indicated that Polhem had planned well for the future. The main reason for the new lock was that sea traffic increased so much that the older lock was not adequate any longer. Then, too, it was difficult to keep it in good repair. Over Polhem's Lock a number of buildings were added, and today it is primarily a regulating canal for Mälaren.

The following works have been used in the preparation of this paper:

  I. The Tröllhattan Canal
      Tröllhattan. Dess kanal-och kraftverk. Historik och beskrifning utgifven af K. Vattenfallsstyrelsen. Del i. Stockholm, 1911.

 II. The Hjälmaren Canal
      Riksarkivet: Riksregistraturet; Äldre handlingar rörande Hjälmare kanal; Riksdagsacta och utskottshandlingar 1726–27.

III. Inland Waterways in Finland
      Kungl. Biblioteket: Chr. Polhems anteckningar om slussar. *Afd. Teknologi.*

 IV. The Karlskrona Naval Station
      K. Flottans arkiv: Skrifvelser till och från K. Amiralitetskollegium; Räkenskaper för Flottans station i Karlskrona.
      Statens sjökrigshistoriska samlingar.
      Stationsingenjörens vid K. Flottans station i Karlskrona arkiv.
      Gynther, Författningssamling för K. Maj:ts flotta. Stockholm, 1851–66.

  V. Technical Work for the Army
      Riksarkivet: Defensionsdeputationens handlingar 1738.
      Kungl. Biblioteket: Handlingar till Polhems biografi; Vetenskapsakademiens handlingar 1747.

 VI. The "Floating Bridge"
      Vetenskapsakademiens handlingar 1742, 1743.

VII. The Water Laboratory
      Vetenskapsakademiens handlingar 1739, 1742: Triewald, Föreläsningar öfwer nya naturkunnigheten. D. 1–2. Stockholm, 1735–36. Hydrografiska byråns årsbok 1908 och 1909. Stockholm, 1911.

VIII. Building and Building Materials
      Kungl. Biblioteket: Chr. Polhems uppsatser om husbyggnad. *Afd. Teknologi.;* Vetenskapsakademiens handlingar, 1739.

 IX. The Construction of the Stockholm Lock
      Stockholms stads arkiv: Akter och handlingar rörande slussbyggnaden i Stockholm, 1724–1747; Räkenskaper för slussen; Äldre ritningar öfver och förslag till områdets mellan Staden mellan broarna och Södermalm ordnande.

225

Stockholms Rådhusarkiv: Magistratens, ekonomi-och byggningskollegii protokoller. Tekniska Högskolans modellsamling.

Kungl. Biblioteket: Handlingar till Chr. Polhems biografi; Chr. Polhems anteckningar om slussar. *Afd. Teknologi;* Elers, Stockholm. D. 1–4. Stockholm, 1800–1801; Ferlin, Stockholm stad. D. 1–2. Stockholm, 1854–1858; Lundequist, Stockholms stads historia. D. 1–3. Stockholm, 1828–1829; Lilienberg, Om strömmarna i Stockholm. Stockholm, 1891; Vetenskapsakademiens handlingar, 1744.

CHAPTER FIVE

A Contribution to a Polhem Bibliography

BY SAMUEL E. BRING

This contribution to a Polhem bibliography contains three major sections. The first is made up of Polhem's published works, which are listed in chronological order according to the date of publication. The second contains a collection, also in chronological order, of books which deal with Polhem's life and his inventions and machines. There is also included a number of papers by Polhem which were published in Swedenborg's *Daedalus Hyperboreus*. These, however, cannot be considered as original works of Polhem, because, with the possible exception of two papers, they were edited and reworked by Swedenborg before they were included in the journal. This contribution to a Polhem bibliography cannot make any claim to completeness, but it is hoped that the major works, books, and articles, have been included. The third section lists Polhem's manuscripts, but this section is less of a contribution than the other two. The reason for this is as follows.

In August of 1878, Baron Carl Adolf Manderström, Christopher Polhem's great-great-grandson, gave Polhem's manuscripts to the Royal Library. They were catalogued according to their content and placed in the proper divisions of the library. For example, the manuscripts which dealt with physics or mechanics were catalogued and placed in the section on physics. The cataloguing procedure was not as intensive and complete as it might have been, particularly in comparison with our modern techniques. Manuscripts dealing with the same subject matter are often separated into different parts of the library. Furthermore, the manuscripts which were deposited in the Royal Library were in extremely poor condition. They were not fastened together in any way, nor were they protected from the elements, with the result that whole sections, as well as individual pages, have been lost. A number of fragments have been collected and arranged according to the subject matter. With the exception of the major works of Polhem, most of the manuscripts are incomplete. A great many of them have the first few pages of the manuscript, but the remaining pages are missing.

A complete cataloguing of Polhem's manuscripts has not been accomplished. This could be done only by a very extensive and thorough arranging of the material, a work which would take a great deal of time and labor and which would still not be fully satisfactory. A number of the fragments could be traced to their original sources, but too many of them have major sections missing which could never be located, and for this reason must remain fragmentary. Furthermore, Polhem never followed any specified plan in his work (as he himself said, "I worked without any order or method"). Many of the manuscripts give the impression that they were written down when Polhem

229

was old, and then only as a form of diversion. Others contain an idea or a proposal which Polhem never completed. Polhem wrote down whatever came into his mind. For that reason, he dealt with many varied subjects in a single paper. Many times he would begin with a philosophical discussion and conclude the same paper with a treatment of a problem in physics or technology. Because of Polhem's many digressions from the subject he was treating, it is difficult and often impossible to follow the continuity of his argument.

It must be recognized, too, that the title of a paper does not always determine its content. It is also not feasible to attempt to work with the manuscripts chronologically, because only a few of them can be dated accurately. Polhem's handwriting does not help, because it is as difficult to read the material he wrote when he was young as it is when he was old.

Within these limitations, I have, nonetheless, attempted (for purely practical reasons) to present a division of his works. I have used the catalogue of the Royal Library, and have made subheadings of them. For every section that I have included, I have indicated the number of volumes of manuscripts and made special reference to those which are the most complete and the most significant. Within every section, the manuscripts have been arranged according to their contents. The choices and arrangement of the subjects are entirely my own and are based solely upon the knowledge I have of the manuscripts. The incompleteness of this listing must therefore be recognized.

Polhem's manuscripts are found in a number of other libraries. Most of these, however, are revisions and copies.

As many as have been found (with the exception of those in the Royal Archives) have been catalogued according to their subject matter. If the original is in the Royal Library, an indication is made where it may be found. Only in one case has a separate division been made. The fragments dealing with typographical subjects, preserved in the library of the Academy of Science, cannot be subsumed under any other heading but must be listed separately.

In reference to the titles of the manuscripts, I have followed as closely as possible Polhem's spelling throughout. However, lower case letters have been used. The spelling ÿ has become y because it corresponds to the Swedish y. Polhem's handwriting is difficult to read and his spelling is usually irregular and inconsistent. In many instances, it is impossible to distinguish an *e* from an *a* or *ä*. The points over *å, ä,* and *ö* are seldom used. When there is a question about the spelling, I have used the customary form.

To catalogue Polhem's manuscripts is a very difficult task and for this reason the collection is necessarily incomplete. The following is only an attempt or an appendix to a chapter on Polhem's life and his scientific ideas. Perhaps it can also be useful to future investigators.*

I. Published Works by Polhem

1. Wishetens andra grundwahl til ungdoms prydnad, mandoms nytto och ålderdoms nöje; lempadt för ungdomen efter theras tiltagande åhr, uti dagliga lexor fördelt. Första boken innehållande en liten försmak af thet, som widare följandes warder; lemnadt af C. P. Upsala, tr. J. H. Werner (1716). (Anon.) lit. 8:0 (4), 12 pp., 1 pl. (vikt större format).
   cf. Stockholmiske kundgiörelser. 1717: no. 14, and Swedenborg's letter to Benzelius, 14–2, 4–3, 1716; 4–4, 1717. in Swedenborg, Opera de rebus naturalibus. 1 (1907), pp. 240, 241, 271. cm. also nos. 245–247.
2. Index experimentorum, quae in montibus vallibusque Laponiae ut instituerentur, digna judicavit Christoph. Polhem reg. coll. commerc. consiliarius d. 15 April 1711.
   in: Acta literaria Sveciae. Vol. 1 (1720–24), pp. 285–289. The original in Codex Bf. 31, Linköpings stiftsbibliotek with the title: Förtekning på några experimenter, som på lapp fiällen och i des dahlar wore nödige att werkställas.
3. Twenne betänkande, det förra angående oeconomien och commercen uti Swerige; det senare öfwer segelfartens inrättande emellan Stockholm och Giötheborg, bägge på sidsta riksdag ingifne åhr 1720. Stockholm, J. H. Werner 1721. 4:0. (2), 43, 25 pp.
4. Duae mensurae novae praxi mechanicae inservientes.
   in: Acta literaria Sveciae. Vol. 2 (1725–29), pp. 108–111.
5. Åtskillige allmänne hushålds förslag, såsom: 1. Om järnbergslagernas förening, at dymedelst slippa taga främmande förlag, samt altid hålla järnet uti skiäligt prijs. 2. Om monopoliernas afskaffande utan någons prejudice. 3. Om upstädernas cultur och tilwäxt. 4. Om åkerbärgningen. 5. Om lijns bråkande och beredande. 6. Om giödselns förökande. 7. Om kiärr och måsars beredande til åker och äng. Wid närwarande rijksdag andras mognare ompröfwande underkastade. Stockholm, tr. Biörkman 1726. 4:0. (2), 28 pp.
6. Kort berättelse om de förnämsta mechaniska inventioner, som tid efter annan af commercie-rådet Christopher Polhem blifwit påfundne och til publici goda nytta och tienst inrättade, sampt om det öde, som en del af dem hafft genom tidernas oblida förändringar. Item anteckning på några in-

* Samuel Bring's "A contribution to a Polhem Bibliography" formed the basis for the work of Henrik Sandblad, Gösta Lindeberg, Axel Liljencrantz and Bengt Löw in the preparation of *Christopher Polhem's efterlämnade skrifter* (vol. i–iv) (Almqvist & Wiksells Boktryckeri, Uppsala and Stockholm) (*Christopher Polhem's Collected Papers*). For this reason, Bring's work, though now dated, has been very important in the development of Polhem research.

ventioner, som ännu ey kommit i practiqve; doch förmodeligen torde kunna lända til landzens stora nytta när det åstundas; så ock en kort underrättelse om de anglers uträknande, som höra til allahanda stångbrått och eljest icke finnes i böcker etc. Stockholm, tr. A. Biörkmans änka 1729. 4:0 (2), 78 pp., 1 pl. (vikt större format).

Polhem's letter to "Wälborne herr kansliråd" from Stjernsund, 12–2, 1729, indicated that it took two years to publish this work. A translation of it never appeared, although one was promised.

7. Epistola ad Andream Celsium de nova sua ignis theoria. Stiernsund d.—an. 1730.

in: Acta literaria et scientiarum Sveciae. Vol. 3 (1730–34), (b), pp. 23–35. Translated into Latin by A. Celsius. See his letter to Polhem dated 11–5 1730. *Biografi P. K. B.*

8. (Tvenne bref till Sedolärande Mercurius rörande järnmanufakturerna.) in: Sedolärande Mercurius, 1731: D. 2, no. 22 (27–4). D. 3, no. 3 (1–6). Signed with the pseudonym Verus Patriota. In reference to the question of the author of this work, I am in agreement with Schaumann's thesis in "Polhem publicist." Compare also the discussion of the same matter in this book.

9. (Bref till Argus angående inrättande af ett assecurants-contoir.) in: Then swänska Argus. 1733: no. 20. Signed V. P. cf. above, no. 8.

10. Om de så kallade elementernes förmon och wärkan i mechaniquen. in: Kongl. swenska wetenskaps academiens handlingar. Vol. 1 (1739–40), pp. 44–51, 1 pl. (tab. 3, fig. 1–2).

11. Tankar, til ytterligare styrkande af Wallerii utgifne rön om rep. *Ibid.*, pp. 65–67. Nils Wallerius' uppsats: "En kort berättelse om rep och tråssars styrka eller sammanhängande kraft, som på almänt sätt ihopwridas. *Ib.*, pp. 52–64.

12. Tankar om hus-byggnad. *Ib.*, pp. 135–159, 1 pl. (tab. 1).

13. Tankar om mechaniquen. *Ib.*, pp. 185–198.

14. Påminnelse wid stål-tilwärkningen, i anledning af 10:de frågan uti 2 qvart. 1739. *Ib.*, pp. 303–309. The question asked by the Academy was "Huru stål må härdas så hårdt, at man dermed kan tälja järn och rista glas."

15. Fortsätning om hus-bygnad. *Ib.*, pp. 343–350. cf. also no. 12.

16. Swar på den andra frågan, i. 2. qvartalet: huruledes säden på en åker må ständigt kunna ökas til 40 kornet. *Ib.*, pp. 354–360.

17. Anmärkningar wid järnberedningen här i Sweriget. in: Kongl. swenska wetenskaps academiens handlingar. Vol. 2 (1741), pp. 30–37.

18. Underrättelse om en qwarn-model som utwisar, huru mycket en qwarn årligen kan mala.

    Ib., 129–131, 1 pl. (tab. 5, fig. 2).

19. Theoriens och practiquens sammanfogning i mechaniquen, och särdeles i ström-wärk.

    Ib., pp. 149–166.

20. Fortsättning om theoriens ock practiquens sammanfogning i mechaniquen.

    Ib., pp. 277–279.

21. Theoretiske uträkningar wid skiut-gewär.

    in: Kongl. swenska wetenskaps academiens handlingar. Vol. 3 (1742), pp. 57–64.

22. Anmärkningar om krokuga liniers tienst i mechaniquen.

    Ib., pp. 114–123.

23. Fortsätning med theoriens ock practiquens sammanlämpning i mechaniquen. (Cap. 4. Om swäng-hiul. Cap. 5. Om hiul och rännor.)

    Ib., pp. 126–132 and 157–171.

24. Anmärkningar wid de prof-skott, som wid artillerie scholan La Fere i Franckrike blifwit giorde i skiutare konsten.

    Ib., pp. 151–153.

    Translated into German in: Beiträge zur Kriegswissenschaft. 2 (1755), nos. 5–6.

25. Fortsättning om husbyggnad, ock denna gången om källare.

    Ib., pp. 233–241.

    Reviewed in: Tidningar om the lärdas arbeten. 1742, pp. 202–203.

26. Nytt påfund at tappa öl ock win up ur källaren, utan at behöfva gå der in.

    in: Kongl. swenska wetenskaps academiens handlingar. Vol. 4 (1743), pp. 169–179.

27. Ny method at pröfva lasten i et skep, til lagom styfhet ock rankning.

    Ib., pp. 270–275.

28. Tal öfver den vigtiga frågan: hvad som vårt kära fädernesland hafver nu mäst af nöden til sin ständig förkofring i längden? Hållit för Kongl. svenska vetenskaps academien, vid praesidii afläggande den 13 octob. 1745. (sic.) Stockholm, tr. L. L. Grefing u. å. 8:0. 24 pp.

    Reprinted in: Bergs-journal for the year 1787, pp. 12–27. The address was read by A. J. von Höpken on October 13, 1744, not 1745, which mistakenly appears on the title page; cf. no. 184.

29. Samtal emellan en swär-moder och son-hustru, om allehanda hushålds förrättningar. Stockholm, tr. L. Salvius 1745 (Anon.). 8:0. 79 pp.

    in *Aurivillius,* Catalogus librorum impressorum Bibl. reg. acad. upsaliensis, 1: 2 (1814), p. 707 refers to a 1750 edition; but none has been found. cf. no. 87.

30. Påfund at förhindra hästarnas skenande för vagnar.

    in: Kongl. swenska wetenskaps academiens handlingar. Vol. 6 (1745), pp. 225–228, 1 pl. (tab. 12).

31. Et nytt sätt på kläde-präss.

    in: Kongl. swenska wetenskaps academiens handlingar. Vol. 7 (1746), pp. 218–220, 1 pl. (tab. 7).

32. Commerce-rådet, riddaren och commendeuren af Kongl. Nord-stjerneorden, Christopher Polhems patriotiska testamente, eller underrättelse om järn, stål, koppar, mässing, tenn och bly för dem, som wilja begynna manufacturer i dessa ämnen. Jemte en förteckning på alla dess mechaniska inventioner. (Utg. af L. Salvius). Stockholm, tr. L. Salvius 1761. (24), 128 pp.

Pp. 3–6 contain L. Salvius' preface; pp. 7–24, the author's; pp. 115–128, Gabriel Polhem's description of the most significant of his father's inventions. Translated into German with the title: Christopher Polhems Patriotisches Testament oder Unterricht von Eisen, Stahl, Kupfer, Messing, Zinn und Bley für diejenigen, welche Manufacturen in diesen Materien anlegen wollen. in: Neue Sammlung verschiedener Schriften der grössten Gelehrten in Schweden. Bd. 1 (1774), pp. 1–118. G. Polhem's descriptions are not found in this edition.

33. Om uhr eller uhrvärk. Jämte en inledning om Polhem och urmakerikonsten af Elis Th. Sidenbladh. Stockholm, tr. S. Stål 1910. 8:0. 34 pp.

Supplement to Svensk urmakeritidning no. 86 (2) 1910.

34. Kort berettelse och anmerckning om slysswerckens inrettning wid Trollhettan, Gullspång etc. (juni 1717).

in: Trollhättan, dess kanal-och kraftverk, utg. af Kungl. Vattenfallsstyrelsen. D. 1 (1911), pp. 323–324. (Bilaga 1).

35. Underdånigt memorial (ang. saltverket och slussbyggnaden. nov. 1717).

Ib., pp. 326. (Bilaga 3).

36. Underdånigt memorial och project (ang. slussbyggnaden dec. 1717).

Ib., pp. 327–329. (Bilaga 4).

37. Det ährnade slusswerket i Göta älf. (maj 1720).

Ib., pp. 330–332. (Bilaga 6).

38. Bref till Eric Benzelius (Stjernsund d. 16–7 1710, d. 10–12 1715, d. 6–3 1716; Falun d. 8–3 1716; Stjernsund d. 18–7 1716; Karlsgraf d. 18–4 1719).

in: Swedenborg, opera de rebus naturalibus. 1 (1907), pp. 205–6, 236–37, 242–43, 244–45, 255, 289–90.

39. Bref till Emmanuel Swedenborg. (Stjernsund d. 7–12, 19–12, 1715; 5–9, sept 1716; d. 27–3, 3–4 1717).

Ib., pp. 235–36, 238, 257–59, 259–62, 269, 270.

The original of the letters of nos. 38 and 39 are to be found in *Codex Bf.* 31, Linköpings stiftsbibliotek, in which Polhem's letters to Benzelius and the members of the *collegium curiosorum* are also located.

II. Published Works about Polhem

40. Giöthe L., Den lilla Astrills strek är liufste juhle-lek, anstält då ehreborne och wählährfarne herr Christopher Påhlhammar, berömlig mechanichus wijd Kongl. Bergz-Collegio, sampt ehreborne och dygderijka jungf. Maria Hoffman, igenom ett oryggeligit echta—förbund blefwo förenade, som skiedde på Rijksteens gård den 28 decembris anno 1691, i hast framwijst af brudefolckens willigste L. Giöthe. U.o.o.å. 4:0. (4) pp.

41. Rudéen, T., Till det wackra och hederwärde brude-paret, herr Christopher Påhlhammar och jungfru Maria Hoffman, då de ett ouplösligit echtaförbund sin emillan ingingo på Rijksteens gård fierde dag juhl anno 1691. U.o.o.å. 4:0. (4) pp.

42. (Swedenborg, E.), Assessor Polhammars instrument at hielpa hörslen.
    in: Daedalus Hyperboreus. 1716: (1), pp. 1–4, 1 pl. (fig. 1, 3).

43. (———), Assessor Polhammars experimenter om liudets beskaffenhet.
    Ib., 6–10.

44. (———), Assess. Chr. Polhammars opfodrings konst wid Blanckstöten.
    Ib., 1716: (2), pp. 25–28, 1 pl. (vikt större format).
    cf. also Polhems letter to Benzelius d. 8–3 1716 in Swedenborg, opera. pp. 244–45 (no. 38).

45. (———), Experimenter som kunna werkstellas i wintertiden, förmedelst wår swenska köld, gifne af åtskilliga wid handen.
    Ib., pp. 30–31.
    Based upon an earlier idea of Polhem and found in: Fölliande experimenter ähre nödige i winter anställass, finnes i *Codex Bf.* 31. Linköpings stiftsbibliotek.

46. (———), Behendigt sett at räkna interessen på interessen, af assessor Polhammar wid handen gifwit.
    Ib., pp. 31–32, 1 pl.

47. (———), Assessor Polhaimers betzmansutdelning.
    Ib., 1716:3, pp. 41–50, i, 1 pl. (vikt större format).

48. (———), Assessor Polheimers wissa anmerckningar om wädretz resistence mot fallande tyngder och areer.
    Ib., 1716:4, pp. 65–79.

49. (———), Commercie rådet Polheimers konstige tapp. (Äfven med latinsk titel och text.)
    Ib., 1717:5, pp. 100–114 (115), 1 pl. (vikt större format).

50. (———), Ett prof at wisa bombers och kulors bogskott: giordt och anstelt af herr commercie-rådet Christ. Polhem.
    Ib., 1717:6, pp. 1–3.
    The articles about Polhem's inventions found in *Daedalus* were probably all (with the possible exception of nos. 47–48) written by Swedenborg. He undoubtedly used material Polhem left, however.

51. (———), Underrättelse, om thet förenta Stiernesunds arbete, thess bruk och förtening. Stockholm, tr. J. H. Werner 1717 (Anon.). 4:0. (4) pp.

52. (———), Underrettelse om docken, slysswercken och saltwercket åhr 1719. (Rubr.). U.o.o.å. (Anon.). 4:0. (8) pp.

53. (———), Triewáld, M., Föreläsningar, på Riddarehuset i Stockholm, öfwer nya naturkunnigheten. D. 1–2. Stockholm 1735–36.
    cf. Kårtt och ungefärlig relation, med des tillhörige rijtningar, angående de fyra af h. directeuren Påhlhammar inventerade och af. h. marscheidern Buschenfelt förfärdigade mechaniske machiner med des experimenter, och bijfogade tabeller; hwilcka af bemelte hr marscheider iempte migh undertechnad och flere äro genomgångne, och sedan efter inventoris egen disposition och underrättelse på föliande sätt deducerade, af Jöran Wallerius Haraldsson. *Codex A 147.* Upsala Universitetsbibliotek.

54. Wallerius, G., Berättelse och beskrifning öfver herr commercie rådet Polhems påfund at inrätta flottbroar på paraboliska spännbogar, til jämnförn-
ing mot det förr brukade sättet i slika flottbroars byggande.
    in: Kongl. swenska wetenskaps academiens handlingar. Vol. 4 (1743), pp.
    13–25, 1 pl. (tab. 1).

55. Tankar, vid vår oförliknelige Polhems död, som timade den 30 Augusti
1751. Stockholm, tr. L. Salvius u. å. 4:0. (4) pp.

56. Twist, P., Äre-stod, efter Kong. Maj:ts tro-man, commercie-råd, riddare
och commendeur af Kongl. Maj:ts Nordstierne-orden, wälborne herr Christopher Polhem, som på sitt 90 års lefnad saligen afsomnade then 30 augusti
1751, wördsamt uprest. Stockholm, tr. J. Merchell u.å. 4:0. (4) pp.

57. König, C. H., Beskrifning öfwer åtskillige af framledne commerce-rådet
Polhem, påfundne machiner.
    in: König, Inledning til mechaniken och bygnings-konsten. 1752, pp.
    155–183, 23 pl. (tab. 6–28).

58. Klingenstierna, S., Åminnelse-tal öfver Kongl. Vetensk. academiens framledne ledamot, commerce-rådet och commendeuren af Kong. Nordstjerne-
orden, herr Christopher Polhem, på Kongl. Vetenskaps academiens vägnar
hållit i stora Riddarhus-salen, d. 25 junii, år 1753. Stockholm, tr. L. Salvius
1753. 8:0. (2), 36 pp.
    Translated into German: Gedächtnissrede über Herrn Christoph Polhem
    . . . welche . . . am 25sten Junii des 1753sten Jahres . . . ist gehalten wor-
    den. in: Stockholmisches Magazin. (Hrsg von C. E. Klein). Th. 2 (1755),
    pp. 79–110. To this is added pp. 160–162.

59. Polhem, G., Beskrifning öfver framledne commerce-rådet och commendeuren Polhems nya påfund af kedje-bommar.
    in: Kongl. svenska vetenskaps academiens handlingar. Vol. 14 (1753), pp.
    48–51, 1 pl. (tab. 3).

60. –––, Beskrifning på en häf-kran, at väga up stubbar och rötter, som
sitta fast i jorden.
    Ib., Vol. 17 (1756), pp. 205–207. 1 pl. (tab. 7). Christopher Polhem was
    the inventor of this "häf-kran."

61. Anmärkningar öfwer det, som i et Tal om Sheldonska ätten blifwit berättadt
om docke-byggnaden i Carlscrona, m.m.
    in: Den nya swenska Mercurius. (Utg. af C. G. Gjörwell). 1761:(2), pp.
    45–49.
    The anonymous articles contain an account of Polhem's work at Lyckeby
    and Karlskrona.

62. (Polhem, G.), Förtekning på de förnämsta inventioner och werk, som framledne commerce-rådet och commendeuren Christopher Polhem, tid efter
annan til publici tjenst uptänkt och werkstält, hwaraf en stor del nu för-
waras i modell-kammaren.
    in: Polhem, Christopher, Patriotiska testamente. 1761, pp. 115–128 (no.
    32).

63. Leben Christoper Polhem's.
    in: Schwedisches Museum, hrsg. von C. G. & C. H. Gröning. Bd. 2 (1784),
    pp. 269–276.

64. Nordin, C. G., Minne af commerce-rådet och commendören af Nordstjerne-orden Christopher Polhem.

in: Svenska academiens handlingar ifrån år 1796. D. 4 (1809), pp. 121–149.

65. Kort berättelse om commerce-rådet Christofer Polhems lefwerne och nyttiga uppfinningar.

in: Läsning för folket. Årg. 1:1 (1835), pp. 84–96.

66. (Bagge, C. A.), Christofer Polhem. Af C.A.B.

in: Svensk folkkalender. Årg. 1: (1838), pp. 41–54.

Republished in: Svenska Familjeboken, utg. af J. G. Carlén. Bd. 3 (1852), pp. 482–490.

67. (Carlén, J. G.), Polhem och hans verk. Till en del eftèr muntliga meddelanden af hans slägtingar.

in: Svea. Årg. 12 (1856), pp. 137–158, 1 pl.

Republished as: Christoffer Polhem och hans werk. En teckning för folket af J. G. C. Med Polhems porträtt och flera illustrationer. Stockholm, A. Bonnier; tr. Hörberg 1861. 16:0. 27 pp. A new addition appeared in 1886.

68. (Berg, P. G.), Kristofer Polhem.

in: Berg, P. G., Skildringar ur svenska mäns ungdomslif. 1873, pp. 93–102.

69. Kristoffer Polhems lärare. (Undert. Hm).

in: Läsning för folket. Årg 64 (F.3:9) (1898), pp. 157–160.

70. Fries, E., Kristoffer Polhem.

in: Fries, E., Den svenska odlingens stormän. 2 (1899), pp. 1–26.

71. (Stiernström, L.), Kristoffer Polhems-lefnadssaga. Berättad för ungdom af Carl Blink.

in: Bilder och minnen (tillägnade J. Bolinder). 1907, pp. 93–104, 1 portr.

72. Kuylenstierna, A., Kristoffer Polhems lif och verksamhet.

in: Kuylenstierna, Svenska bragder och stordåd. 1908, pp. 112–124.

73. Sellergren, G., Polhemsminnets firande.

in: Teknisk Tidskrift. Årg. 39 (1909), Allm afd., pp. 86–87.

74. Schauman, G., Polhem publicist.

in: Aftontidningen. 1910: no. 173 (26–7).

75. ———, Studier i frihetstidens nationalekonomiska litteratur. Idéer och strömningar 1718–1740. Helsingsfors 1910.

Pp. 9–19 behandlar Polhems nationalekonomiska skrifter.

76. Nyberg, E., När föddes Kristoffer Polhem? Några anteckningar om Polhem och hans släkt.

in: Gotlands Allehanda. 1910: no. 82 (12–4) med tillägg i no. 83 (13–4).

77. Bring, S. E., Trollhätte kanals historia till 1844.

in: Trollhättan, dess kanal-och kraftverk, utg. af Kungl. Vattenfallsstyrelsen. D. I. (1911). Kap. 2. Den Polhem-Wimanska perioden 1716–57, pp. 59–126, 2 portr.

78. (Meijer-Granqvist, P.), Christofer Polhems afkomlingar 1661–1911 . . . för Aftonbladet och Dagen af P.M.G.

in: Aftonbladet. 1911: no. 209 (6–8).

III. Polhem's Manuscripts

A. Biographical Material

There is material in two folio volumes which deals with Polhem's biography from the years 1694–1730. The one volume contains letters of appointment, edicts, letters from Karl xii, Ulrika Eleonora, Fredrik i, from *bergskollegium, kommerskollegium,* and other officials; as well, there are letters from individuals, Casten Feif, N. Stromberg, Carl Cronstedt, Augustin Ehrensvärd, Charles Sheldon, and rough drafts of Polhem's answers to these letters. The material is arranged chronologically, and an index in the beginning of the volume facilitates its use. In the second volume, there are a number of official documents, some notes about the life of Polhem, as well as rough copies of these. A few of them are handwritten, undoubtedly by Gabriel Polhem, others by Reinhold Rückersköld. There is also Gabriel Polhem's catalogue of his father's inventions (no. 62), and a copy of Jonas Norberg's catalogue of the machines in the *laboratorium mechanicum* (1739). Polhem's own manuscripts include a number of drafts for letters and memoranda and other fragments.

79. C.R.C.P. lefwerness beskrifning af sonen G.P. 4:0. (16) pp.
    Incomplete, ends with the year 1691. As the title indicates, the autobiography contains Gabriel Polhem's name. However, in a number of references Christopher Polhem has forgotten this fact and wrote in the first person. This material can be considered to be a plan for an autobiographical sketch which the Academy of Science required; cf. below, nos. 85–86.
80. Berettelse om min tienst och löön. 4:0. (4) pp.
    Incomplete.
81. C. P. byggnad och inventioner utom Fahlun. 4:0. (4) pp.
82. (Berättelse till rikets ständer) för huad iag åtniutit min löön. 4:0. (8) pp.
    A fragment, six pages, without a beginning.
83. (Berättelse om laboratorium mechanicum). Fol. (11) pp.
    Without a title and a beginning.
84. En liten upsattz på det förnämbsta, hwar till undertecknad blifwit brukat, och hwad der wid är wordet uträttat. Fol. (4) pp.
    A copy; another copy (4 pages) in the collection (T), (3 parts, containing Polhem's manuscripts, most of which have been copied by J. Troilius, rector in Husby). *Teknologi.*
85. Commercie-rådets herr Christ. Polhems lefwernes lopp i korthet af honom sielf upsatt. 4:0. (10) pp.
    Revision in the library of the Academy of Science. Another edition of this autobiography, which concludes with the period in Fållnäs, is in the possession of Miss G. Polheimer in Falun.

86. Till Hans Kongl. Maij:tz och fäderneslandetz tiänst, enär påfordras, har undertecknad giort sig kunnig i fölljande wettskaper. 4:0. (4) pp.

Copy in the collection (T). *Teknologi*. Contains thirty items. It is undoubtedly the list of inventions that Polhem sent to Casten Feif in Bender to be shown to Karl xii.

B. *Economic*

Divided into three volumes, two in *folio* and one in *quarto,* which deal primarily with household matters, agriculture, and the saltworks which Polhem hoped to build in Bohuslän.

87. Ett samtahl emellan en swährmohr och sohn hustru om alla handa hussholdz förrettningar. 4:0. (52) pp.

The manuscript is made up of pp. 1–30, the work: Samtal emellan en swär-moder och son-hustru (no. 29); there are two fragments added to this, but the content of the chapters is different from the published work.

88. Hussreglor för ungt och nygifft folk. Fol. (88) pp.

Incomplete.

89. Ett lijtet samtahl om alla handa nödiga huss holdz saker som ungt folk som nyss sätta boo, har att lära något af till well-ment tienst lemnad af comercierådet Christoff. Polhem. 4:0. (16) pp.

Incomplete.

90. C. R. C. P. Husshåldz book lempat till ungdomenss tienst wijd scholor och accademier och under wissa frågor och swahr framstelt. 4:0. (24) pp.

91. Några små anmerkningar för ungt och nygifft folk sampt nysatta husshollen. 4:0. (37) pp.

92. Coloquium oeconomicum eller ett lijtet samtahl om de algemenaste husshåldz sysslor, som för ungdomen i gemen kan wara nyttigt att läsa och lära. 4:0. (38) pp.

Cf. no. 11 in the earlier numbering.

93. Samtahl emellan (en) fadren och sin sohn om alle handa husshåldz saker och wettskaper. Fol. (137) pp.

Cf. no. 17 in the earlier numbering.

94. Om lantculturens inrettning. 4:0. (28) pp.

95. Naturliga egenskaper om åkerbruk. 4:0. (32) pp.

Cf. no. 58 in the earlier numbering.

96. Några anmerkningar wijd åkerbruk, som befinnes haa sin wisshet. 4:0. (7) pp.

97. Anmärkningar wijd de twene (?) inventioner af tufplog och spanmåhlss bod som I, mina herrar behagat låta mig tillskicka att fella mina tankar der wed. 4:0. (16) pp.

Address in the Academy of Science?

98. Mina högt ährade herrar af den ber(ö)melige Wettskapz accademien i Stokholm. 4:0. (12) pp.

99. Om salt siuderi her i Swärie. 4:0. (24) pp.

100. En lijten och kort beskrifning om salt-och victriolss siuderi. 4:0. (15) pp.

Cf. no. 18 in the earlier numbering.

101. Tankar om saltsiuderi. Fol. (20) pp.
     Cf. no. 26 in the earlier numbering.
102. Att salt siuderi här i Swärie serdeless i Båhuss län icke kan wara aldeless omöieliget och onyttigt det kan så någorlunda prefwass af efter fölliande skiehl. Fol. (3) pp.
103. Några oförgrijpelig(e) anmerkningar wijd hr. consul Backmansons tankar om saltsiuderi i Swerie. 4:0. (8) pp.
     Nos. 102–103 are directed toward Andreas Bachmanson (Nordencrantz) who believed that Sweden could not produce an adequate supply of salt without grievous damage to herself, cf. his work, Arcana oeconomiae et commercii (1730), Chapter 12, pp. 330–362.

C. Philosophy

Both in folio and in quarto volumes, dealing with many different philosophical subjects. For a fuller understanding of Polhem's philosophical position, there is material in the Linköpings stiftsbiblioteket, *Codex Bf.* 31 and the material in the listing "natural science."

104. Tankar om Dippels philosophia. 4:0. (20) pp.
105. Tankar om Dippels nyia philosophia. Fol. (12) pp.
106. Nääseglass för hr. Dippel. 4:0. (24) pp.
     Cf. no. 46 in the older numbering. There are also a copy and three fragments dealing with the same material.
107. Förundran öfwer Dimorti löjliga philosophi. Fol. (6) pp.
     Incomplete.
108. De principiis philosophiae. 4:0. (16) pp.
109. Tankar om andarnass warelsse. 4:0. (16) pp.
110. Om lijfandar. 4:0. (35) pp.
     Cf. no. 57 in the earlier numbering. It was written before 1710, and may be found also in a copy by J. Troilus in the collection (T), *Teknologi*.
111. Discurs om spiritibus och dess egenskaper generaliter. 4:0. (11) pp.
     Cf. no. 54 in the earlier numbering. There are two copies, one of which is in the collection (T), *Teknologi*.
112. Discurs om spiritibus och dess egenskaper specialiter. 4:0. (15) pp.
     Cf. no. 33 in the earlier numbering. There are two copies, one of which is in the collection (T), *Teknologi*.
113. Samtahl emellan naturen och konsten om den wärdzlige wijssheten. 4:0. (52) pp.
     Contains five conversations, and a fragment which might possibly be a sixth.
114. Tankar om werdzenss uphof. Fol. (12) pp.
     Cf. no. 2 in the earlier numbering.
115. (Att Gud alzmächtig åhr hela naturens uphof, skapare och herre). 4:0. (32) pp.
     Incomplete. The title is taken from the beginning of the work.
116. Om werldeness upprettelse effter Phaetons förstöring. 4:0. (52) pp.
     Incomplete. The title is crossed out.

240

117. Officia scientiarum eller wettskaperness nambn och gangn under en kort-
willig historia förestelt. 4:0. (101) pp.

Copy. The title is in Polhem's handwriting, as well as the notations in
the text. Only A–D, E, Z, Y, Aa–Ff.

118. Samtahl emellan naturen, konsten och wanan om meniskornass högsta goda
i lijfwet. Fol. (12) pp.

Incomplete.

119. De causis rerum humanarum eller ett samtahl emellan naturen och konsten
om de ting, som dem strijdigt eller lerachtigt kan förekomma. 4:0. (16)
pp.

Incomplete. There is also a similar incomplete manuscript with almost
the same title.

120. Samtahl emellan den andelige siehlen och det jordiske förnufftet om kroppen och dess slätta willkor. Fol. (16) pp.

121. Samtahl emellan kroppen och siehlen. Fol. (19) pp.

122. Ett lijtet samtahl emellan naturen och konsten om menniskorness wäsende
och hanteringar. Fol. (20) pp.

Incomplete.

123. Comedia om den meniskelige felachtigheten. 4:0. (7) pp.

Incomplete. There is a fragment in 16:0 format with almost the same
title.

D. Medicine

Two volumes in quarto; a detached manuscript which contains
advice about health and diet and a discussion of the causes of various
illnesses.

124. Naturens kiening i de ting som wår helssa och lijfz lengd angå. Fol. (14)
pp.

Cf. no. 15 in the earlier numbering.

125. Discurs emellan naturen och konsten om meniskornass hellssa och lijfzlängd.
4:0. (10) pp.

Incomplete. Cf. no. 43 in the earlier numbering. A large fragment included.

126. Några anmerkningar om helssan. 4:0. (8) pp.

Written after 1735.

127. Anmarkning wid helssens bjbehållande. 4:0. (42) pp.

Cf. no. 22 in the earlier numbering.

128. Allmän orsak till meniskornass ohellssa. 4:0. (38) pp.

Cf. no. 51 in the earlier numbering.

129. Om några siukdomerss orsaker. 4:0. (10) pp.

Contains a note of Polhem, "Biheng uti en almnake."

130. Questio huru wijda bara wattn i stellet för öhl och wijn, ähr nyttigt och
skadeliget att dreka för gamelt folk som anorlunda i från sin ungdom sig
want. 4:0. (16) pp.

Cf. no. 74 in the earlier numbering.

131. Tankar om koppors och messlingz uphof och orsak. 4:0. (8) pp.

Cf. no. 20 in the earlier numbering.

132. Fråga huad monde orsaken ware till barna messlingen eller kopporna? 4:Q. (4) pp.

133. (Samtal) Emellan en patient af tandwerk och en doctor. 4:0. (16) pp.
Not finished.

134. C:P: Pulspendel bequeml. för den som eij hafwa tijd ware siuke. 4:0 (18) pp.
Among the fragments, a large untitled work in 4:0 must be mentioned. It ends in the middle of chapter 19 and is made up of 80 pages.

E. Public Administration

Two volumes in folio and three in quarto, containing manuscripts and fragments dealing with national and economic matters.

135. Discurs om rikzenss handel och husshållning. Fol. (31) pp.
Cf. no. 11 in the earlier numbering. According to a later notation, written in 1719.

136. Oförgrijpelige tankar och förslag om det som syness tiena till rikzenss welstånd. 4:0. (22) pp.

137. En lijten discurs och rådslag emellan Swäriess oeconomia och comercen, angående rikzenss wellferd till florizant wellstånd. 4:0. (68) pp.
Cf. no. 8 in the earlier numbering.

138. Oeconomia publica i frågor och swar ställd. 4:0. (20) pp.
Cf. no. 12 in the earlier numbering.

139. Några anmerkningar i allmen(a) oeconomien. 4:0. (28) pp.
Cf. no. 70 in the earlier numbering.

140. Discurs emellan Swäriess oeconomie och commercie om rikzenss slätta tillstånd och dess uprättelse. 4:0. (32) pp.
Incomplete.

141. Felix quem faciunt aliena pericula cautem. 4:0. (24) pp.
Cf. no. 49 in the earlier numbering.

142. Pro memoria (angående rikzenss oeconomia). 4:0. (30) pp.

143. Lista uppå de förnembste kiennemerken som skilja bättre och sämbre husshållningen i från huar andra uti ett land och rijke. Fol. (12) pp.
Cf. no. 3 in the earlier numbering.

144. Sweriess förnembste siukdomar. Fol. (15) pp.
Cf. no. 28 in the earlier numbering.

145. Oeconomia publica i frågor och swar stelt. Smal fol. (52) pp.
Incomplete.

146. Upmuntring och förslag til federness landetz reparation. Fol. (60) pp.
Cf. no. 23 in the earlier numbering.

147. Några frågor, för huad orsak och nytta skull fölliande punkter ähro i bruk. Fol. (28) pp.

148. Oeconomiske öfwerwägningar. Fol. (56) pp.
Cf. no. 37 in the earlier numbering.

149. Utlenska rådslag och maximer emot de swänska och dess oeconomie. Fol. (48) pp.
Incomplete.

242

150. Memorial angående rikzenss cultur och dess nyttigheter. Fol. (32) pp.
   Cf. two manuscripts dealing with "Rikzenss cultur." *Codex Bf.* 31, pp.
   515–526, Linköpings stiftsbibliotek.

151. Swärjess sanskyliga welstånd. 4:0. (32) pp.
   Cf. no. 59 in the earlier numbering. Incomplete.

152. Så ähr då sådane manufacturer onödige som betarfwa utrijkess materialer?
   4:0. (18) pp.

153. Om Sweriess fiskerie. Fol. (48) pp.
   Cf. no. 18 in the earlier numbering.

154. Discurs om närwarende Swäriess comercie anförd under små frågor och
   swahr och nyttig för ungdomen. 4:0. (48) pp.
   Cf. no. 16 in the earlier numbering.

155. Är det nyttigt äller skadeligit för et regemente och land, at bönder och
   gemene man undertryckes til trälar eller fattigdom? 4:0. (76) pp.
   With the year 1722. Copy. A work which is written in question and answer form. The first question serves as the title.

156. Om städerss privileger och inrättningar. 4:0. (23) pp.
   Cf. no. 17 in the earlier numbering.

157. Tankar om rikzenss allmäna husshollning under ett samtahl mellan landzenss inbyggrar och stedernass handelssmän. 4:0. (12) pp.
   Cf. no. 72 in the earlier numbering.

158. Discurs emellan en ståndzperson och rikzbetient. Fol. (4) pp.

159. Samtahl emellan politia och oeconomia om städerss cultur. Fol. (32) pp.
   Incomplete.

160. Samtahl emellan politia och oeconomia om rikzenss cultur. Fol. (56) pp.

161. Discurs om landzenss och städernass prerogativ. 4:0. (14) pp.
   Incomplete.

162. Discurs emellan upstäderna och stapelstäderna i rijket. 4:0. (6) pp.
   Cf. no. 73 in the earlier numbering.

163. En lijten träta emellan en stapelstadzborgare och en upstadz, angående derass borgerliga stånd till sammanss på herdagarne. 4:0. (4) pp.
   Incomplete.

164. Discurs emellan ständerna och Fahluns magazin. 4:0. (15) pp.
   Cf. no. 24 in the earlier numbering.

165. (Samtal mellan en köpman och en landtman). 4:0. (72) pp.
   The beginning and the end are missing.

166. Discurs emellan en landtbo och stadzbo om landet bör wara för sterna (!)
   skull eller stederna för landet skull. 4:0. (8) pp.
   Incomplete.

167. Swar på den gångbara fråga om manufacturer bör gå för lantbruket eller
   lantbruket för manufacturer. 4:0. (12) pp.
   Incomplete.

168. Om lant-colegers inrettning. 4:0. (13) pp.
   Cf. no. 13 in the earlier numbering.

169. Om manufacturers nytta. 4:0. (35) pp.
   Cf. no. 71 in the earlier numbering.

170. Medel att få manufacturer i landet inrettade. 4:0. (31) pp.
   Cf. no. 15 in the earlier numbering.

171. Allmän manufactur ordning för hant wärkrane. 4:0. (19) pp.
    Cf. no. 14 in the earlier numbering. There are also two different plans and designs, one in folio, 15 pp. with no. 22, the other in folio, 12 pp. with no. 7.

172. Samtahl emellan oeconomien, naturen, och konsten om inrikess jernmanu-facturer. 4:0. (32) pp.
    Cf. no. 19 in the earlier numbering.

173. Discurs emellan A. och P. om nyia manufacturer. Fol. (20) pp.
    Cf. no. 8 in the earlier numbering.

174. Historia om manufacturer. Fol. (12) pp.
    Incomplete.

175. Handelss compagnetz inrettning. 4:0. (21) pp.

176. Förteckning på de nyttigheter och skador som ett allment handelss com-pagni skulle kuna förorsaka om det här i landet blefwe inrättad(t). 4:0. (27) pp.
    Cf. no. 10 in the earlier numbering.

177. Werk- och wettskapz skohla för Sweriess rikess ungdom. Fol. (4) pp.
    Incomplete. Cf. no. 218.

178. General instruction för alla wåra consuler, expeditorer, factorer, köpmän och betienter, som under wårt handelss compagnie sortera och på åtskilliga orter kuna wara förordnade och wistande. Fol. (12) pp.
    Cf. no. 30 in the earlier numbering.

179. Anmärkning om mynt. 4:0. (40) pp.
    Cf. no. 7 in the earlier numbering. Incomplete. Cf. the two manuscripts, Landzenss mynt and Skillie mynt och plåter, which were added to Pol-hem's letter from Stjernsund, May 17, 1720 to Landtmarskalken of the parliament of 1720. *Riksdagshandlingar* 1720. Riksarkivet; cf. also, two smaller manuscripts on coinage, *Codex Bf.* 31, pp. 447–455; Linköpings stiftsbibliotek.

180. Discurs om mynt, i frågor och swar. Fol. (7) pp.
    Cf. no. 31 in the earlier numbering.

181. C. P. mening, huru rijket tyckess kuna komma till tienl. och gångbart mynt. 4:0. (16) pp.
    Incomplete.

182. Till minnes om koppar myntning. Fol. (14) pp.
    Revised with annotations by Polhem. Also in copy, 24 pp. in *Codex W.* 361. Upsala Universitetsbibliotek. A notation reads "afskrifwit effter h. autoris concept d.9 decemb. 1715."

183. Discurs emelan hela rijket i gemen och Fahluns bergzlag om koppar myn-tetz wicht och wärde. Fol. (23) pp.
    Cf. no. 32 in the earlier numbering.

184. Tahl (i Vetenskapsakademien vid praesidiets nedläggande). Fol. (15) pp.
    Incomplete. Printed with changes; cf. no. 28.

185. Tahl pä Riddarhuset. 4:0. (20) pp.

186. Samtahl emellan Argj discipel och Argj correspondenter om de materier som på det 51 arket stå antecknad. Fol. (4) pp.

187. Förklaring på mitt förra till Argus angående barnafostran till dygden. 4:0. (4) pp.

188. (Bref till Argus). Fol. (2) pp. 4:0. (4), (4), (4), pp.
    Two of these lack material.

189. Samtahl emellan politia och oeconomia om riksens cultur. 4:0. (235) pp.
    Copy in collection R, which is a collection made up of Polhem's written manuscripts. In the possession of C. A. E. Reuterholm. *Teknologi* cf. no. 160.

190. En discurss emellan oeconomien och comercien uti Swerige af assess. h. Chri. Pollhamer författat uti septembris & octobris månader åhr 1716. 4:0. (193) pp.
    Copy in *Codex W.* 361. Upsala Universitetsbibliotek. Another copy in collection R. *Teknologi*.

191. Oförgripeligit förslag, huruledes oeconomien och commercien i Swerige kunde och borde ändras. Till andra rättsinniga partrioters närmare skärskådande och ompröfwande lemnat af Christopher Polhem. 4:0. (100) pp.
    Copy in collection R. *Teknologi*. Printed in Tvenne betänkande 1, cf. no. 3.

192. Ett förslag, tienande till fiendens twång och skada, sampt wårt landz conservation och wählfärd. 4:0. (11) pp.
    Written in October 1717. Copy in *Codex W.* 361. Upsala Universitetsbibliotek.

193. Anmarkningar wijd nyia manufactures anleggande. Fol. (8) pp.
    Rålamb collection. Fol. 117. The discussion of linen manufacturing refers to Floor in Hälsingland.

F. Swedish History

Two volumes of handwritten material; one in folio, the other in quarto. They contain papers on politics and parliamentary matters, particularly from the period of peace during Polhem's lifetime. There are also papers dealing with national and economic matters.

194. Dialog emellan en stadz borgare och en herdagz man. Fol. (22) pp.
    Cf. no. 21 in the earlier numbering.

195. Discurs emellan en adelss man och en bonde om rikzen(s) tillstånd. 4:0. (28) pp.
    Cf. no. 9 in the earlier numbering.

196. Samtahl emellan en adelss man och en präst wid rikz-dagen. 4:0. (60) pp.
    Copy. There are only 8 pages in folio remaining.

197. En härdagz man tahl. 4:0. (8) pp.
    Also a fragment with almost the same title.

198. Disqution om olijka regementzformer. 4:0. (8) pp.
    Cf. no. 73 in the earlier numbering.

199. Regement byggnad. 4:0. (4) pp.

200. En lijten discurs, om Nimbrodz upstijgande till det monarkiske herra wäldet. 4:0. (32) pp.
    Cf. no. 65 in the earlier numbering.

201. Discurs emellan en machiavelist och en god patriot om ett rikess skada och wellstånd. Fol. (16) pp.

202. Rikzenss frijhet. Fol. (16) pp.
    Cf. no. 10 in the earlier numbering.

203. Quaestio om krigetz framhärdande med ryssen kan försäkra bettre fredz willkor framdeless än nu för tijden. Fol. (4) pp.

Incomplete. Written before 1721.

204. Om fred med rikzenss grannar. 4:0. (3) pp.

Written about 1720.

205. Discurs om närwarande frijd och frijhet. 4:0. (6) pp.

Cf. no. 37 in the earlier numbering.

206. Samtahl emellan krig och fred. 4:0. (12) pp.

Cf. no. 7 in the earlier numbering. The year 1739 is in the title. Incomplete. Also the conclusion of a conversation between pax and bellum; 8 pp.

G. Science of Language

Manuscripts and fragments, one in folio, dealing primarily with Polhem's *lingua philosophica.*

207. C. P. Project till ett nytt universalt språk huar igenom alla slagz meningar kuna med bättre tydelighet och mindre ord utförass, så at med mindre möda och tijd spillan läress än elliest wanl. 4:0. (23) pp.

Cf. no. 271 in the earlier numbering. An additional fragment; cf. no. 265.

208. Project till ett fundamentalt språk el. skrifkonst. Fol. (20) pp.

Contains a description of Stjernsund, etc.

209. Försök till en ny och kort skrifkonst. 4:0. (12) pp.

Incomplete.

210. Nomina rerum naturalium per philosophicam novam. 4:0. (24) pp.

211. Signatura rerum natur(a)lium eller de naturliga tingenss korta anteckning. 4:0. (13) pp.

Two fragments with similar titles.

212. Nya tiender uthur månan. Fol. (12) pp.

Cf. no. 13 in the earlier numbering.

H. Education

Manuscripts dealing with the training and rearing of children; one in quarto volume.

213. Om barna fostran. Fol. (12) pp.

Incomplete. An additional fragment in 4:0, 12 pp., with a similar content.

214. Om barns upfödande etc. 4:0. (16) pp.

Cf. no. 6 in the earlier numbering. Title rewritten later. Probably part of a larger work.

215. Ett samtahl emellan naturen och konsten om meniskorness opfostring, nering och bergning, frijd och frihet. 4:0. (9) pp.

216. Minnesslista upå de wettskaper som ungdomen har att lära i skohlorna till allmena bästass tienst och sin egen nytta och prydnad, antecknad med swenska nambn af —. 4:0. (16) pp.

Cf. no. 66 in the earlier numbering.

246

217. Samtahl emellan en fader och en preceptor om sin sohn och dess studier. 4:0. (20) pp.
   Cf. no. 39 in the earlier numbering.
218. Om wärk skohlor i Swärie. Fol. (4) pp.
   Cf. no. 177.
219. Method att få lerd(t) folk till konungss tienster. 4:0. (24) pp.
220. (Undervisningsplan för dottersönerna till "mechaniske wettskaper och öfningar.") 4:0. (6) pp.
221. (Förslag till en svensk fakultet i ekonomi, manufaktur och kommers.) 4:0. (12) pp.
   Without beginning or end.
222. Discours om ungdomens första information. 4:0. (51) pp.
   Copy in collection R. *Teknologi*.
223. Ett sätt, att lätteligen bringa mechaniske studier och wettenskapper i flohr och gång. 4:0. (7) pp.
   Written in October 1716. Copy in *Codex W.* 361. Upsala Universitets-bibliotek.

I. *Literary Works*

One volume in quarto.

224. Historia om Folke. 4:0. (23) pp.
   Cf. no. 69 in the earlier numbering.
225. (Fragment af ett drama.) 4:0. (16) pp.
   Begins with the fifth scene of the second act, and concludes with the first scene of the fourth.
226. (Epigrammer.) 4:0. (8) pp.
   Six belong to Polhem; the others have been written by someone else.

J. *Natural Science*

Seven volumes, six volumes in quarto, one in folio, which deal with many different topics in the general area of natural science. There are manuscripts dealing with problems in physics, botany, magic, as well as a rough draft for a book in mathematics.

227. Philosophia naturalis, artificalis et experimentantur (!) till den mognare ungdomenss tienst. 4:0. (384) pp.
   Cf. no. 83 in the earlier numbering. Incomplete.
228. Orda tecken på naturens materialer och dess egenskaper. 4:0. (123) pp.
   Cf. no. 60 in the earlier numbering.
229. Kunskap om naturens och konstens wässende. 4:0. (136) pp.
   Cf. no. 86 in the earlier numbering. Incomplete.
230. En lijten förklaring öfwer skapelsse historien (jämte företal). 4:0. (128) pp.
   Cf. no. 25 in the earlier numbering.
231. En kort manuduction och inledning till philosophicam naturalem af C. P. Fol. (20) pp.
   Cf. no. 24 in the earlier numbering. There are a number of fragments with a similar content among the philosophical manuscripts.
232. Några quaestioner om naturens egenskaper i gemen. 8:0. (36) pp.

247

233. (Discours emellan mechaniqven och chymien om naturens wäsende.) 4:0. (19) pp.

Incomplete, only the conclusion remains. Found also in a complete copy (25 pp.), probably by Swedenborg, in the section *Fysik,* with the number 42.

234. Discurs om motu et materia. 4:0. (13) pp.

Cf. no. 27 in the earlier numbering. Also a copy in the collection T. *Teknologi.*

235. Discurs om dhe 4 elementerna eld, weder, watt(en) och jordh. 4:0. (16) pp.

Cf. no. 28 in the earlier numbering. Also a copy in the collection (T). *Teknologi.*

236. Discurs om rarefactione. 4:0. (12) pp.

Cf. no. 31 in the earlier numbering. Also a copy.

237. Discurs om naturens fördolda egenskaper stält under korte frågor och swar med sina mechaniske experimenter och resoner. 4:0. (16) pp.

Cf. no. 55 in the earlier numbering. Incomplete.

238. Discurs om eldenss och wattnetz strijdigheeter. 4:0. (16) pp.

Cf. no. 32 in the earlier numbering.

239. Discurs om forma och figura, spatium och materia i genere. 4:0. (16) pp.

Copy. Cf. no. 42 in the earlier numbering. Also a copy in the collection (T). *Teknologi.*

240. Förslag till nyia namm uti botanicen. 4:0. (24) pp.

The subject: "Förslag på nyia ordatecken till örterss kiening."

241. Förslag till sådana tillnamn på örter och gräss, som kuna i korthet utmerka derass dygd och egenskaper i gemen. 4:0. (10) pp.

Incomplete.

242. Discurs om träenss och örterss generation och wäxt. 4:0. (8) pp.

Cf. no. 30 in the earlier numbering. Copy in the collection (T). *Teknologi.*

243. Mathematiskt och mechaniskt bewijss att guldmakeri artificcaliter per lapidem philosophorum ähr omöjeliget i wår horizont. 4:0. (8) pp.

Incomplete.

244. Swar om lapide philosophorum. 4:0. (12) pp.

Incomplete. Cf. no. 47 in the earlier numbering.

245. Wijsshetenss andra grundwahl til ungdomss prydnad, mandomss nytta och ålderdomss nöje, bestående i räkna, mäta, jemföra, figurera och sammanfoga alla synbara ting i naturen, til federnesslandetz ungdomss tienst, kortel. sammanfattat af C. P. 4:0. (16) pp.

Incomplete. It appears to be a first draft of the published work with the same title (no. 1).

246. Andra boken af wijsshetenss andra grundwahl, inehollandes ett kort memorial af de nyttigeste och cureusa wettskaper som den studerande ungdomen har att lera på dena grundwahlen, wellment uptecknad af C. P. 4:0. (20) pp.

Additional six drafts or plans, two of which deal with mathematics, with the same title.

247. Tredie delen af wijsshetenss andra grundwahl, inehollandess i sig ett kort memorial på dee förnembste wettskaper, regler och proportioner, som en mechanicus bör kuna, af C. P. 4:0. (17) pp.

K. Astronomy

One paper in one quarto volume. It is possible that it was not written by Polhem. The title is:

248. En uhrmaakaress bewijss, att första timan effter middagen bör reknass emellan klockan 12 och kl. 1 och eij, some em annan uhrmaakare will meena, emellan klockan 1 och kl. 2, referreras af Pytagaros. 4:0. (28) pp.

   The title is from Polhem, as well as the notations in the text, but it was written by someone else.

L. Physics

One volume in folio and six in quarto, which deal with physical, theoretical, and mechanical subjects. A number of manuscripts with similar topics are located in the section "Natural Science."

249. Mechaniske definitioner eller utydning och förklarning på dee ord och termer, som i mechanicen brukass jempte superficiel underrettelsse om dee nödigeste wettskaper, som der till höra. 4:0. (75) pp.

   Cf. no. 61 in the earlier numbering.

250. Inledning till mechanicen, så som fundament iempte geometrien och rekenkonsten, till oeconomien. Fol. (21) pp.

   Cf. no. 36 in the earlier numbering.

251. Den andra mechanske delen inehålländendess (!) de nödigeste wettskaper, reglor, proportioner och uträkningar, som practicen behöfwer betiena sig utaf utur theorien. 4:0. (24) pp.

   Incomplete.

252. Om dee egenskaper huar uppå mechaniquen sig förnembligst grundar. 4:0. (28) pp.

253. Huru fördelass mechaniquen generaliter. 4:0. (6) pp.

254. Mechaniska wettskaper. Fol. (78) pp.

   Cf. no. 43 in the earlier numbering; as well, there is a small incomplete manuscript (16 pp.) with the same title.

255. Mechanica naturalis eller naturens konstiga sammanhang, framstelt under små frågor och swar af C. R. C. P. Fol. (52) pp.

   Incomplete. Cf. C. Polhem's mechania naturalis; 4:0. (16) pp. Copy in *Codex A* 133 Upsala Universitetsbibliotek.

256. Mechanica naturalis, bestående i definitioner, proportioner och constructioner. Fol. (32) pp.

   Incomplete.

257. Om naturens mechanique. 4:0. (24) pp.

   Cf. no. 30 in the earlier numbering. Also ten lesser, fragmentary manuscripts with almost the same title.

258. Pars mechanica. 4:0. (23) pp.

259. Mechaniske experimenter med sina tillhörige resoner frågwiss förestelt. 4:0. (16) pp.

260. Mandata memoriae mechanicorum el. de förnembste principia, egenskaper, proportioner, reglor och utrekningar, som en ferdig mechanicus altijd bör weeta och minass utan till, så frampt han skall kuna finna reson och orsak

till alt, huadh som i practicen ähr möjeliget och omöjel. att wärkstella, den studerarnde ungdomen till tienst af Christoph. Polhamer. 4:0. (38) pp.

Cf. no. 31 in the earlier numbering. Incomplete.

261. Lista på de förnemste och nödigaste wettskaper, som en incipient i mechanicen har att lära och minass wijd all sina förrättningar. Fol. (12) pp.

Cf. no. 35 in the earlier numbering.

262. Samtahl och discurs emellan theoria och praxis om mechanske och physiccalske saker, huar igenom ungdomen, som der till har lust, kan lära något. Fol. (40) pp.

Cf. no. 20 in the earlier numbering.

263. Mechaniske handgrep och wettskaper för ungdomen i scholorne, som der till lust hafwa. Fol. (12) pp.

Incomplete.

264. Mechanisk öfning för ungdomen. 4:0. (40) pp.

265. Mathematisk och mechaniskt bewijss att ingen materia i naturen äger huarken tyngd eller letthet wijdare än i anseende till dess particlarss samansettning och dess skingrande huar för sig. 4:0. (24) pp.

Incomplete.

266. Om de rörelsserss afmätningar, som naturen medelar, och tiena för fundament och hielpreda i alla slagz machiners och strömwärkz utrekningar. Fol. (8) pp.

Cf. no. 42 in the earlier numbering.

267. Om rörelssenss qualiteter. 4:0. (8) pp.

268. Physicco-mechanica. 4:0. (36) pp.

Cf. no. 56 in the earlier numbering.

269. Physiccalske grundsattzer som rationaliter, mathematice och mechanice kuna demonstreras. 4:0. (28) pp.

Cf. no. 50 in the earlier numbering.

270. Pes mechanicus finness sålunda. 4:0. (39) pp.

Cf. no. 21 in earlier numbering.

271. Physcalska reisonamenter om naturens operationer mechanice. 4:0. (8) pp.

272. Responsio de coloribus. 4:0. (16) pp.

Incomplete; cf. Responsio brevissima de coloribus. *Codex Bf. 31*, pp. 495–498. Linköpings stiftsbibliotek.

273. Discurs om jordenss och planeternas lopp. 4:0. (15) pp.

Cf. no. 52 in the earlier numbering. Copy in the collection T. *Teknologi.*

274. De gravitate et compressione aeris. Fol. (5) pp.

275. Discurs om gravitate. 4:0. (15) pp.

Cf. no. 26 in the earlier numbering. Also two smaller papers with almost the same content; cf. the copy in the collection T, *Teknologi.*

276. Orsaken till lufftenss förändringar. Fol. (4) pp.

Cf. Discurs om storm och blåsväder; copy in the collection T, *Teknologi.*

277. Gissningz tankar om orsaken till lufftens och magnetre (?) förandringar utan wiss ordning. 4:0. (20) pp.

Incomplete.

278. Barometer. 4:0. (8) pp.

279. Anledning till wederleekarss uthrekning. 4:0. (7) pp.

Cf. no. 23 in the earlier numbering. Cf. Om wädrets egenskap i synnerhet; copy in collection T, *Teknologi.*

280. Orsak till wattnetz stigande i osynlig ijma och fallande i synligit regn. 4:0. (12) pp.

> Cf. no. 6 in the earlier numbering.

281. Tankar om eldenss uphof, warelsse och wärkan, mechanice demonstrerat. Fol. (4) pp.

> Cf. Förklaring på anmerkningarna mot eldeness warelsse, och det i samma ordning punctwijss. *Codex Bf. 31,* pp. 507–514. Linköpings stiftsbibliotek, cf. no. 7.

282. Om pendlarss vibrationer och resistentia aeris i stigandet. 4:0. (12) pp.

> Cf. no. 68 in the earlier numberings.

283. Om rullande kuhlorss egenskaper. 4:0. (35) pp.

> Only the title in the first part of the work.

284. Kuhlorss rörelsser. 4:0. (12) pp.

285. (Större fragment) Fol. (48), (22) pp.

> Both with no. 33 in the earlier numbering.

286. Om linia projectorum. (nr. 1). De motu et resistentia mediorum. Nr. 2. Om skått och bog linier. Nr. 3. Continuatio de motu et resistentia mediorum, men i synnerhet om pendlars vibrationer, och resistentia aëris i stigandet. Nr. 4. Continuatio ejusdem. Om lijka fart i stigande och fallande, när materia och superficies ell. storlek äro olijka. 4:0. (48), (16), (15), (11), (14) pp.

> *Codex N. 13.* Linköpings stiftsbibliotek. (Gammalt signum LXXIV: 4 och B. 73. d.) Written by Benzelius: "Directeurn hr Christopher Polhammar de linea projectorum — de motu resistentia mediorum." Revision. The first part is written by Polhem and includes, "Stiernsund d. 6 maij 1711. Christopher Polhammar." The work was read in the *collegium curiosorum* on June 20, 1711.

287. Om linea musica. 4:0. 43 pp.

> *Codex N. 12.* (Gammalt signum LXXIV: 3 och B. 73. c.) Written by Benzelius, "Directeurn hr Christopher Polhammar de linea musica cum annotatis professoris Haraldi Vallerii; item Joh. Cahman artis construendorum organorum musicorum magistri."
> Revision. See Polhem's letter to H. Wallerius 1711 and to J. Wallerius 6–3, 1711 in *Codex Bf.* 31. Linköpings stiftsbibliotek.

288. Christopher Polhems anmärckningar om barometerns stigande och fallande på följande luftens förändringar. 4:0. 156 pp.

> Copy in collection R. *Teknologi.* There are also a number of handwritten annotations (20 pp.), or an appendix which Polhem later added. The major manuscript is found also in copy in *Codex A* 210 and *Codex N* 526, Uppsala Universitetsbibliotek; cf. also, Discurs om barometerens stigande och fallande, 8 pp., copy in the collection T, *Teknologi.*

289. Christopher Polhem om elementernas jämn-wigt. 4:0. (13) pp.

> Copy in *Codex A* 1429 Uppsala Universitetsbibliotek.

290. Commercie råd Polheims inledning til mechaniquen. 4:0. (13) pp.

> Copy in *Codex A* 128 Uppsala Universitetsbibliotek.

291. Christ. Polheim: Mechaniske defi(ni)tioner. 319 blad.

> *Svedsk.* Q. X. 1. Kejserliga biblioteket. St. Petersburg.

292. Polheim: Mecanique. 97 blad.

> *Svedsk.* Q. X. 3, Kejserliga bibliotekset. St. Petersburg. Dr. F. Hjelmqvist,

Lund, has very kindly informed me about these last manuscripts. I have not had opportunity to interpret their contents.

M. Mathematics

Three volumes, one in folio, two in quarto. There are papers among the volumes in quarto on measurement, standards, weights, and the others are on arithmetic, stereometry, geometry, analysis, and other similar topics.

293. Om swenska footenss fullkomlighet. 4:0. (15) pp.
294. Bessmåhl. 4:0. (9) pp.
295. Frågass huru en pyndare bör wara utdelt till skepundz wicht, frågass huru dess delning bör wara inrettad till pund, marker och lod. 4:0. (4) pp.
296. (Större fragment angående besman). 4:0. (24) pp.
    Cf. no. 47.
297. Några reglor och utrekningar i den allmena practicen, och icke ähro i Agrels rekenbok införde, de unga och cureusa huss hållrar till tienst af C. R. C. Polhem. 4:0. (4) pp.
298. Frågor om algebra. 4:0. (24) pp.
299. Om linea logarithmica. 4:0. (4) pp.
300. Stereometria. 4:0. (8) pp.
    Cf. no. 75 in the earlier numbering.
301. Puncters bruk, nytta och förklaring i practicen. 4:0. (8) pp.
302. Förklaring om figurers bruk och nytta. 4:0. (8) pp.
303. Elementa geometriae. 4:0. (4) pp.
304. En lijten, dåck grundel. underre(te)lsse, om analysis infinitorum eller den sinrijka räkenkonsten, som tiena kan, icke allenast för en brynsteen att wässa hiernan uppå, utan och för en god probersten att finna huilka hiernor som till höga studier ähro bequema. Till ungdomenss tienst af C. R. C. P. Fol. (27) pp.
    Cf. no. 14 in the earlier numbering.
305. Compendium mathematicum eller ett kort begrep af det som pryder ung-domen, gangnar mandomen och förnöjer ålderdomen, lempat till ungdon-menss åhr och ålder af C. P. 4:0. (19) pp.
    Another work with a similar title.
306. (Arbete utan titel, behandlande hufvudsakligen geometri och stereometri). 4:0. (66) pp.
    Cf. no. 43 in the earlier numbering. The heading reads "Cap. 1 om grad-bogen och dess bruk."
307. (Arbete utan titel, behandlande aritmetik, geometri, stereometri, trigono-metri, geografi, astronomi, astrologi, mekanik, statik, hydrostatik.) Fol. (84) pp.
    Cf. no. 25 in the earlier numbering.

N. Technology

Eleven volumes in quarto, and five in folio, made up the most part of Polhem's written manuscripts. A number of manuscripts are based upon Polhem's papers. They can be divided up in the following way:

1. Mining and Metalworking

One volume in quarto, mostly fragments dealing with mining techniques, the preparation of iron and steel, testing of tin, etc.

308. Wägwijssare till bergz mechaniquen. 4:0. (16) pp.
     Incomplete.
309. Examen för en bergz mechanicus eller den som skall göra tienst för berg mestare, konstmestare och marcheider. 4:0. (12) pp.
     Incomplete.
310. Mechanske begrep om gruf machiner. 4:0. (23) pp.
     Cf. no. 63 in the earlier numberings.
311. Några mechanska reglor wed malmgrufworss brännande och brytande till förekeomande af dhe olägenheter som her wed i längden gemenl. pläga före möta. Fol. (4) pp.
312. Om ståhl. Fol. (12) pp.
     Cf. no. 12 in the earlier numberings.
313. Kunskap om jern tillwekning för inrijkess manufacturer. 4:0. (20) pp.
     Incomplete. Cf. no. 4 in the earlier numberings.
314. Orsaken till det mesta stång iernetz oduglieghet her i landet. 4:0. (20) pp.
     Cf. no. 2 in the earlier numberings.
315. Om hamarsmijde specaliter. 4:0. (24) pp.
     Cf. no. 3 in the earlier numberings.
316. En kort underrettelsse att profwa ten med wattuwegning. 4:0. (8) pp.
     Cf. no. 64 in the earlier numberings. Incomplete.
317. Om mässing. 4:0. (4) pp.
     Copy in the collection T; *Teknologi*.

2. Handicrafts

One volume in quarto.

318. Tunbinnarefrågor. 4:0. (4) pp.
319. Swarfwarefrågor. 4:0. (24) pp.
320. Att slijpa glass till glassögon, perspectiver med mera. 4:0. (8) pp.
321. Lantmätarefrågor. 4:0. (12) pp.
322. Klockgiutarefrågor. 4:0. (11) pp.
323. Tengiutarefrågor. 4:0. (4), (8) pp.
324. Kopparslagarefrågor. 4:0. (12), (4) pp.
325. Frågor om wangzjuhl. 4:0. (12) pp.
326. Frågor om alla handa låss. 4:0. (16) pp.
327. Bergzmanssfrågor. 4:0. (16) pp.
328. Uhrmakarefrågor. 4:0. (16) pp.
329. Orgbyggarefrågor. 4:0. (8) pp.
330. Klockegiutarefrågor. 4:0. (8) pp.
331. Muhrmestarefrågor. 4:0. (16) pp.
332. Om tegelslageri. 4:0. (4) pp.
333. Guldsmedzfrågor. 4:0. (6) pp.
334. Fråga om wattuspanter och dess utrekningar. 4:0. (6), (4), (4), (12) pp.
     Four manuscripts with similar titles.
335. Frågor om tryckwärk att föra wattnet up i högden. 4:0. (4) pp.

253

3. Miscellaneous writings, dealing with various kinds of handicrafts

One volume in quarto, mostly in fragment form, dealing with organ building, threshing machines, locks, bellows-making, coopering. Most of them are incomplete.

336. Muscicalisk instrumentmakeri. 4:0. (8) pp.
　　　Also two fragments with similar titles.
337. Swar på några frågor, som orgbyggaren h. Daniel Stråhle begert af mig underre(ttel)se om. 4:0. (13) pp.
　　　Also two plans.
338. Om mathematiske instrumentmakeri. 4:0. (17) pp.
　　　Incomplete. Above the title, "Det 5 capitlet," complete copy, (41 pp.) in *Codex A* 128 Upsala Universitetsbibliotek. Another copy in the volume "Uppsatser i teknologi och praktisk mekanik."
339. Om snickare hantwerket. Fol. (12) pp.
　　　Above the title "4 capit."
340. Belljmakarefrågor. 4:0. (20) pp.
341. Perlstijkare arbete. 4:0. (3) pp.
342. C. P. Om de fundamental wettenskaper, som höra till instrumentmakerijet. 4:0. (14) pp.
　　　Copy in *Codex A* 128 Upsala Universitetsbibliotek.

4. Housebuilding

One volume in quarto, dealing with building in general, as well as roofs, foundations, earthenware, brewhouses, poultryhouses, sheep- and cowhouses, etc. It probably belongs to a rough draft of a larger work "Allmän huss håldz byggnad," which Polhem wrote in 1710 and sent to the *collegium curiosorum* (cf. no. 335).

343. Samtahl emellan fröken theoria och byggmästar practicus om sitt förehafwande. 4:0. (92) pp.
344. Anmerkningar wijd huss byggnan. 4:0. (28) pp.
　　　Cf. no. 14 in the earlier numberings.
345. Mechanica practica eller fundamental byggarekonst. 4:0. (24) pp.
　　　Cf. no. 36 in the earlier numberings.
346. Om huss håldz byggenskap. 4:0. (32) pp.
347. Byggningz memorial emot de feel och olägenheter som i alla handa huss håldz byggnader i bland plä yppass. 4:0. (68) pp.
　　　Incomplete.
348. En kort underrettelse och anledning till den swänske byggningz och byggare konsten, framstelt i små frågor och swar. 4:0. (14) pp.
　　　Cf. no. 35 in the earlier numberings.
349. Byggningz- och reparations memorial wijd kiörkor och andra byggnader som fodra en bestendig warachtighet i längden. 4:0. (9) pp.
　　　Above the title: C. R. C. P.
350. Om muhr mestare konsten. 4:0. (12) pp.
　　　Incomplete.

351. Anmerkningar wijd tegelslageri. Fol. (7) pp.
    Cf. no. 19 in the earlier numberings.
352. Steenhuss grund. 4:0. (7) pp.
353. Jern-kakelugn. 4:0. (8) pp.
354. Frågor om ungnar och eldzwärk. 4:0. (8) pp.
355. Allmän huss håldz byggnad, så rörlige af quarnar, som orörl, aff huss bygg-
    nad, med sina mathematiske, mechaniske och physicalske anmerkningar,
    reglor och proportioner, saman hemptat och ut gonget aff colegio curioso-
    rum upsaliensi, till wårt kära fäderness landz nytta och tienst. 4:0. (146) pp.
    Codex E. 3. Linköpings stiftsbibliotek — Gammalt signum LXXIV: 1 and B.
    73. By Benzelius "H:r Pohlhammars om hus hållz-bygnad skrifwit. 1711."
    Above the title in Benzelius' hand, "Skrifvit 1710 d. 31 december." The
    work is divided into nine different numbers, of which several have
    appendices. Some of these are in copy.
    Found also in copy in the collection R. *Teknologi;* another copy in *Codex
    A* 128 Upsala Universitetsbibliotek.
356. Memorial om stadzbyggnad i Swärie. Stjernsund d. (5) maj 1711. Fol. (4) pp.
    Biografi P. (no. 80); also in copy in the collection T; *Teknologi.*
357. Om leer. 4:0. (5) pp.
    Copy by J. Troilius in the collection T; *Teknologi;* another copy in the
    collection R: *Teknologi.*
358. Om mur-leer. 4:0. (5) pp.
    Copy by J. Troilius in the collection T; *Teknologi;* another copy in the
    collection R; *Teknologi.*
359. Om tegel. 4:0. (7) pp.
    Copy by J. Troilius in the collection T; *Teknologi;* another copy in the
    collection R; *Teknologi.*

5. Papers on bellcasting and bells

One volume in quarto, appears to be almost complete.

360. Mathemathisk och mechanisk wettskap om klåckor. 4:0. (102) pp.
    Cf. no. 86 in the earlier numberings.

6. Papers dealing with windmills

Two volumes, one in folio and one in quarto, made up mostly of
fragments.

361. Om quarndammar. Fol. (21) pp.
    Cf. no. 38 in the earlier numberings.
362. En kort dock grundel. underrettelsse om allahanda quarnar och större wärk.
    Fol. (4) pp.
    Incomplete.
363. Fundamental kunskap om alla handa quarnarss inrettningar. Fol. (4) pp.
364. Theoretiska anmärkningar wijd quarnbyggnad. 4:0. (47) pp.
365. Om miöhl quarnar. 4:0. (20) pp.
    The last 13 pages contain a scientific treatise on language. Also two
    manuscripts with similar titles, one 12 pp., the other 7.

366. Några mathematiska utrekningar som wijssa huar uti den mechaniska practicen har theoriens handräkning af nöden, och för dena gången om miöhlquarnar allenast så som mest brukelige. 4:0. (32) pp.

Above the title, no. 1; incomplete.

367. Frågor om gryn quarnar. 4:0. (4) pp.
368. Frågor om såg quarnar. 4:0. (4) pp.

7. Smaller papers dealing with problems in practical mechanics

One volume in quarto, made up primarily of fragments.

369. Elementa mechanicae practicae. 4:0. (12) pp.
Incomplete.

370. Om rörelssernass egenskaper i alla rörliga machiner och quarnwärk och strömwärk. 4:0. (24) pp.
Cf. no. 67 in the earlier numbering.

371. Om fiedrar. Tvär. 4:0. (14) pp.
Cf. no. 40 in the earlier numbering.

372. Några allmena wettskaper som höra till rullspehlss inrettningar. Fol. (8) pp.
Cf. no. 16 in the earlier numbering.

8. Papers on locks and lockmaking

One volume in quarto.

373. Om uhr eller uhrwärk. Fol. (36) pp.
Cf. no. 4 in the earlier numberings. Published in 1910 by E. Sidenbladh (no. 33).

374. (Större arbete utan titel). 4:0. (102) pp.
The work is divided into four parts with the contents listed on the first two pages; the chapter appears to be incomplete.

375. Anledning till uhrmakeri konsten sampt dess bruk och wijdmacht hållande. 4:0. (24) pp.
Cf. no. 20 in the earlier numberings. Incomplete.

376. Anmerkningar wijd uhrmakeri. 4:0. (8) pp.

377. En lijten berettelsse och kunskap om uhrmakeri. 4:0. (7) pp.
Several fragments with a similar title.

378. Om uhrmakare konsten. 4:0. (122) pp.
Written in August 1726.
Codex E. 16. Linköpings stiftsbibliotek. (Gammalt signum LXXIV: 2 och B. 73. b.) Revision with corrections and additions by Polhem. By Benzelius: "Directeuren Hr Christopher Polhemmar om uhrmakarekonsten." Also in copy in the collection R. Teknologi. Another copy in Codex A. 128 Upsala Universitetsbibliotek and in Engeström's collection. C.X., 1, 24; made up of 46 and 20 pages, incomplete.

9. Technology and practical mechanics

One volume in quarto, all copies. It is questionable whether they all come from Polhem. However, it is questionable whether even those copied fragments which are found among Polhem's papers in a folio volume under the title "Mechaniske frågor och resolutioner" are also his. Because there is no conclusive proof, they have not been included. In the first volume, there are included only those which are *not* listed in other sections.

379. Om swarfware konsten. 4:0. (23) pp.
380. Om smeds hantwärket. 4:0. (24) pp.
381. Om furubräder. 4:0. (2) pp.
    Another copy in the collection T. *Teknologi,* in connection with a paper on pine wood.
382. Om stångjerns beredning. Fol. (17) pp.

10. Waterworks and canals

Two volumes, one in folio, and one in quarto; made up of papers dealing with canals, locks, dams, water-wheels, etc. Among the many fragments, three chapters (3, 4, 8) are especially noteworthy, of a large work on hydrology. Also of importance are his papers dealing with the subject of a waterway between Stockholm and Göteborg, one of which is a sketch in a note about the canals in Finland. There is also a volume in a folio which contains notes of the lock in Stockholm; this contains only two papers, one of which is by another person (Klingenstierna?), as well as a description of the Stockholm lock itself.

383. Theoria practica de motu sive lapsu aquarum eller fundamental wettskap om wattufall, wattujuhl och rännor etc., nödig för dem att lära som will låta bygga quarnar, och andra wärk i en ström huarest knapp wattudrecht finness. I discursiva frågor och swar framstelt af C. P. directeur öfwer den swänske bergwerkz mechanicen. 4:0. (64) pp.
    Cf. no. 34 in the earlier numberings.
384. Om wattufall, rennor och juhl etc. Fol. (28) pp.
    Incomplete.
385. Pars mechanica om wattujuhl och rennor. 4:0. (31) pp.
386. Pars mechanica om wattudrijfwande wärk i gemen. 4:0. (31) pp.
387. Pars mechanica om wattuwärk i gemen och i synnerhet. 4:0. (16) pp.
    A number of other fragments with almost the same title.
388. Theoria aquatica eller de wettskaper om wattn, som kuna betiena de hantwärkrar som omgå med damar, slyssar, dockor, spring- eller lustwärk i trägårdar, wattusprutor (?) och huad mera dylikt. 4:0. (43) pp.
389. Mechaniske afmätningar och utrekningar i practicen. 4:0. (16) pp.
390. Om slussar. 4:0. (32) pp.
    Incomplete.
391. Slusswärk. Fol. (4) pp.
    Incomplete.
392. Memorial el:r instruction wid nya slussbyggnaden i Stockholm som företogs d. 15 maj 1744, författat af com. rådet Christ. Polhem. Fol. (14) pp.
    Copy.

393. Om hålldamar. 4:0. (32) pp.
394. Om stenbroar. 4:0. (4) pp.
   Incomplete.
395. Om hengbroar. 4:0. (4) pp.

11. Remarks on mechanical science, directions, rules, and measurements

One volume in quarto, made up of one fragment of 36 pp.

396. En lijten anledning till mechaniske wettskaper, handgrep, reglor och proportioner som i den dagliga praxi kan förekoma, tienlig så well för hussål-
lare i gemen, att kuna sluta contracter om alla handa arbeten och pröfwa
dess godhet, som för incipienter i synnerhet som sig i sådhana wettskaper
öfwa will, (i) wellment upsatt af C. P. 4:0. (190) pp.
   Incomplete.

12. Papers dealing with Polhem's activity in the Falun mine

One volume in folio, made up of documents and papers dealing
with Polhem's hoisting machine in King Fredrik's mine, a number of
which are handwritten, R. Rückerskiöld's notes, and letters and
drafts, letters from the authorities and other people to Polhem, most
of which are copies. There are several accounts of Polhem's activity in
the Falun mine. The most important of these are:

397. Angående com:r. Polhems konstbyggnader och projecterade desseiner samt
nyttiga förslager wid Stora Kopparbergz grufwa etc. Fol. (24) pp.
   Cf. no. 5 in the earlier numberings. The title was written by someone else.
398. Ödmjukt och oförgripjpeliget förslag om Fahluns grufwass beständiga up-
rätthållande. Fol. (8) pp.
   Cf. no. 6 in the earlier numberings.
399. Upfodringz wärk i Fahlun. Fol. (16) pp.
400. Berättelse om Fahlu grufvas tilstånd. 4:0. (78) pp.
   Cf. no. 62 in the earlier numberings. The title by someone else. Cf. Kort
   berettelse om Fahluns grufwa (no. 129). Fol. 8 pp. *Biografi* P.

13. Papers dealing with Stjernsund

A volume in folio, made up of "papers dealing with Stjernsund's
manufacturing work," most of which is in fragments, notes, memoranda, contracts, etc., dealing with the operation of the manufactory.

401. En kort berettelsse för samptl. rikzenss ständer om jern manufacturiet
Stiernsund, huru wijda det till närwarande tijd avancerat och huad till dess
wijdare befrämiande fodrass. 4:0. (28) pp.
402. En kort relation om Stiernsundz manufacturs beskaffenhet och närwarande
tillstånd. Fol. (4) pp.

1730 is the year indicated. There is a revision with a similar content (cf. no. 46).

403. Memorial wijd det förtenta jern arbete i från Stiernsundz manufactur. Fol. (6) pp.

Cf. another edition.

404. Anmärkningar wijd contracterna. Fol. (8) pp.

405. Lista på de wärk och machiner son wijd manufacturwärket Stiernsund ähro inrettade. Fol. (4) pp.

406. Ödmiuk berättelse om manufactur werket Stiernsund och thess tillstånd. 4:0. (13) pp.

From the middle of the 1730's. Copy in the collection R, *Teknologi*. Possibly an addition to Polhem's letter to N. Reuterholm, 27–3 1734; cf. no. 208.

O. *Nautical subjects*

Made up of small papers on the subject of navigation and ship-building.

407. Ett nytt sätt att retardera skiep i stark storm och till den ort, dijt man intet will, när ankar grund feelar. 4:0. (11) pp.

408. Ett nytt påfund att retardera skiep utan anckare. 4:0. (11) pp.

409. En ny method att finna skieppens retta under- och öfwerlast, att de icke blij för styfwa eller för ranka i storm wäder. 4:0. (4) pp.

P. *Typography*

410. Discurs om de latinska och tyska tryckstijlar. 4:0. (20) pp.

Incomplete. Vetenskapsakademiens bibliotek. On the last page by someone other than Polhem, "Polhems tankar om latinska caracterer d. 22 sept. 1739."

This limited edition of
5,000 copies
was designed by
Asher T. Applegate
and printed by
Connecticut Printers, Incorporated.
The type is Baskerville
The paper is Hermes E. F. 60 lb.
Binding by Russell-Rutter, Inc.